Shakespeare
the
Wars of the Roses
and the
Historians

WILLIAM SHAKESPEARE
the WARS OF THE ROSES
and the HISTORIANS

Keith Dockray

First published 2002

PUBLISHED IN THE UNITED KINGDOM BY:

Tempus Publishing Ltd
The Mill, Brimscombe Port
Stroud, Gloucestershire GL5 2QG
www.tempus-publishing.com

PUBLISHED IN THE UNITED STATES OF AMERICA BY:

Tempus Publishing Inc.
2 Cumberland Street
Charleston, SC 29401
(Tel: 1-888-313-2665)

www.tempuspublishing.com

British Library Cataloguing in Publication Data.
A catalogue record for this book is available from the British Library.

ISBN 0 7524 2320 7

Typesetting and origination by Tempus Publishing.

PRINTED AND BOUND IN GREAT BRITAIN.

CONTENTS

ACKNOWLEDGEMENTS

Charles Ross first fired my enthusiasm for fifteenth-century England, and interest in the influence of William Shakespeare's history plays on the century's historiography, in the 1960s. Alan Sutton encouraged me to embark on this particular book in 1999 and has maintained a lively interest in its progress (or otherwise) ever since. Peter Fleming has been a constant source of inspiration and advice, while Peter Allender, Ann Rippin, fellow real ale drinkers and staff at *The Sportsman and Annexe Inn*, Bristol, have all helped sustain me as well. I would also like to thank Richard Bray and Jonathan Reeve of Tempus Publishing for their hard work in seeing this book through to publication. Its many faults, needless to say, are entirely my own.

Keith Dockray
Bristol, April 2002

THE DYNASTIC DIMENSIONS OF THE WARS OF THE ROSES

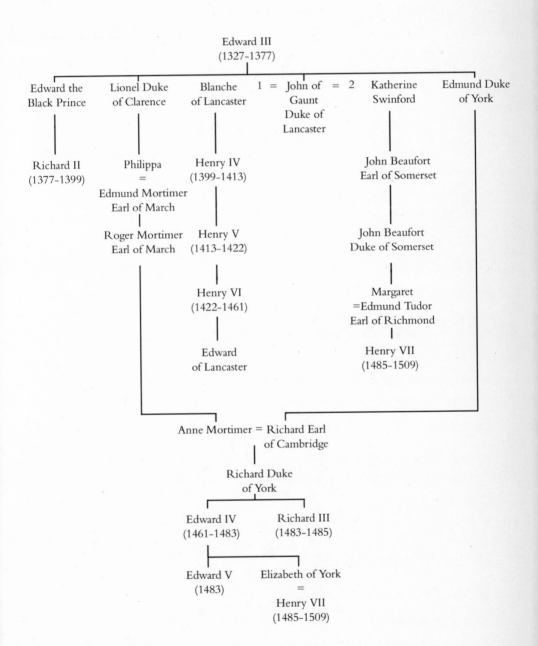

Edward III
(1327-1377)

Edward the Black Prince

Lionel Duke of Clarence

Blanche of Lancaster

1 = John of Gaunt Duke of Lancaster

= 2 Katherine Swinford

Edmund Duke of York

Richard II
(1377-1399)

Philippa
=
Edmund Mortimer
Earl of March

Henry IV
(1399-1413)

John Beaufort
Earl of Somerset

Roger Mortimer
Earl of March

Henry V
(1413-1422)

John Beaufort
Duke of Somerset

Henry VI
(1422-1461)

Margaret
=Edmund Tudor
Earl of Richmond

Edward
of Lancaster

Henry VII
(1485-1509)

Anne Mortimer = Richard Earl
of Cambridge

Richard Duke
of York

Edward IV
(1461-1483)

Richard III
(1483-1485)

Edward V
(1483)

Elizabeth of York
=
Henry VII
(1485-1509)

INTRODUCTION

For historians of the Wars of the Roses William Shakespeare is both a curse and a blessing: a curse because he immortalised Tudor spin on fifteenth-century civil wars that helped justify Elizabeth I's legitimate occupation of the English throne; a blessing because, without Shakespeare's history cycle, hardly anyone beyond the confines of a few elite schools, universities and the Richard III Society would even know of their existence.

The great Elizabethan dramatist has traditionally been acknowledged as author of no fewer than eight history plays covering the era of Plantagenet rule in England from Richard II to Richard III. Four of them date from the early 1590s and explore personalities, politics and war during the reigns of the third Lancastrian king, Henry VI (1422-1461), and the two Yorkists Edward IV (1461-1483) and Richard III (1483-1485). *Henry VI Part 1* is concerned, very loosely, with the first couple of decades of the king's reign and *Henry VI Part 2* with the sequence of events that culminated in the first battle of St Albans in 1455, conventionally regarded as the beginning of the Wars of the Roses. *Henry VI Part 3* highlights the bloodfeuds characterising the wars, the role of Henry VI's queen, Margaret of Anjou, both before and after her husband's deposition in 1461, the overweening ambitions of Warwick the Kingmaker and their consequences, the pleasure-loving Edward IV, and the emergence on to the political stage of his ruthless and entirely self-seeking brother, Richard of Gloucester. The dramatic climax of the cycle, *Richard III*, charts Richard of Gloucester's bloody progress to the throne, his defeat and death at Bosworth in 1485, and the ending of the wars once Tudor rule was inaugurated by Henry VII. Then, in the later 1590s, Shakespeare added a further four plays, concentrating on the deposition of Richard II (1377-1399) in 1399, the turbulent times of Henry IV (1399-1413) and the military triumphs of his once wayward son Henry V (1413-1422): *Richard II, Henry IV Parts 1 & 2* and *Henry V*.

All these plays can, of course, be seen in their own right and they are formidable products of the dramatist's art. But they are dramas not histories and Shakespeare was perfectly willing to take liberty with what he found in his sources. Chronology was certainly not sacrosanct, nor was the telescoping of events to facilitate narrative development and heighten dramatic tension in any way out of order. For instance, *3 Henry VI* opens with the parliament of 1460 (as though it immediately followed the Yorkist victory at St Albans in 1455) and, thereafter, much that happened in the 1460s is ignored in the interests of highlighting Edward IV's wooing of Elizabeth Grey (Woodville), his quarrel with Warwick the Kingmaker, the restoration of Henry VI in 1470, and the ruin of both Warwick at Barnet and the Lancastrian cause at Tewkesbury in 1471; throughout the play, moreover, Richard of Gloucester is, quite unhistorically, a key figure, an essential prelude to the full treatment of this crook-backed, cruel and ruthless schemer in *Richard III*. The plays are littered with factual errors and, indeed, whole scenes unknown to history. Thus, in *1 Henry VI*, the memorable sequence where rival Lancastrian and Yorkist leaders distribute red and white roses to their followers is completely fictitious while, in *2 Henry VI,* William de la Pole Duke of Suffolk is erroneously presented as Margaret of Anjou's lover. In *3 Henry VI* Richard of Gloucester participates in the battles of Mortimer's Cross and Towton even though he was a mere child and not even in England at the time and in *Richard III*, Gloucester's wooing of Anne Neville in the presence of the corpse of Henry VI (in whose recent murder, and that of Anne's husband Prince Edward of Lancaster, he has played a leading role) is entirely the product of Shakespeare's vivid imagination. Even more strikingly, Shakespeare had no qualms when it came to enhancing or altering the characters of historical men and women. Did the real Margaret of Anjou, for instance, bear more than a passing resemblance to the entirely formidable harridan of *3 Henry VI* and *Richard III*? Did Henry VI actually hang around battlefields wringing his hands at the horrors of civil war? And, most crucially and controversially of all, was Richard III anything like the monster of Tudor tradition?

Since Shakespeare's time, indeed, virtually everything pertaining to the Wars of the Roses has provoked controversy, even the very term itself. Yet, although modern historians have occasionally quibbled, the red rose had certainly been an emblem of the house of Lancaster in the later fourteenth century (and was shrewdly employed again by Henry VII), the white rose was a Yorkist badge and, in 1486, a contemporary chronicler remarked that at Bosworth the previous year 'the tusks of the boar [Richard III] were blunted and the red rose, avenger of the white, now shines upon us'. The humanist historian Polydore Vergil, in the early sixteenth century, learned that 'the white rose was the emblem of one family and the red rose of the other' while Sir John Oglander referred to 'the quarrel of the warring roses'. Later, in 1762, David Hume coined the phrase 'wars of the two roses' and, in his 1829 novel *Anne of Geierston*, Sir Walter Scott highlighted 'the civil discords so dreadfully prosecuted in the wars of the White and Red Roses'. Surely, with so distinguished a historical pedigree, the term Wars of the Roses deserves a better fate than its current and misleading application to Lancashire/Yorkshire cricket confrontations?

Later fifteenth-century commentators were strongly inclined to seek the seeds of civil strife in the upheavals attendant on the deposition of Richard II and usurpation of Henry IV in 1399. Tudor chroniclers, too, felt powerfully drawn to 1399 as the starting point for almost a century of domestic turmoil, an interpretation enthusiastically taken on board by William Shakespeare. William Denton in 1888, and even A.L. Rowse in 1966, remained confident that the struggles of Lancaster and York could indeed be traced back to the dynastic drama of 1399. Most twentieth-century historians settled on the first battle of St Albans in May 1455 as the beginning of the Wars of the Roses proper, although other events and dates did find favour as well: Jack Cade's rebellion in 1450, for instance, Richard of York's armed challenge to the Lancastrian regime at Dartford in February 1452, the Percy/Neville confrontation on Heworth Moor near York in August 1453 and, a case powerfully argued by A.J. Pollard, the battles of Blore Heath and Ludford in the autumn of 1459.

There is no real agreement, either, on when the Wars of the Roses ended. For centuries the defeat and death of Richard III remained the favoured option since, not only did it bring the great Tudor dynasty to the throne, it marked the end of the Middle Ages as well. Yet, insofar as the Wars of the Roses were dynastic wars fought between the houses of Lancaster and York, they ended in 1471, while, arguably, Henry VII's possession of the crown only began to look reasonably secure once he had won the battle of Stoke in June 1487.

For Tudor commentators, and William Shakespeare, the Wars of the Roses resulted in appalling carnage and destruction, massive dislocation of people's lives and, most particularly, bloody vendettas among the aristocracy. Here, too, many recent historians have been inclined to be critical, pointing out that the wars were, in fact, much more limited in both scale and impact. Most people never became involved in the fighting, there was relatively little looting or material destruction, agriculture and trade were only minimally disrupted, and religious and cultural life continued to flourish almost as if the wars were invisible. The ruling elite, particularly families having royal blood flowing through their veins, bore the brunt of it all, but even they often displayed considerable reluctance to take up arms. Many nobles were either killed in the fighting or faced execution for having backed the wrong side but few, if any, prominent families became extinct directly as a result of civil strife. Rarely were noble houses split and bloodfeuds, although not unknown, were very much the exception rather than the rule.

However, it would be a mistake to play down unduly the impact and significance of civil war in the later fifteenth century, particularly between 1459 and 1461 and, again, from 1469 to 1471. England, described as 'out of all good governance' in 1459, certainly suffered considerably in 1460/61, especially the northern counties which seem to have degenerated into a condition of near anarchy. Then, between 1469 and 1471, at least six separate rebellions occurred in northern England, four major battles were fought and, in 1471, there was even a short-lived siege of London. Certainly, too, a high percentage of the nobility did become involved in these wars at one time or another; many gentry, however reluctantly, found themselves drawn in as well; and the English countryside provided most of the fighting men. The fate of leading Lancastrian magnates at St Albans in 1455, in particular, may well have sparked a series of vendettas that resurfaced with a vengeance at the battles of Wakefield and Towton in 1460 and 1461, as William Shakespeare highlighted so dramatically in *3 Henry VI*. Clearly, his plays cannot be regarded as history; nevertheless, rather more than many recent historians have been inclined to admit, Shakespeare did adapt for the stage not only a powerful Tudor tradition about the Wars of the Roses but an interpretation already firmly embedded in contemporary and near-contemporary sources.

1

WILLIAM SHAKESPEARE, THE LATER PLANTAGENET KINGS AND THE WARS OF THE ROSES

ELIZABETH I, COURTLY POLITICS AND THE ENGLISH RENAISSANCE

Queen Elizabeth I, England's last and most revered Tudor monarch, ascended the throne – in a blaze of publicity and to the relief of most of her new subjects – on 17 November 1558. William Shakespeare, eventually to become the most distinguished of English playwrights, was born in deep obscurity at Stratford-upon-Avon, Warwickshire, on or about 23 April 1564. The queen died, a mere shadow of her former self, on 24 March 1603. Shakespeare lived on, retired and back in his home town, until he too died on 23 April 1616. By then both their reputations were assured and, oddly enough, irrevocably intertwined.

Elizabeth I, Henry VIII's unwanted daughter by Anne Boleyn, was hardly an odds-on favourite to succeed to her father's throne at the time of her birth in 1533. Yet following the deaths in rapid succession of the bombastic Henry himself in 1547, his precocious son Edward VI in 1553 and his bigoted daughter Mary I in 1558, the English crown did indeed become hers. It was not an easy legacy but the queen and her spin doctors rose to the challenge splendidly. And they did so by deliberately encouraging the idolisation of her person and projecting an image of Elizabeth as the visible embodiment of the state and guardian of its wellbeing.

Clearly, the queen enjoyed flattery and welcomed it and it was the mark of a successful Elizabethan courtier that he could please her by his attentions. Indeed, in October 1572, Edward Dyer specifically urged his fellow courtier Christopher Hatton to employ flattery in order to retain the queen's favours:

> Never seem deeply to condemn her frailties, but rather joyfully to commend such things as should be in her, as though they were in her indeed.

Hatton obviously took such advice to heart, not least in a letter to Elizabeth dated June 1573:

> This is the twelfth day since I saw the brightness of that sun [the queen] that gives light to my sense and soul… Live forever, most excellent creature…

And when, in 1592, Sir Walter Raleigh found himself temporarily excluded from the queen's presence (for getting a female courtier pregnant, apparently), he penned an even more fawning missive, addressed to Robert Cecil but no doubt meant for the queen's eyes:

> I that was wont to behold her riding like Alexander, hunting like Diana, walking like Venus, the gentle wind blowing her fair hair about her pure cheeks like a nymph, sometimes sitting in the shade like a goddess, sometimes singing like an angel, sometimes playing like Orpheus. Behold! The sorrow of the world, once amiss, has [now] bereaved me of all.

The queen, incidentally, was almost sixty years old at the time.

Elizabeth I was certainly very well aware of the political advantages that might result from a successful projection of her own charismatic personality. 'I know I have the body but of a weak and feeble woman', she declared when confronted by the Spanish Armada in 1588, 'but I have the heart and stomach of a king, and of a king of England too'. No less graphically, in 1601, she assured parliament that 'no prince loves his subjects better' and, 'though God has raised me high, this I count the glory of my crown – that I have reigned with your love'. Elizabeth was certainly adept at exploiting the mystique of monarchy: the elaborate and magnificent ritual of her court, its extreme formality and strict etiquette, greatly impressed visiting dignitaries and was meant to do so. This is particularly evident in a German envoy's picture of Elizabeth and her court at Greenwich in 1599:

> The queen, in the sixty-fifth year of her age, was very majestic… As she proceeded to chapel in all magnificence, she spoke very graciously, first to one, then to another, whether foreign visitors or native courtiers, in English, French or Italian… Whoever spoke to her, it was kneeling, but –

now and then – she raised some with her hand... Wherever she turned her face, everybody fell down on their knees.

Moreover, wherever the queen happened to be such pageantry and ceremony was maintained, most notably during her regular summer progresses through the southern shires of the realm.

Court pageantry and progresses apart, literature and art provided the other major means by which Elizabeth I was idolised and the cult of Gloriana promulgated. For William Shakespeare the queen was 'a pattern to all princes living and all that shall succeed'; Ben Jonson hailed her as 'queen and huntress, chaste and fair'; and the playwright Thomas Dekker fancifully represented her as a goddess and her court as a temple where she could be adored. Portraits, miniatures, engravings and woodcuts of the queen seem to have been in considerable demand; men and women displayed them in their homes and even carried medallions on their persons as symbols of loyalty; and not only did Sir Francis Drake and Sir Francis Walsingham (both prominent courtiers and servants of the queen) have portraits painted of themselves wearing such medallions, even an aged William Cecil Lord Burghley (Elizabeth's chief minister for most of her reign) had himself portrayed with a cameo of the queen in his hat. No wonder Elizabeth I, ever since, has enjoyed such an unrivalled reputation.

The royal court was the centre of political life in Elizabethan England and a magnet for men anxious to benefit from the queen's bounty and secure political advancement. Inevitably, this resulted in the growth of factions, groups of men surrounding leading figures at court who enjoyed easy access to the queen and her patronage, and bound together by personal and material self-interest. Equally inevitably, factional rivalries flourished, particularly during the 1590s when Burghley's son Robert Cecil and Robert Devereux Earl of Essex became locked in competition for the now elderly Elizabeth's favour. Indeed, according to a court insider, by 1599 it had become 'a very dangerous time for, the heads of both factions being here, a man cannot tell how to govern himself'. Moreover, although the queen remained a formidable figure, she was clearly hard-pressed to maintain control; Burghley backed his son's political aspirations for all he was worth; and Essex, strong-willed, greedy for power and oblivious to court conventions, had a positive genius for disruption. Eventually, Essex completely over-stepped the mark, fomented rebellion in 1601 and earned himself a traitor's death. By then, however, the court, riven by factional rivalry for almost a decade, had become a veritable political minefield. Yet the 1590s also saw the greatest flowering of the so-called Elizabethan Renaissance.

Clearly, the Elizabethan court could and did exercise a powerful influence on cultural life as it was not only a fount of political patronage but also a vital source of sponsorship for the arts. Elizabeth I was able to attract the best minds of the day to court and she herself was no intellectual slouch;

she encouraged the formation of a company of actors and the resulting Queen Elizabeth's Men performed at court from Christmas 1583, as well as touring the country; and, apparently, the queen kept a collection of miniatures in her own bedchamber. Vernacular pastoral and love poetry, especially sonnets, obviously had a great appeal to the men and women who peopled Elizabeth I's court. Prominent Elizabethan courtiers could and did sponsor prose writers, poets, playwrights and artists: Robert Dudley Earl of Leicester, like the queen, backed a company of actors; Henry Wriothesley Earl of Southampton was a patron of William Shakespeare; and Sir Philip Sidney managed to combine the roles of poet, patron and eminent man of affairs, even defending poetry on the grounds of its political utility. Painters, engravers and miniaturists of ability, too, found employment at court, not least the still much admired Nicholas Hilliard. Perhaps it is legitimate to discern a veritable Elizabethan Renaissance and, in the 1590s, its greatest star was William Shakespeare.

WILLIAM SHAKESPEARE, ELIZABETHAN ENGLAND AND THE LONDON STAGE

Virtually nothing is known of William Shakespeare until he began to make his mark as an actor and playwright in the early 1590s. Even the exact date of his birth is uncertain, although tradition has it that his life both began and ended on St George's Day (23 April). His father was John Shakespeare, a prosperous Stratford-upon-Avon glovemaker and trader, his mother Mary Arden, daughter of a well-to-do local farmer, and his baptism – on 26 April 1564 - is recorded in the local parish register. Interestingly enough, his fellow dramatist Christopher Marlowe, son of a Canterbury shoemaker, was also born in 1564 but, whereas Marlowe's classics-dominated schooldays in his home town and university career at Cambridge, where he studied rhetoric, logic and philosophy, are beyond dispute, Shakespeare's education must remain a matter for speculation. Certainly, he did not enjoy the benefits of a university education and, later on, Ben Jonson scathingly mocked his small Latin and even less Greek. Yet, as his plays so clearly indicate, he must have acquired some education, probably at Stratford Grammar School in the 1570s where he would have received a solid grounding in Latin language and literature and, perhaps, a smattering of Greek as well. Also, both before and after he embarked on his writing career, he must surely have been a voracious reader. His plays demonstrate, in particular, an extensive knowledge of Plutarch's *Lives* of famous Greeks and Romans – no doubt obtained from Sir Thomas North's English translation of 1579 – and the *Chronicle of Raphael Holinshed* (prime source for the Plantagenet cycle of history plays).

Hard facts remain elusive however, apart from Shakespeare's marriage to Anne Hathaway in 1582. Even the date of his arrival in London is not known for certain. Perhaps he first took up residence in the capital in 1587 or 1588 but it was not until 1592 that his blossoming career as actor-playwright was sneeringly acknowledged by rival dramatist and pamphleteer Robert Green:

> There is an upstart crow, beautified with our feathers, that with his *tiger's heart wrapped in a player's hide* [a parody of a line in *3 Henry VI*] supposes he is well able to bombast out a blank verse as the best of you, and being an absolute Johannes-factotum in his own conceit the only Shakes-scene in a country.

Since Green also attacked Christopher Marlowe for his 'diabolical atheism', however, he can hardly be regarded as an impartial commentator on the contemporary theatrical scene.

Soon after his arrival in London, William Shakespeare became an actor and continued to perform even after he had established himself as a play-wright. In 1598, for instance, he appeared as a 'principal comedian' and, in 1603, a 'principal tragedian'. Perhaps he began his acting career as a member of Robert Dudley Earl of Leicester's company of players at the *Theatre* in Shoreditch, built by James Burbage (the leading member of Leicester's troupe) in 1576, or maybe its rivals the *Curtain* or the *Rose*. Indeed, a visiting Dutchman, Johannes de Witt, noted the existence of at least four London theatres in about 1596, the *Theatre* and the *Curtain* north of the Thames, the *Rose* and the *Swan* south of the river:

> There are four ampitheatres in London of notable beauty... In these each day a different play is performed for the people. The two more splendid of them are situated across the Thames to the south, and from the signs hanging before them are called the *Rose* and the *Swan*... The grandest and largest of all the theatres [is] the *Swan* [which] accommo-dates three thousand people in its seats...

Meanwhile, in 1594, Shakespeare became a founder member of the Lord Chamberlain's Men, a theatrical company which, early in James I's reign, obtained royal patronage and changed its name to the King's Men. In 1594 he and his fellow actors moved into their own newly built theatre south of the Thames and it was probably there, at the *Globe*, that his play *Henry V* was first performed:

> Can this cockpit hold
> The vasty fields of France? Or may we cram

> Within this wooden O the very casques
> That did affright the air at Agincourt?

Towards the end of 1599 a Swiss visitor, Thomas Platter, not only saw Shakespeare's *Julius Caesar* at the *Globe* –'the house with the thatched roof' – but also recorded enthusiastically that:

> ...every day at two o'clock in the afternoon in the city of London sometimes two, sometimes three, plays are given in different places, which compete with each other and those which perform best have the largest number of listeners. The [playing] places are so constructed that [the actors] play on a raised scaffold, and everyone can see everything... The actors are dressed in a very expensive and splendid fashion...

For more than a decade, until he returned to Stratford in around 1611, Shakespeare probably acted regularly at the *Globe* (often in his own plays) and, even after that, he seems to have paid frequent visits to the capital. By the time of his death in April 1616 he had clearly become both a highly acclaimed playwright in London and a wealthy, well-respected citizen in his home town.

During the 1590s William Shakespeare wrote all his Plantagenet history plays and they certainly reflect the politics and society of late Elizabethan England. These were years of economic depression, rising inflation and serious outbreaks of plague (particularly in London where, in 1593, even theatres were closed to help prevent the spread of infection). So widespread was poverty and vagrancy that the dangers of riot and civil disorder seemed ever more threatening.

Politically, too, the 1590s were fraught with difficulties as Elizabeth I aged. Factional rivalries disrupted the royal court, the war with Spain showed no signs of coming to an end, and the question of who would succeed the queen still remained unresolved. No wonder such characteristically Tudor notions as the God-given powers exercised by reigning monarchs, the doctrine of non-resistance to rulers, the sinfulness of rebellion and the potential horrors of civil war were so powerfully voiced in political circles. No wonder either that Shakespeare should have found such appreciative audiences for plays deliberately exploring issues so seemingly relevant to their own times. Why did he choose, specifically, to write about the deposition of Richard II, the troubled times of Henry IV, the patriotic exploits of Henry V, the pious but ineffectual Henry VI, the monstrous Richard III and the Wars of the Roses? The most convincing answer is that he believed *contemporary* problems and issues could be dramatically highlighted in political plays focusing on the familiar, but now safely remote, era of Lancaster and York. Indeed, Elizabethan men and women might even learn valuable lessons from them about the nature of kingship, the exercise of political power and its consequences for society.

Significantly, Shakespeare began with the long and disastrous reign of the last Lancastrian king. Just when the three parts of *Henry VI* were written, and in what order, has been much debated and even Shakespeare's authorship of the trilogy has been disputed. Common sense, if nothing else, points to their composition in chronological order and, although Shakespeare may not have been the sole author (at any rate of *1 Henry VI*), his was surely the dominant hand throughout. Almost certainly, too, when writing the *Henry VI* sequence, Shakespeare already had *Richard III* in mind as the climax of the tetralogy. Perhaps he began the *Henry VI* cycle in 1590 and completed *Richard III* before the end of 1591. If so, the *1 Henry VI* text that has actually come down to us is probably a revised version put together early in 1592. Certainly, a play highlighting John Talbot Earl of Shrewsbury's gallant, if ultimately unsuccessful, efforts to defend Henry VI's French provinces would have had an obvious popular appeal at a time when Robert Devereux Earl of Essex also failed to achieve military objectives across the Channel. Moreover, since Talbot's endeavours had been seriously undermined by political divisions among the English nobility, there was a clear lesson to be learned. Indeed, the Elizabethan satirist, Thomas Nashe – here, surely, responding to *1 Henry VI* – made this only too explicit:

> How it would have joyed brave Talbot – the Terror of the French – to think that after he had lain two hundred years in his tomb he should triumph again on the stage, and have his bones new embalmed with the tears of ten thousand spectators at least, who, in the tragedian that represents his person, imagine they behold him fresh bleeding.

2 Henry VI picked up where *1 Henry VI* ended (the king's marriage to Margaret of Anjou), concentrating on the personality and political role of the queen herself, the rise of Richard Duke of York and the deepening rivalries among the nobility that eventually resulted in the battle of St Albans. *3 Henry VI*, much the best play in the Henry VI trilogy, is dominated by the dynastic struggle of Lancaster and York, unfettered aristocratic ambitions, bloodfeuds and, most of all, the horrific battles of the Wars of the Roses. Again, the lesson to Elizabethan audiences is clear: civil war must be avoided at all costs. The message is finally hammered home in *Richard III*, a play culminating in the evil tyrant's defeat and death at Bosworth, the accession of Henry VII and the promise of restored political stability and peace under the new Tudor dynasty.

William Shakespeare probably had no intention in 1592/93 of adding to his Wars of the Roses history cycle. Indeed, drama itself seemed ever more seriously threatened. As early as 1583, the Puritan pamphleteer Philip Stubbes had delivered a blistering attack on the theatre and lambasted its promotion of immorality; London's ruling elite had been instrumental in preventing the building of theatres within the city's walls; and, now, plague brought the closure of playhouses even in Shoreditch and Bankside. During the plague years, moreover, Shakespeare himself seems to have been much preoccupied in writing narrative poems and sonnets for his new courtly patron Henry Wriothesley Earl of Southampton, specifically dedicating *The Rape of Lucrece* to him in notably fulsome fashion:

> The love I dedicate to your lordship is without end; whereof this pamphlet, without beginning, is but a superfluous moiety. The warrant I have of your honourable disposition, not the worth of my untutored lines, makes it assured of acceptance. What I have done is yours; what I have to do is yours; being part in all I have, devoted yours. Were my worth greater my duty would show greater; meantime, as it is, it is bound to your lordship, to whom I wish long life, still lengthened with happiness.

Perhaps courtiers such as Southampton also helped secure the reopening of theatres but why, in 1595, did Shakespeare embark on a second tetralogy of Plantagenet history plays? Topicality may once more be the key, particularly as far as *Richard II*, the first of the new sequence, is concerned. There followed, in 1597/98, the two parts of *Henry IV* and, in 1599, *Henry V*. Clearly Shakespeare, in common with most Elizabethans, regarded Henry IV as a usurper: hence why that king's reign, ever overshadowed by the events of 1399, proved so strife-ridden. Henry V, by contrast, might be regarded as the very embodiment of English patriotism, at a time when the Elizabethan people seemed sorely in need of a nationalistic clarion call. Indeed, in what is generally held to be a reference to Robert Devereux Earl of Essex (who, in March 1599, left London to put down a rebellion in Ireland), *Henry V* even contains a direct response to current events:

> Were now the General of our gracious Empress –
> As in good time he may – from Ireland coming,
> Bringing rebellion broached on his sword,
> How many would the peaceful city quit
> To welcome him!

The most topical of all Shakespeare's history plays, arguably, is *Richard II*, since contemporaries probably appreciated only too well the ominous similarities between the fourteenth-century Plantagenet king's later years and their own increasingly crisis-ridden times. Perhaps the play was even conceived as a deliberate political allegory, a timely warning to Elizabeth I of what might yet befall her if she failed to solve the many problems posed by expensive warfare, growing factional rivalry at court and mounting economic and social distress in the country, particularly if parallels were drawn between the rebellious usurper Henry Bolingbroke in 1399 and the frustrated Robert Devereux of the mid-1590s, let alone the challenge posed by Ireland to the last Tudor monarch no less than her hapless predecessor Richard II. Significantly, too, when *Richard II* appeared in print in 1597 the deposition scene was omitted. A few years later, in 1601, Richard II's fate became even more worryingly topical. The Earl of Essex, after returning in disgrace from Ireland and failing to persuade even an infatuated queen of his unimpaired merit, fomented a rebellion in London. When his efforts proved futile, his condemnation and execution as a traitor rapidly followed. Interestingly enough, a faction of Essex's own supporters had commissioned a performance of *Richard II* by the Lord Chamberlain's Men on the very eve of his rising, while Elizabeth I herself is convincingly reported as declaring at one point, 'I am Richard II, know ye not that?'

SHAKESPEARE'S HISTORY PLAYS

In his Plantagenet history plays William Shakespeare, adding generous dramatic licence to fruitful quarrying of largely Tudor sources, certainly told a series of gripping tales of personality, politics and warfare. Moreover, he was by no means the only later Elizabethan playwright to find inspiration in Lancastrian and Yorkist triumphs and disasters. Chronicle plays – often reflecting the patriotic, even jingoistic, sentiments unleashed by the defeat of the Spanish Armada in 1588 – could clearly attract enthusiastic audiences in the 1590s, and he may well have drawn himself on such anonymous examples of the genre as the *Famous Victories of Henry V* (1593) and *True Tragedy of Richard III* (published in 1594 but written some years earlier). Perhaps he consulted, as well, the likes of Samuel Daniel's *First Four Books of the Civil Wars between the Houses of Lancaster and York* (1595).

However, the most important of Shakespeare's sources for the history plays was probably the *Chronicle of Raphael Holinshed*, compiled by a syndicate of writers of whom Holinshed was one, and available to the play-wright in its second edition (published in 1587). Holinshed's *Chronicle* is not renowned for its originality, however, since its authors, even more than most Tudor writers, happily plagiarised earlier works, most notably the very substantial accounts of fifteenth-century English political history penned by Edward Hall in his *Union of the Two Noble and Illustrious Families of Lancaster and York* (published in 1548).

Shakespeare, too, depended heavily on Hall as well as Holinshed, taking from Hall's *Chronicle* the general framework for his history plays – the notion of a fifteenth century dominated by prolonged dynastic conflicts as Lancaster and York fought for possession of the throne. Indeed, many scenes and characterisations – for instance, his portrayals of Henry VI, Margaret of Anjou and Richard III – can confidently be traced back to Hall and, most importantly, his vision of the nature of the Wars of the Roses. Among the sources most obviously influencing Hall, and heavily plagiarised by him, was the Italian Renaissance humanist historian Polydore Vergil's *English History* (written during the reigns of Henry VII and Henry VIII). Moreover, even if he did not consult Vergil directly, Shakespeare certainly took on board much of his interpretation via Hall and Holinshed. He may also have drawn, again most probably indirectly, on Robert Fabian's *New Chronicles of England and of France* and Sir Thomas More's *History of King Richard III* (both of early Tudor date). For particular plays, he might even have accessed more strictly contemporary sources (for instance, for *Richard II*, Jean Froissart's *Chronicle*, in John Bourchier Lord Berner's early sixteenth-century English translation).

By the time he commenced work on *Richard II* in the mid-1590s William Shakespeare probably already had in mind the two parts of *Henry IV* and *Henry V* as well, for Richard II's deposition dogs the entire reign of the first Lancastrian king and it is only when Henry V embarks on his French adventures that the shadow of 1399 is temporarily lifted. The personal and political shortcomings of the king, leading inexorably to Henry Bolingbroke's usurpation in 1399, provide the central theme of exploration throughout *Richard II* (although only the last two years of the reign figure in the action). There is plenty of opportunity, too, for Shakespeare to examine the nature of kingship, the awesome challenge of reigning successfully and the dire consequences of royal failure, not least via the medium of Richard II's own speeches. Here, for instance, is Richard's firm statement of a king's divinely ordained right to rule:

> Not all the water in the rough rude sea
> Can wash the balm off from an anointed king;
> The breath of worldly men cannot depose
> The deputy elected by the Lord.

Yet, a little later, he ruminates gloomily on what fates might nonetheless await a king:

> For God's sake let us sit upon the ground
> And tell sad stories of the death of kings;
> How some have been depos'd, some slain in war,
> Some haunted by the ghosts they have depos'd,
> Some poison'd by their wives, some sleeping kill'd,
> All murder'd. For within the hollow crown

> That rounds the mortal temples of a king
> Keeps Death his court.

Significantly, *Richard II* ends with Henry IV's pledge to undertake a pilgrimage as a penance for his predecessor's violent deaths:

> I'll make a voyage to the Holy Land,
> To wash this blood off from my guilty hand.

And, at the beginning of *1 Henry IV*, he makes a heart-felt plea for peace and stability:

> No more the thirsty entrance of this soil
> Shall daub her lips with her own children's blood;
> No more shall trenching war channel her fields,
> Nor bruise her flow'rets with the armed hoofs
> Of hostile paces. Those opposed eyes
> Which, like the meteors of a troubled heaven,
> All of one nature, of one substance bred,
> Did lately meet in the intestine shock
> And furious close of civil butchery,
> Shall now in mutual well-beseeming ranks
> March all one way, and be no more oppos'd
> Against acquaintances, kindred and allies.

Such hopes proved in vain since, ever overshadowed by the events of 1399 and despite all the king's efforts, Henry IV's reign (and Shakespeare's *1 Henry IV* and *2 Henry IV*) was dominated by rebellion, warfare and even the unruly behaviour of his son and heir. Finally, struck down by terminal illness, Shakespeare's Henry IV voices a truly poignant lament:

> How many thousand of my poorest subjects
> Are at this hour asleep? O sleep, O gentle sleep,
> Nature's soft nurse, how have I frighted thee,
> That thou no more wilt weigh my eyelids down,
> And steep my senses in forgetfulness?...
> Canst thou, O partial sleep, give thy repose
> To the wet sea-boy in an hour so rude;
> And in the calmest and most stillest night,
> With all appliances and means to boot,
> Deny it to a king? Then, happy low, lie down!
> Uneasy lies the head that wears a crown.

Henry V is surely the oddest of Shakespeare's history plays as the playwright, for once, turned his talents to portraying a veritable hero-king. Indeed, only by employing his military talents in a glorious and successful war against England's traditional enemy (the French) can the second Lancastrian king, at last, rise above the legacy of 1399. And, although the play is more than a simple glorification of the archetypal warrior king, no patriotic Elizabethan could fail to respond to such uplifting speeches as Henry V's to his troops at Agincourt:

> This day is called the feast of Crispian.
> He that outlives this day and comes safe home,
> Will stand a tip-toe when this day is nam'd
> And rouse him at the name of Crispian...
> Old men forget; yet all shall be forgot,
> But he'll remember, with advantages,
> What feats he did that day...
> This story shall the good man teach his son;
> And Crispin Crispian shall ne're go by,
> From this day to the ending of the world,
> But we in it shall be remembered –
> We few, we happy few, we band of brothers;
> For he today that sheds his blood with me
> Shall be my brother; be he ne're so vile,
> This day shall gentle his condition;
> And gentlemen in England now a-bed
> Shall think themselves accurs'd that were not here,
> And hold their manhoods cheap whiles any speaks
> That fought with us upon Saint Crispin's day.

In the three parts of *Henry VI* and *Richard III* William Shakespeare charts how, once Henry V's crown passed to his hapless son and successor Henry VI, unfettered aristocratic ambitions and rivalries brought the loss of the Lancastrian empire in France, bloody civil war in England and, eventually, the rise and fall of the murdering tyrant Richard III. *1 Henry VI*, narrating the dismal story of English failure in France, is clearly a young man's play but it does present a compelling picture of John Talbot Earl of Shrewsbury, whose admirable patriotism and noble military endeavours are fatally under-mined by aristocratic back-biting and discord, and Joan of Arc, whose own courage and nationalistic fervour are set at naught by the immorality and 'devilish witchcraft and sorcery' which, eventually, bring her to the stake as both a strumpet and an enchantress. Here, too, are to be found the first hints of the imminent Wars of the Roses, the origins of which provide the central theme for *2 Henry VI*. Opening with the arrival of Queen Margaret of

Anjou in England in 1445 and ending with Richard Duke of York's victory at the battle of St Albans in 1455, *2 Henry VI* is clearly superior to *1 Henry VI* in construction and more sophisticated in both its delineation of personality (for instance, Henry VI's domineering and ruthless queen) and the handling of dramatic action. Not only does Shakespeare cover political intrigue and aristocratic discord at the highest level as Henry VI's government disintegrates, he also highlights the mounting social discontent fuelling Jack Cade's rebellion. Very much reflecting his own age's fear of popular unrest and its potentially dire consequences, however, he depicts Cade's men as a 'rabblement', an ignorant mob who threaten the country's social stability, just as a quarrelling nobility disrupts its political well-being, and he certainly has no sympathy for Jack Cade himself:

> Die, damned wretch, the curse of her that bare thee!
> And as I thrust thy body in with my sword,
> So wish I might thrust thy soul to hell.
> Hence will I drag thee headlong by the heels
> Unto a dunghill, which shall be thy grave,
> And there cut off thy most ungracious head,
> Which I will bear in triumph to the King,
> Leaving thy trunk for crows to feed upon.

3 Henry VI, a fast-moving and action-packed narrative play, tells the story of the Wars of the Roses from 1460 to 1471. Richard of York's regal ambitions are dashed when he loses his life at Wakefield but realised by his son when he seizes the throne as Edward IV; the new king's ill-advised marriage to Lady Grey alienates the Earl of Warwick who then engineers the restoration of Henry VI; Edward IV, in response, rallies his own supporters and wins the battles of Barnet and Tewkesbury; and Lancastrian hopes are finally destroyed by the ruthless murder of both Henry VI himself and his only son. By assigning a prominent role in these dramatic events to Edward IV's brother, Richard Duke of Gloucester, Shakespeare also sets the scene for *Richard III*:

> ...since this earth affords no joy to me
> But to command, to check, to o'erbear such
> As are of better person than myself,
> I'll make my heaven to dream upon the crown,
> And whiles I live t'account this world but hell,
> Until my misshap'd trunk that bears this head
> Be round impaled with a glorious crown.

The playwright's maturing confidence and skill at his craft, already evident in

2 Henry VI and *3 Henry VI*, are even more apparent in *Richard III*. Indeed, this play was probably Shakespeare's first major success and creating the title role also made the reputation of the actor Richard Burbage (son of James who, in 1576, had built the *Theatre* in Shoreditch). Extending from Edward IV's triumph over the Lancastrians in 1471 to Henry Tudor Earl of Richmond's victory at Bosworth in 1485, it chronicles the sequence of political intrigues and string of murders (including his own brother Clarence, his nephews, even his wife) whereby Richard III first secured, then sought to consolidate his hold upon, the English throne. Shakespeare's second longest play (only *Hamlet* is longer), it is dominated throughout by the evil, ruthless yet curiously engaging king himself, until the monstrous tyrant's ignominious death on the battlefield at last opens up the prospect of 'smooth-fac'd peace', 'smiling plenty' and 'fair prosperous days'.

KINGS, QUEENS AND MAGNATES IN SHAKESPEARE'S HISTORY PLAYS

Although traditionally acknowledged as author of plays about King John and Henry VIII, and more recently Edward III as well, William Shakespeare can most confidently be credited with dramatic portrayals of Richard II, Henry IV, Henry V, Henry VI, Edward IV, Richard III and their times. Moreover, when bringing the turbulent politics and endemic warfare of fifteenth-century England to the Elizabethan stage, he clearly regarded the unfolding of events as very much governed by the characters and choices of individual men and women.

Richard II is very much the central figure of the play that bears his name and Shakespeare was all too evidently fascinated by the enigmatic personality he found in his sources. Was he, perhaps, a man whose flawed character and impossibly high kingly ideals spawned the tyrannical behaviour that eventually brought his deposition? Or was he a tragic victim of circumstances beyond his control? Shakespeare's Richard II is certainly acutely aware of his God-given regality, as he makes clear when addressing a rebellious Henry Percy Earl of Northumberland:

> We are amaz'd; and thus long have we stood
> To watch the fearful bending of thy knee
> Because we thought ourself thy lawful King;
> And if we be, how dare thy joints forget
> To pay their awful duty to our presence?
> If we be not, show us the hand of God
> That hath dismiss'd us from our stewardship;
> For well we know no hand of blood and bone

> Can grip the sacred handle of our sceptre,
> Unless he do profane, steal or usurp.

'My master, God omnipotent', he further asserts:

> Is mustering in his clouds on our behalf
> Armies of pestilence; and they shall strike
> Your children yet unborn and unbegot,
> That lift your vassal hands against my head
> And threat the glory of my precious crown.

For much of the play, Richard II's personal shortcomings and political mistakes, although not unduly dwelt upon, are nevertheless evident enough, and the reasons why most of the nobility choose to back Henry Bolingbroke are only too apparent. When news of John of Gaunt's death reaches him, Northumberland declares:

> The King is not himself, but basely led
> By flatterers; and what they will inform
> Merely in hate, 'gainst any of us all,
> That will the King severely prosecute
> 'Gainst us, our lives, our children and our heirs.

And Lord Ross, in turn, remarks:

> The commons hath he pill'd with grievous taxes;
> And quite lost their hearts; the nobles hath he fin'd
> For ancient quarrels and quite lost their hearts.

Richard II's surrender, abdication and death clearly arouse a real measure of sympathy in Shakespeare, however, as well as inspiring poetic lyricism of a very high order. At the end, indeed, the king becomes a truly tragic figure, melancholic and genuinely dignified in defeat:

> I give this heavy weight from off my head,
> And this unwieldy sceptre from my hand,
> The pride of kingly sway from out my heart;
> With mine own tears I wash away my balm,
> With mine own hands I give away my crown.

The Lancastrian king of *1 Henry IV* and *2 Henry IV* can never rise above the circumstances of his accession or cast aside his responsibility for Richard

II's death. 'So shaken as we are, so wan with care' are his very first words in *1 Henry IV* and when, later in the play, his son Prince Henry's wild behaviour is causing concern, he addresses him more in sorrow than in anger:

> I know not whether God will have it so,
> For some displeasing service I have done,
> That, in his secret doom, out of my blood,
> He'll breed revengement and a scourge for me;
> But thou dost in thy passages of life
> Make me believe that thou art only mark'd
> For the hot vengeance and the rod of heaven
> To punish my mistreadings.

Moreover, although Henry IV strives throughout to be a conscientious and just ruler, his rebellion-packed reign and his son's apparent lack of aptitude for future regality ensure he never finds peace of mind. Eventually, exhausted by strife and fatally weakened by sickness, he dies prematurely and, right to the end, remains haunted by his earlier sin of usurpation. 'God knows my son', he muses to Prince Henry as he contemplates imminent death in *2 Henry IV*:

> By what by-paths and indirect crook'd ways
> I met this crown; and I myself know well
> How troublesome it sat upon my head.

In *1 Henry IV* and *2 Henry IV* William Shakespeare, very much in line with chronicle tradition, paints a portrait of Prince Henry as a wild and headstrong youth, albeit a young man always rather aloof from his rumbustious companions and well aware of his future responsibilities:

> I know you all, and will a while uphold
> The unyok'd humour of your idleness;
> Yet herein will I imitate the sun,
> Who doth permit the base contagious clouds
> To smother up his beauty from the world,
> That, when he please again to be himself,
> Being wanted, he may be more wond'red at
> By breaking through the foul and ugly mists
> Of vapours that did seem to strangle him.

Long before his father's death there are strong hints of sterling qualities and, once king himself, they rapidly manifest themselves:

> The tide of blood in me
> Hath proudly flow'd in vanity till now.
> Now doth it turn and ebb back to the sea,
> Where it shall mingle with the state of floods,
> And flow henceforth in formal majesty.

In *Henry V* Shakespeare, probably not very comfortably, allows the king to blossom into the epic embodiment of military heroism so dear to the hearts of Tudor myth-makers, the 'mirror of all Christian kings': serious minded, concerned for the welfare of his subjects and, above all, an archetypal man of action. Such, certainly, is the Henry V who so compellingly inspires his troops at the siege of Harfleur:

> Once more unto the breach dear friends, once more;
> Or close the wall up with our English dead...
> Stiffen the sinews, summon up the blood,
> Disguise fair nature with hard-favour'd rage...
> Now set the teeth and stretch the nostril wide;
> Hold hard the breath, and bend up every spirit
> To his full heart. On, on, you noblest English...

'And you, good yeomen', he continues as the oration reaches its climax:

> Whose limbs were made in England, show us here
> The mettle of your pasture; let us swear
> That you are worth your breeding – which I doubt not;
> For there is none of you so mean and base
> That hath not noble lustre in your eyes.
> I see you stand like greyhounds in the slips,
> Straining upon the start. The game's afoot:
> Follow your spirit; and upon this charge
> Cry 'God for Harry, England and Saint George!'

Yet Henry V's French campaigns may, in part at least, be seen as the product of an urgent need to win honour and renown so as to offset his questionable right to the English throne and, certainly, however glorious his achievements in life, they are doomed to be sadly squandered after his death by his pious and pacific son, Henry VI.

Far from dominating the three plays that bear his name, Shakespeare's Henry VI, described in life as 'gentle, mild and virtuous', becomes, in death:

> Poor key-cold figure of a holy king,
> Pale ashes of the house of Lancaster.

A truly dramatic contrast to his warlike father, he is a highly gullible, easily led man, always inclined to peace rather than war and, indeed, horrified by bloodshed. He fails to prevent the loss of Henry V's lands in France and, worse still, presides over England's subsequent and relentless descent into civil war. When confronted by the upheavals of Cade's rebellion in *2 Henry VI*, he remarks prophetically to Margaret of Anjou:

> Come, wife, let's in and learn to govern better;
> For yet may England curse my wretched reign.

Later, in *3 Henry VI*, bemoaning the chaos, confusion and outright civil war his rule has duly brought, he laments:

> O God! methinks it were a happy life
> To be no better than a homely swain;
> To sit upon a hill, as I do now…
> O piteous spectacle! O bloody times!
> Whiles lions roar and battle for their dens,
> Poor harmless lambs abide their enmity.

And Lord Clifford, mortally wounded in battle, certainly places the blame firmly on Henry VI's shoulders:

> …hadst thou sway'd as kings should do,
> Or as thy father and his father did,
> Giving no ground unto the house of York,
> They never then had sprung like summer flies!
> I and ten thousand in this luckless realm
> Had left no mourning widows for our death.

All Shakespeare's history plays feature powerful magnates sometimes supporting, often resisting, occasionally even deposing, reigning kings. Frequently, too, we are treated to the spectacle of ambitious aristocrats at odds with one another. *Richard II* opens with the quarrel of Henry Bolingbroke, son of 'Old John of Gaunt, time-honoured Lancaster', and Thomas Mowbray Duke of Norfolk; it ends with Bolingbroke, now in rebellious alliance with Henry Percy Earl of Northumberland, seizing the crown for himself. *1 Henry IV* is dominated throughout by armed resistance to the first Lancastrian king, Northumberland's son Hotspur playing a particularly prominent role until his death at the battle of Shrewsbury. Indeed, the vigorous and warlike Hotspur even inspires Henry IV to castigate his own son and heir Prince Henry for his very lack of such sterling qualities:

> Now, by my sceptre and my soul to boot,
> He hath more worthy interest to the state
> Than thou the shadow of succession;
> For of no right, nor colour like to right,
> He doth fill fields with harness in the realm;
> Turns head against the lion's armed jaws;
> And, being no more in debt to years than thou,
> Leads ancient lords and reverend bishops on
> To bloody battles and to bruising arms.

In *Henry V* the new king faces an aristocratic conspiracy on the very eve of his invasion of France but, in contrast to his father, his reaction is confident, swift and merciless:

> Get you therefore hence,
> Poor miserable wretches, to your death;
> The taste whereof God of his mercy give
> You patience to endure, and true repentance
> Of all your dear offences. Bear them hence.
> Now, lords, for France; the enterprise whereof
> Shall be to you as us like glorious.

However, it is in the three parts of *Henry VI* that Shakespeare most thoroughly explores the personal ambitions of powerful magnates and the dire consequences for the country of a lethal combination of dynastic rivalry and aristocratic feuding. In *1 Henry VI* John Talbot Earl of Shrewsbury gallantly dons the mantle of leadership but the probable outcome of his endeavours is already becoming apparent when he confronts Joan of Arc at Orleans:

> Where is my strength, my valour, and my force?
> Our English troops retire, I cannot stay them;
> A woman clad in armour chaseth them…
> Hark, countrymen! Either renew the fight
> Or tear the lions out of England's coat…

Perhaps if all the English nobility had been like Talbot, the results might have been different, both in France and England. Unfortunately, they are seriously divided amongst themselves. Early in *2 Henry VI*, indeed, 'Good

Duke Humphrey' of Gloucester, the king's uncle and an undoubted patriot, is overthrown and murdered by his enemies (headed by the grasping Cardinal Beaufort and self-seeking Duke of Suffolk) while, even before that, the ambitious and calculating Richard Duke of York has proclaimed his objective of claiming Henry VI's throne for himself once the time is ripe:

> Then will I raise aloft the milk-white rose,
> With whose sweet smell the air shall be perfum'd,
> And in my standard bear the arms of York,
> To grapple with the house of Lancaster;
> And force perforce I'll make him yield the crown,
> Whose bookish rule hath pull'd fair England down.

When sent to Ireland to put down a rebellion, he realises his opportunity has now arrived:

> Whiles I in Ireland nourish a mighty hand,
> I will stir up in England some black storm
> Shall blow ten thousand souls to heaven or hell;
> And this fell tempest shall not cease to rage
> Until the golden circuit on my head,
> Like to the glorious sun's transparent beams,
> Do calm the fury of this mad-bred flaw.
> And for a minister of my intent
> I have seduced a headstrong Kentishman,
> John Cade of Ashford,
> To make commotion, as full well he can,
> Under the title of John Mortimer.

Cade's rebellion fails but York's ambitions remain undaunted and *2 Henry VI* ends with his victory over the Lancastrians at the battle of St Albans. At the beginning of *3 Henry VI* York formally sets out his claim to the crown in parliament but, although he accepts a compromise whereby Henry VI can remain a nominal king for the rest of his life, Margaret of Anjou is not prepared to countenance her son's exclusion from the succession. The resulting battle of Wakefield culminates in Richard of York's humiliation and death, while Margaret of Anjou revels in her triumph:

> Off with his head, and set it on York gates;
> So York may overlook the town of York.

Queens, indeed women generally, play relatively minor roles in Shakespeare's history plays, apart from Joan of Arc in *1 Henry VI* and, of course, the domineering and single-minded Margaret of Anjou. Richard II's queen is a sorrowing observer of her husband's downfall but little more; Henry IV's never appears at all; and, although Henry V woos the French princess who is soon to become his wife, she is a mere foil for the king's amorous advances. Several decades later, Lady Grey allows herself to be cajoled into marriage by Edward IV (in 3 *Henry VI*), while the king's brothers are clearly angered by her dubious political and social credentials and, later, her behaviour as queen. Richard of Gloucester in *Richard III*. for instance, blames her for Clarence's arrest and imprisonment:

> ...this is when men are rul'd by women:
> 'Tis not the King that sends you to the Tower;
> My Lady his wife, Clarence, 'tis she
> That tempers him to this extremity.

And the queen herself, in turn, complains of Gloucester's 'interior hatred' for herself, her brothers and her children:

> My Lord of Gloucester, I have too long borne
> Your blunt upbraidings and your bitter scoffs.
> By heaven, I will acquaint his Majesty
> Of those gross taunts that oft I have endur'd.
> I had rather be a country servant-maid
> Than a great queen with this condition –
> To be so baited, scorn'd and stormed at.

After her husband's death, she becomes an even more implacable critic, particularly once Richard III has murdered her young sons:

> Th'imperial metal, circling now thy head,
> Had grac'd the tender temples of my child;
> And both the Princes had been breathing here,
> Which now, two tender bedfellows for dust,
> Thy broken faith hath made the prey to worms.

As for Richard III's own queen, after a macabre wooing beside the coffin of her murdered father-in-law, Henry VI, she is scarcely heard of again until, on the very eve of Bosworth, her spirit returns to haunt her husband's dreams:

> Richard, thy wife, that wretched Anne thy wife
> That never slept a quiet hour with thee
> Now fills thy sleep with perturbations.
> Tomorrow in the battle think on me,
> And fall thy edgeless sword. Despair and die.

Queen Margaret of Anjou, a central figure in Shakespeare's Wars of the Roses plays, is formidable indeed. Energetic, single-minded, ruthless, cruel and pitiless in pursuit of her overtly political objectives, she soon seeks consolation for her pathetic husband's inadequacies in the arms of the Duke of Suffolk and, once her son has been born, becomes a truly unbending champion of the house of Lancaster. The 'She-wolf of France', judged even by her opponent Richard of York to possess a 'tiger's heart wrapt in a woman's hide', she is forever railing at Henry VI, particularly once he has acquiesced in Prince Edward of Lancaster's disinheritance:

> Ah, wretched man! Would I had died a maid
> And never seen thee, never borne thee son,
> Seeing thou hast prov'd so unnatural a father!
> ...Ah, timorous wretch!
> Thou hast undone thyself, thy son and me;
> And given unto the house of York such heed
> As thou shalt reign but by their sufferance.
> ...I here dissolve myself
> Both from thy table, Henry, and thy bed,
> Until that act of parliament be repeal'd
> Whereby my son is disinherited.

Once 'proud ambitious Edward Duke of York' has usurped the 'regal title and seat' of 'England's true-anointed lawful king', moreover, she is even prepared, in her son's interest, to back her erstwhile foe the Earl of Warwick. And when, in the aftermath of Edward IV's victory at Tewkesbury, both her husband and her son are murdered, Margaret's implacability towards the house of York knows no bounds, especially once Shakespeare has made her the prophetess of vengeance against Richard III:

> ...at hand, at hand,
> Ensues his piteous and unpitied end,
> Earth gapes, hell burns, fiends roar, saints pray,
> To have him suddenly conveyed from hence.
> Cancel his bond of life, dear God, I pray,
> That I may live and say 'The dog is dead'.

Edward IV, unlike his brother and eventual successor Richard III, receives relatively scant attention from William Shakespeare and, of course, no Shakespearian play actually bears his name. Indeed, the king tends to be pushed into the background by both his greatest subject, the Earl of Warwick (the 'Kingmaker') and his younger brother, Richard of Gloucester. When news of his father's death at Wakefield reaches young Edward Earl of March, he promptly turns to Warwick for sympathy and support:

> Lord Warwick, on thy shoulders will I lean;
> And when thou fail'st – as God forbid the hour! –
> Must Edward fall, which peril heaven forfend.

'Proud setter up and puller down of kings', Margaret of Anjou later dubs him, and certainly, in *3 Henry VI*, Warwick's role is pivotal in enabling his young protégé to seize the crown. Edward IV himself, by contrast, is the 'lascivious Edward', the king who marries 'more for wanton lust than honour' or the 'strength and safety of our country', and who loses Warwick's backing, even temporarily the throne, as a result. Nevertheless, he manages to win back his crown and can now confidently anticipate a return to the pleasures of former times:

> And now what rests but that we spend the time
> With stately triumphs, mirthful comic shows,
> Such as befits the pleasures of the court?
> Sound drums and trumpets. Farewell, sore annoy!
> For here, I hope, begins our lasting joy.

In his last years, however, Edward IV becomes 'sickly, weak and melancholy', having 'kept an evil diet long' and 'overmuch consum'd his royal person', and, early in *Richard III*, his 'sickly heart' finally fails him.

Richard III is William Shakespeare's first great villain and his portrayal of the king, very much reflecting the Tudor sources he drew upon, can be regarded as the magnificent dramatic climax of almost a century of ever-growing denigration. Not only does the king dominate *Richard III*, moreover, he threatens to take over *3 Henry VI* as well, and, more often than not, he is both an evil ruthless plotter and a man who takes a positive delight in his own wickedness. In a splendid soliloquy towards the end of *3 Henry VI* he declares unequivocally:

> I am myself alone.
> Clarence, beware; thou keep'st me from the light;
> But I will sort a pitchy day for thee;

> For I will buzz abroad such prophecies
> That Edward shall be fearful for his life;
> And then to purge his fear, I'll be thy death.
> King Henry and the Prince his son are gone.
> Clarence, thy turn is next, and then the rest;
> Counting myself but bad till I be best.

And, again, at the beginning of *Richard III*:

> Plots have I laid, inductions dangerous,
> By drunken prophecies, libels and dreams,
> To set my brother Clarence and the King
> In deadly hate the one against the other.

Throughout, too, Shakespeare makes much of Richard III's physical deformities since, in the plays, his monstrous appearance is very much an outward manifestation of the king's warped character. In *3 Henry VI* he remarks that, 'since the heavens have shap'd my body so, let hell make crook'd my mind to answer it', while, in the opening soliloquy of *Richard III*, he represents himself as:

> Cheated of feature by dissembling nature,
> Deform'd, unfinish'd, sent before my time
> Into this breathing world scarce half made up,
> And that so lamely and unfashionable
> That dogs bark at me as I halt by them.

Therefore, he continues, since he cannot play a lover, he is 'determined to prove a villain'. As for Richard III's critics, they variously describe him as the crook-back, the 'foul misshapen stigmatic', the 'elvish-marked abortive rooting hog', the 'bottled spider' and the 'poisonous bunch-backed toad'. Temperamentally, the king is 'the dreadful minister of hell' who, 'having neither pity, love nor fear', can 'smile and murder while I smile'. First appearing in *2 Henry VI* as the Duke of Somerset's slayer at the battle of St Albans (when the *historical* Richard III was not yet three years old), his catalogue of crimes in *3 Henry VI* and *Richard III* is impressive indeed, most notably the elimination of Prince Edward of Lancaster (stabbed after Tewkesbury), Henry VI and Clarence (killed in the Tower of London) and, of course, his own nephews the Princes in the Tower. Magnates standing in his way – Hastings, Rivers, Grey, Vaughan and Buckingham – all bite the dust as well. And, on the very eve of Bosworth, the ghosts of no fewer than eleven of his victims deliberately disturb his uneasy slumbers. No wonder, since Shakespeare's portrayal of Richard III's character and behaviour is so devastating, it has become virtually synonymous with popular perceptions of England's last Plantagenet king.

THE WARS OF THE ROSES IN SHAKESPEARE'S HISTORY PLAYS

On the verge of death in *Richard II* the elderly John of Gaunt Duke of Lancaster conjures up the spirit of an England that William Shakespeare and many patriotic Elizabethans might well have wished to see recreated in their own troubled, post-Spanish Armada times:

> This royal throne of kings, this scept'red isle,
> This earth of Majesty, this seat of Mars,
> This other Eden, demi-paradise,
> This fortress built by Nature for herself
> Against infection and the hand of war,
> This happy breed of men, this little world,
> This precious stone set in the silver sea,
> Which serves it in the office of a wall,
> Or as a moat defensive to a house,
> Against the envy of less happier lands;
> This blessed plot, this earth, this realm, this England...

If such an idyllic vision had any reality at all in the later fourteenth century, it was rudely shattered when John of Gaunt's son deposed Richard II and seized the English crown for himself. Indeed, as Shakespeare and his contemporaries saw it, the events of 1399 precipitated almost a century of dynastic conflict, political turmoil and, eventually, bloody civil war, a coherent and compelling theme for an eight play Plantagenet history cycle.

Clearly, in Tudor times, the usurpation of Henry IV tended to be regarded as a sacrilegious act interrupting the divinely laid down succession of God's anointed, a kind of original sin for which England and her rulers inevitably suffered greatly in the years to come. Thus, in *Richard II*, the Bishop of Carlisle predicts (on the occasion of the king's deposition) that:

> The blood of English shall manure the ground,
> And future ages groan for this foul act;
> Peace shall go sleep with Turks and infidels,
> And in this seat of peace tumultuous wars
> Shall kin with kin and kind with kind confound;
> Disorder, horror, fear, and mutiny,

> Shall here inhabit, and this land be call'd
> The field of Golgotha and dead men's skulls.

On the very eve of Agincourt, in *Henry V*, the king is haunted by the events of 1399:

> Not today, O Lord,
> O, not today, think not upon the fault
> My father made in compassing the crown!
> I Richard's body have interred new,
> And on it have bestow'd more contrite tears
> Than from it issu'd forced drops of blood.

The sin of Henry IV is certainly visited on his hapless grandson Henry VI when Richard of York challenges his right to the throne and the Wars of the Roses result. As the Yorkist leader puts it in *2 Henry VI*:

> From Ireland thus comes York to claim his right
> And pluck the crown from feeble Henry's head.
> Ring bells aloud, burn bonfires clear and bright,
> To entertain great England's lawful king.

'I am far better born than is the king', he adds, 'more like a king, more kingly in my thoughts', and, addressing Henry VI personally:

> King did I call thee? No, thou art not king;
> Not fit to govern and rule multitudes...
> That head of thine doth not become a crown;
> Thy hand is made to grasp a palmer's staff,
> And not to grace an awful princely sceptre.
> That gold must round engirt these brows of mine...
> Here is a hand to hold a sceptre up,
> And with the same to act controlling laws.
> Give place. By heaven, thou shalt rule no more
> O'er him whom heaven created for your ruler.

When Richard of York's son seizes the crown as Edward IV he, too, breaches a solemn oath and pays the price when his brother not only murders Edward's sons but also usurps the throne himself. In William Shakespeare's *Richard III*, in fact, the inexorable sequence of events stemming from 1399 reaches its climax, culminating in Richard III's defeat and death at Bosworth and Henry Tudor Earl of Richmond's taking of the crown, as prophesied by his Lancastrian predecessor in *3 Henry VI* when he meets the young Henry:

> Come hither, England's hope. If secret powers
> Suggest but truth to my divining thoughts,
> This pretty lad will prove our country's bliss.
> His looks are full of peaceful majesty;
> His head by nature fram'd to wear a crown,
> His hand to wield a sceptre; and himself
> Likely in time to bless a regal throne.

Only with Henry VII's accession and his marriage to Edward IV's daughter Elizabeth of York (uniting, at last, the two warring dynasties) is the sorry saga of the Wars of the Roses brought to an end and the way cleared for the glories of Tudor rule. Indeed, at the end of *Richard III*, Richmond triumphantly proclaims:

> We will unite the white rose and the red —
> Smile heaven upon this fair conjunction,
> That long have frowned upon their enmity…
> O, now, let Richmond and Elizabeth,
> The true successors of each royal house,
> By God's fair ordinance conjoin together…
> Now civil wounds are stopp'd, peace lives again —
> That she may long live here, God say amen!

The Wars of the Roses themselves are portrayed by William Shakespeare as a depressing catalogue of battles, executions, murders, treachery and unrivalled lust for power, dominated, in particular, by bloodfeuds and their consequences. Thus Margaret of Anjou has Richard of York killed and, in revenge, York's sons murder her son, Prince Edward of Lancaster and her husband, Henry VI. The killers of Edward IV's brother George Duke of Clarence tell him that he deserves God's punishment for breaking a solemn oath and stabbing Prince Edward and Richard, similarly, must pay with his life for causing the deaths of his brother, his nephews, his wife and his closest associates. Shakespeare explores this theme most graphically in the great battle scenes in *3 Henry VI*. Following the battle of St Albans, Henry VI declares:

> Earl of Northumberland, he [York] slew thy father,
> And thine, Lord Clifford; and you both have vow'd revenge
> On him, his sons, his favourites and his friends.

At Wakefield, Clifford, to avenge his father's death, seeks out York's son Rutland and kills him, declaring as he does so:

> Had I thy brethren here, their lives and thine
> Were not revenge sufficient for me;
> No, if I digg'd up thy forefathers graves
> And hung their rotton coffins up in chains,
> I could not shake mine ire nor ease my heart.
> The sight of any of the house of York
> Is as a fury to torment my soul;
> And till I root out their accursed line
> And leave not one alive, I live in hell.

Then, at Towton, there is the famous scene where a son kills his father and a father his son: 'I, who at his hands receiv'd my life', cries the son, 'have by my hands bereaved him'; 'O boy, thy father gave thee life', echoes the father, 'and hath bereft thee of thy life too late'. Henry VI, sadly viewing all this, comments bitterly:

> O that my death would stay these rueful deeds –
> O pity, pity, gentle heaven, pity! –
> The red rose and the white are on his face,
> The fatal colours of our striving houses…

And, in his valedictory speech at the end of *Richard III* Richmond declares:

> England hath long been mad, and scarr'd herself;
> The brother blindly shed the brother's blood,
> The father rashly slaughter'd his own son,
> The son, compell'd, been butcher to the sire;
> All this divided York and Lancaster.

2

RICHARD II, HENRY IV AND THE ESTABLISHMENT OF THE LANCASTRIAN DYNASTY

LATER MEDIEVAL KINGS, POLITICS AND WAR

William Shakespeare, in his eight play Plantagenet history cycle, chose to focus on kings, magnates and the importance of crown/baronial relations in later medieval England, while warfare (whether at home or abroad) and its consequences provided a no less central dramatic theme. Clearly, the playwright very much reflected here both the historical stance of his Tudor sources and the need, as an up-and-coming dramatist, to appeal to Elizabethan audiences. Even so, such a portrayal of the English realm was by no means wide of the mark and historians, too, have always been inclined to highlight the pivotal role of kings, magnates and war in fourteenth and fifteenth-century English politics and society.

Political power in the later medieval English state remained, as it had long been, very much concentrated in the crown and the consequences could be catastrophic if a monarch proved unfit to rule. Here, indeed, is the key to much of the political turbulence and social disruption during times when, whether by reason of tender years, personal ineptitude or mental incapacity, kings too often proved singularly ill-equipped for the job they had to do, most notably Edward II, Richard II and, worst of all, Henry VI. Such rulers, inevitably, had problems when it came to controlling political society in general and the great landed aristocracy in particular. The monarchy found itself having to resist the claims and contain the ambitions of nobility and greater gentry while, at the same time, being quite unable to function effectively without their support, especially when it came to fighting the French and the Scots. In fact, success or failure at ruling in the later Middle

Ages is almost indistinguishable from success or failure in handling the magnates. Thus, in the fourteenth century, two kings who failed to get on with the baronage – Edward II and Richard II – were deposed and, indeed, murdered, while a third – Edward III – who, for most of his reign, managed to achieve an effective working relationship with his great men, was still England's unchallenged ruler at his death. Similarly, in the fifteenth century, the military achievements of Henry V in France depended on his ability to work hand-in-glove with the nobility, while Henry VI's failure to contain baronial rivalries eventually brought him to the same fate as Edward II and Richard II. Indeed, so great was Henry VI's incompetence, and so powerful the feuding nobility, that England dissolved into full-scale civil war. Even the first Tudor monarch, Henry VII, for all his reputation as the king who put an end to dynastic strife and perhaps even laid the foundations of Tudor despotism, had no choice but to secure and hold the loyalty of the English nobility and gentry.

Scarcely less significant as a determinant of monarchical success or failure was warfare. Medieval kings were expected to lead their great men in war and if they did so triumphantly their reputations were assured. Both Edward III and Henry V secured notable successes against the French – including victory in great pitched battles like Crécy (1346), Poitiers (1356) and Agincourt (1415) – and these ensured an enthusiastic verdict in many contemporary and near-contemporary sources. Edward II, by contrast, failed dismally against the Scots at Bannockburn (in 1314), while Richard II's predilection for peace rather than war mightily aroused the misgivings of his magnates. Henry VI, too, had no aptitude or enthusiasm for war: indeed, his pursuit of peace at any price in the 1440s eventually brought the end of the Lancastrian empire in France. War, moreover, whether successful or not, frequently brought financial problems for later medieval governments and these, in turn, proved a major factor in the evolution of parliament as a means of raising extra cash through the medium of taxation. Later medieval governments, by and large, had an appalling record in matters financial. Even Henry V was heavily in debt by the time of his death, while Henry VI's government failed dismally on the financial front and was virtually bankrupt by the 1450s. Only during the reigns of the Yorkist kings Edward IV and Richard III did royal finances show real signs of improvement and Henry VII was able to build on Yorkist financial foundations. Parliament particularly flourished when kings were inept and government weak: in 1376, for instance, the Commons in parliament launched a vigorous attack on royal ministers and corruption now Edward III was too senile to lead and rule; Henry IV, an insecure usurper of the throne, had no choice but to make concessions to parliament; and the shortcomings of Henry VI and his government provoked much criticism, even resistance, in parliament in the 1440s and 1450s. Even Edward IV, in his penurious early years, had to handle parliament with considerable care. Only when effective government and a sound financial base began to be restored by the Yorkists (after 1471) and Henry VII did parliament become more quiescent and co-operative.

What of the law, and law and order? Kings were seen as the fount of justice and, as far as most people were concerned, justice meant maintaining law and order in the country and enabling men and women to follow their lawful pursuits in peace. Certainly, royal justice became increasingly sophisticated, with professional judges both sitting in great central law courts and perambulating around the country dispensing justice, while these centuries also saw the growing use of influential country gentry in the shires as justices of the peace. Just how effective justice was, and how far law and order was indeed maintained, again owed much to the king himself and the quality of leadership he provided.

EDWARD II, EDWARD III AND THE HUNDRED YEARS WAR 1307-1377

Although William Shakespeare never tackled the turbulent reign of Edward II (1307-1327), Christopher Marlowe did. His play *Edward II* was probably first performed in 1592. Central to the play, and its driving force, is Edward II's wilful yet indomitable character: frivolous, foolish and petulant, fatally susceptible to flattery by ill-chosen friends, incapable of placating baronial enemies and devoid of all military prowess, his manifold personal defects lead inexorably to deposition and death. Such a portrayal, moreover, very much reflects contemporary and near-contemporary judgements on the king. According to one anonymous chronicler, it was 'commonly reported' that Edward II:

> ...devoted himself privately from his youth to the arts of rowing and driving chariots, digging pits and roofing houses, [and] other mechanical arts, besides other vanities and frivolities unbecoming in a king's son.

During the king's own lifetime, a perceptive and well-informed biographer recorded that:

> ...if he had followed the advice of the barons, he would have humiliated the Scots with ease. If he had habituated himself to the use of arms, he would have exceeded the prowess of King Richard [the Lionheart]. Physically this would have been inevitable, for he was tall and strong, a fine figure of a handsome man... If only he had given to arms the

labour that he expended on rustic pursuits, he would have raised England aloft; his name would have resounded throughout the land.

No less reprehensible, this commentator believed, was Edward II's devotion to unworthy and unpopular favourites, particularly, during his early years as king, Piers Gaveston. Despite being a 'humble squire' and an 'alien of Gascon birth', he declared indignantly, Gaveston:

> ...accounted no one his fellow, no one his peer, save the king alone... His arrogance was intolerable to the barons and a prime cause of hatred and rancour... Piers alone received a gracious welcome from the king and enjoyed his favour to such an extent that if an earl or baron entered the king's chamber to speak to the king, in Piers' presence the king addressed no one, and to no one showed a friendly countenance save to Piers only... Indeed I do not remember ever hearing that one man so loved another. Jonathan cherished David, Achilles loved Patroclus. But we do not read that they were immoderate. Our king, however, was incapable of moderate favour, and on account of Piers was said to forget himself...

Gaveston met a violent death in 1312 and so, in 1327, did another royal favourite, Hugh Despenser, when, according to the later fourteenth-century French chronicler Jean Froissart, his private parts were cut off because he had been 'guilty of unnatural practices, even with the king'. As for Edward II himself, the Oxfordshire cleric Geoffrey le Baker (writing in the 1340s) tells us that, deposed and incarcerated in Berkeley castle:

> ...he was shut up in a secure chamber where he was tortured for many days [until, finally, he was] seized on the night of 22 September [1327] as he lay sleeping in his room. There, with cushions heavier than fifteen strong men could carry, they held him down, suffocating him. Then they thrust a plumber's soldering iron, heated red hot, guided by a tube inserted into his bowels, and thus they burnt his innards and vital organs.

So loud were his howls of agony, the chronicler added, that 'many heard him cry, both within and without the castle, and knew it for the cry of a man who suffered violent death'. Fortunately, as contemporaries saw it, his son and successor Edward III (1327-1377) could hardly have been a greater contrast.

Recently, William Shakespeare himself has been credited with the authorship (in whole or in part) of a rather mundane play *Edward III*, first printed in 1596, and very much focusing on the king's just claims to hegemony in France and his victorious exploits there. For instance, he vigorously challenges the French king's right to his throne:

> ...the crown that he usurps is mine.
> And where he sets his foot, he ought to kneel;
> 'Tis not a petty dukedom that I claim,
> But all the whole dominions of the realm;
> Which if with grudging he refuse to yield,
> I'll take away those borrowed plumes of his
> And send him naked to the wilderness.

And, remembering Crécy on the eve of his own great victory at Poitiers, Edward III's son, the Black Prince, remarks:

> At Cressy field our clouds of warlike smoke
> Chok'd up those French mouths and dissever'd them.

Whether Shakespeare actually wrote this play remains a matter for debate but, clearly, the Edward III of the play is a king very much to be admired. Did the real Edward III either attract, or deserve, such admiration? Interestingly enough, when about to embark on his French adventures in 1337, the king himself declared in parliament:

> Among the marks of royalty, we consider it to be the chief that, through a due distribution of positions, dignities and offices, it is buttressed by wise counsels and fortified by mighty powers.

Moreover, for much of the ensuing three decades he acted in accordance with this dictum. Unlike his father, he maintained an effective and productive relationship with his magnates, managed to inspire his fighting troops and certainly won the admiration of the continental chronicler Jean le Bel:

> When this noble King Edward first gained England in his youth, nobody thought anything of the English and nobody spoke at all of their valour or their hardiness but now, as the king has so often put them to work, they have learnt to bear arms and they are the most noble and most daring soldiers known.

Indeed, 'it is impossible to honour too highly' this king who:

> ...always accepted wise advice in his undertakings, always loved his knights, squires and men, and always did honour to each according to his estate; always defended his kingdom against its enemies and gained conquests from them; always fearlessly risked his own life with the lives of his followers both at home and abroad; and always paid the wages of his armed men and gave generously of his own wealth.

Everything depended, however, on Edward III's continued vigour and leadership, and on maintaining his record of successful campaigning in France. When, in his last years, the French began rolling back English territorial advances and the king himself became ever more senile, political corruption and baronial rivalry (so rife under Edward II) once more became all too evident. As the St Albans' monastic chronicler, Thomas Walsingham, sadly recorded:

> ...just as at first both grace and prosperity made King Edward renowned and illustrious, so in his old age and declining years, with his sins, little by little that good fortune diminished, and many misfortunes and difficulties arose which, alas, tarnished his reputation.

When he finally died, moreover, 'that infamous whore Alice Perrers', the king's mistress, dragged the very rings from his fingers and even deserted the royal corpse!

RICHARD II 1377-1399

Central to William Shakespeare's *Richard II* is the king's enigmatic character but, since the play covers only his last traumatic months on the throne, the evolution of a complex personality is compressed, by dramatic licence, into less than two years. When Richard II became England's king in 1377, he was a mere ten years old. His father the Black Prince had died only the year before and, during his early years on the throne, royal uncles very much held sway both at court and in government. Perhaps, as contemporary and near-contemporary commentators suggest, it was the Peasants' Revolt of 1381 that first brought the young king firmly into the political arena. The well-informed *Anonimalle Chronicle*, for instance, tells how, during the rebel occupation of London, he:

> ...came to Mile End [where] the commons all knelt down to him, saying: 'Welcome our lord King Richard, if it pleases you, and we will have no other king but you'. Wat Tyler, their leader and chief, prayed to him in the name of the commons that he would suffer them to take and hold all the traitors who were against him and the law... And at this time the king caused a proclamation to be made before them that he would confirm and grant them their freedom and all their wishes generally, and that they should go through the realm of England and catch all the traitors and bring them to him in safety, and that he would deal with them as the law required.

Perhaps, indeed, the dramatic events of 1381 were pivotal in helping determine how Richard II, in the years to come, would not only behave as king but also choose to exercise his royal powers. Even as a boy, the sacred and unique nature of his office was clearly impressed upon him. Once he began to exercise power himself, moreover, he seems deliberately and self-consciously to have set out to create a new image of kingship, an image almost certainly designed to distance the crown from its subjects. Every opportunity was taken, in fact, to emphasise the monarch's special status as the Lord's anointed, not least by means of elaborate court etiquette and ceremonial. Contemporary portraits, most notably the *Wilton Diptych*, tended to depict the king in Christ-like isolation, carefully elevated above those he ruled; the use of words like 'majesty' and 'highness' was much encouraged; and even Westminster Abbey came to be promoted as a veritable shrine to royalty. In practice, however, Richard II's personal predilections and petulant political behaviour ensured that, in the end, monarchical imagery could never be translated into regal reality.

Like his great-grandfather Edward II, the young king soon began to display a penchant for favourites deemed entirely unsuitable by his great magnates and the crown/baronial consensus, already cracking in the 1370s, completely fell apart during the 1380s. Robert de Vere Earl of Oxford, in particular, attracted fierce criticism, as the chronicler Thomas Walsingham recorded:

> King Richard, lest he should appear to be idle, now [in 1386] elevated Robert de Vere, lately Earl of Oxford but created Marquis of Dublin in the recent parliament, to the rank of Duke of Ireland, to be raised later from duke to king if fortune favoured him. This action demonstrated the depth of King Richard's affection for this man, whom he cultivated and loved, not without a degree of improper intimacy or so it was rumoured. It also provoked discontent among the other lords and barons who were angry that a man of such mediocrity should receive such promotion, for he was not superior to the rest of them in either nobility of birth or gifts of character.

Walsingham, like most contemporary and near-contemporary chroniclers, had little sympathy for Richard II but he was surely right to identify Robert de Vere as a prime cause of discontent. Michael de la Pole Earl of Suffolk, perhaps less justifiably, also attracted hostility in 1386. Indeed, according to the contemporary chronicler Henry Knighton, parliament refused to co-operate with the king:

> ...as long as he [Suffolk] remained in the chancellor's office. The king was moved to anger and ordered them to be silent about this, and to make haste and proceed with the business of parliament, saying that he would not remove the meanest scullion in his kitchen from office at their request.

Such petulance got the king nowhere. Suffolk was not only dismissed from the chancellorship but impeached for treason as well, while Richard II himself was forced to approve new councillors appointed by parliament. When, in 1387, he rehabilitated Suffolk, refused to submit to his new council's wishes and continued to rely instead on unpopular favourites, he provoked an even more dramatic reaction, culminating in the Merciless Parliament of 1388 where three of the most powerful magnates in the land – Thomas Woodstock Duke of Gloucester, the king's own uncle, Richard Fitzalan Earl of Arundel and Thomas Beauchamp Earl of Warwick – secured the exile, imprisonment or execution of his five leading supporters.

In 1389, however, Richard II (now aged twenty-two) successfully confronted his critics at a council meeting when, according to Thomas Walsingham, he declared theatrically:

> ...I have for long been ruled by tutors and it was not possible for me to act at all, or hardly at all, without them. Now, henceforth, I will remove these men from my council and, as heir of lawful age, I will appoint whom I wish to my council, and conduct my own affairs.

This time the royal stratagem worked and now, having finally grasped the reins of power, the way was at last open for the king to pursue his own political agenda for good or ill.

What did motivate Richard II in the 1390s? Was he fired primarily by deep-rooted resentment at his earlier treatment and near-fanatical determination to get his revenge? Did he set his sights on becoming an absolute ruler and embrace whatever measures he deemed necessary, however tyrannical, in order to achieve this overriding aim? Alternatively, did an impossibly romantic and impractical conception of kingship, when combined with growing mental instability, help spawn the high-handed and arbitrary behaviour that ultimately cost him the crown? Or perhaps, as the king's most recent biographer Nigel Saul has persuasively argued, Richard II was actually aiming at the creation of a *new*, more overtly royalist, political consensus than had hitherto prevailed, albeit a consensus very much tailored to his own interests and on his own terms. Hence his determination to secure a permanent end to Anglo-French hostilities, free himself from financial dependence on parliamentary taxation, and resist the complaints and demands of his subjects. Hence, too, his projection of himself as a veritable father of the nation, entitled, in this paternal role, to both the loyal obedience of his people and their ready submission to his laws. Yet Richard II's quest for such a consensus eventually proved fatal to him: his personal persuasions and political actions clearly challenged vested interests, particularly those of the higher nobility, and his manipulative behaviour also created dissension in local society. In his last years, moreover, he increasingly lost touch with the real world and, when confronted by Henry Bolingbroke Duke of Lancaster in 1399, contrived to lose the support of all but a few die-hard royalists.

Certainly, during the 1390s, Richard II remained as determined as ever to choose his own friends and councillors; he sought Anglo-French amity with some vigour; and, in 1397, he finally obtained revenge on his leading opponents of a decade earlier (when Warwick was exiled, Arundel executed and Gloucester probably murdered). Indeed, so Walsingham tells us, the king:

> ...demanded great sums of money from seventeen shires of the realm, under fear of death, charging them that they had supported the Duke of Gloucester, and the Earls of Arundel and Warwick, in their opposition to him... The clergy and the commonalty, and the temporal lords of the shires, were compelled to pay to the king insupportable sums of money, to recover his favour. The king desiring, as it was said, to subdue and oppress the people of his realm, directed letters patent to all shires of his realm, and induced them by terror, both temporal and clerical subjects, to swear unaccustomed oaths of a kind which could really cause the final destruction of his people... He compelled them to affix their seals to blank charters so that, as often as he might wish to proceed against them, he should have the opportunity to oppress them, singly or together.

Richard II's increasing remoteness, by 1398, is nicely highlighted by another commentator:

> [The King] ordered a throne to be set up in his chamber on which he would sit after dinner, showing himself. He would talk to no one but would look at people, and whoever he looked at, whatever his rank, had to genuflect.

Clearly, Richard II's arbitrary behaviour, especially during the last two or three years of his reign, lost him a good deal of popular as well as aristocratic support, but the revolution of 1399 was not the product of a popular uprising against the king. Rather, it was precipitated by his decision, following John of Gaunt's death, to seize the Duchy of Lancaster for the crown. Gaunt's exiled son Henry Bolingbroke invaded England and announced, initially, that he had merely come to take possession of his rightful inheritance. Many of the nobility, perhaps fearful for the security of their own estates, no doubt sympathised with his dilemma and, in the end, concurred in Richard II's deposition and Henry IV's accession as the best solution to an impossible situation. Most chroniclers accepted the official line, as promulgated in parliament, that the king's tyrannical rule had brought about his downfall and such, indeed, is the thrust of Richard II's abdication speech:

> ...I confess, acknowledge, consider and truly judge from sure knowledge that I, in the rule and government of [my] realms and lordships and all pertaining to them, have been and am wholly insufficient and useless, and because of my notorious deserts am not unworthy to be deposed.

For the chronicler Adam of Usk, though, the king's eventual fate had been foreshadowed even at his coronation:

> Firstly, in the procession he lost one of his coronation shoes; whence, in the first place, the commons who rose up against him hated him ever after his life long. Secondly, one of the golden spurs fell off; whence, in the second place, the soldiery opposed him in rebellion. Thirdly, at the banquet a sudden gust of wind carried away the crown from his head; whence, in the third and last place, he was set aside from his kingdom and supplanted by King Henry.

Once deposed, Richard II was imprisoned in Pontefract castle where, if we are to believe Thomas Walsingham, he 'killed himself by voluntary starvation' the following year, while Adam of Usk specifically linked the king's death to his disappointment at the failure of an early rebellion against Henry IV:

> Now those in whom Richard, late king, did put his trust for help were fallen. And when he heard this, he grieved more sorely and mourned even to death, which came to him most miserably on the last day of February [1400], as he lay in chains in the castle of Pontefract, tormented by Sir [Thomas] Swinford with starving fare.

For the only clearly anti-Lancastrian chronicler whose work has come down to us, however, blame for Richard II's death – indeed, murder – could be laid firmly at the door of Henry IV himself, and he certainly tells a dramatic tale:

> In January 1400 Henry IV, facing a rising in support of King Richard, ordered a knight, Sir Peter Exton, to go and put an end to the days of 'John of London' as Richard was known. [At Pontefract while Richard II was at dinner] in rushed Sir Peter Exton and seven men, every one of them armed with an axe. When Richard saw them, he threw back the table, jumped in amongst the armed men, and snatched an axe from one of his would-be murderers. He now set about defending

himself with great courage and strength, killing four of the eight, but Sir Peter had leapt on to the king's dining chair and waited, axe in hand, until Richard came near. It was astonishing how long Richard managed to hold out against all the armed men and he did so like a true and loyal knight until at last, defending himself, he stepped back towards the chair where Sir Peter was waiting. Sir Peter brought his axe down with such force that Richard staggered backwards shouting, 'Lord have mercy on me', and fell dead to the ground.

HENRY IV 1399–1413

On 13 October 1399, reported the St Albans' chronicler Thomas Walsingham, Henry Bolingbroke was crowned King Henry IV at Westminster, 'a year to the day after he had been sent into exile', an event 'thought to have been a miracle sent by God'. More colourfully, Adam of Usk recorded that, after his anointing, 'there ensued such a growth of lice, especially on his head, that he neither grew hair nor could he have his head uncovered for many months'. Already in his early thirties by 1399, the new king's military credentials were impressive: he had a well-established reputation as a jouster; he had participated in a crusade against pagan Slavs in eastern Europe; and he had even made a pilgrimage to the Holy Land. As a result, so the French chronicler Jean Froissart tells us, he had attracted much admiration as 'an amiable knight, courteous and pleasant to all'. As a man he was deeply pious and, once England's king, soon proved his Christian orthodoxy by vigorously targeting the native Lollard heresy; yet he was also unusually well educated for a great magnate, possessed a genuine interest in literature and enjoyed both listening to music and participating in its performance. Moreover, when an Augustinian friar, John Capgrave, penned a series of lives of illustrious Henrys in the 1440s, he judged Henry IV a king who:

> ...followed the paths of justice, greatly honoured the servants of God and, drinking from the fountain of Scripture, did not go away thirsty. I knew highly educated men who enjoyed his company and said that he had a very able mind and an excellent memory, so that he spent a lot of the day in solving and unravelling problems.

Clearly, Henry IV lacked the conventional background, upbringing and experience for a future king but he did have many promising qualities, most notably courage, energy and a real sense of purpose. Unfortunately, as William Shakespeare so rightly emphasised, the circumstances of his accession ensured his reign would be a turbulent and uneasy one. Even after the failure of a rebellion by Richard II's former supporters in 1400 and the king's death in Pontefract Castle, rumours persisted that he was still alive. For instance, there is this almost certainly imaginary conversation between Richard Frisby (who was tried for treason against Henry IV in 1402) and the king, preserved in the annals of a contemporary Franciscan friar:

The King: Did you say that King Richard is alive?

Frisby: I do not say that he is alive, but I do say that if he is alive he is the true King of England.

The King: He abdicated.

Frisby: He did abdicate, but under compulsion while in prison, and that is not a valid abdication.

The King: He abdicated right willingly.

Frisby: He would never have resigned had he been at liberty. And a resignation made in prison is not a free resignation.

The King: Even so, he was deposed.

Frisby: While he was king, he was captured by force of arms, thrown into prison, while you usurped his crown.

The King: I did not usurp the crown but was duly elected.

Frisby: An election is null and void while the legitimate possessor is alive. And if he is dead, you killed him. And if you are the cause of his death, you forfeit all title and any right which you may have to the kingdom.

The King: By this head of mine, thou shalt lose thine!

Henry IV was certainly very different from Richard II and, in the end, he did succeed in establishing the Lancastrian dynasty on a sound footing. In order to do so, however, he had to tread a long and difficult path. Lack of enthusiasm for Richard II in 1399 did not necessarily add up to positive commitment to Henry IV and the king, in fact, had to make an all-out effort to widen the basis of his support during the early years of the reign, not least by frequently consulting the nobility and generous political patronage. Financial problems also made for difficulties with parliament and, although Henry IV was not the premature advocate of constitutional monarchy he has sometimes been portrayed as, he had no alternative but to make concessions to the Commons on more than one occasion.

Most seriously, Henry IV had to face a string of rebellions during his early years, as well as the threat of foreign intervention in English affairs. There seemed a very real possibility of a French invasion; the Scots were notably aggressive (at any rate until a Scottish army was defeated by Henry Percy Earl of Northumberland and his son Hotspur at the battle of Homildon Hill in 1402 and James I of Scotland was captured by the English in 1406); and there was a prolonged revolt in Wales led by Owen

Glendower. In England itself, moreover, Henry IV had to face no fewer than three Percy-inspired rebellions. Both Henry Percy Earl of Northumberland and his eldest son had been prominent supporters of the successful Lancastrian challenge to Richard II in 1399 but, by 1403, such were their ambitions, and grievances against the new regime, that they came out in open rebellion. Fortunately for Henry IV, the rebels were defeated at the battle of Shrewsbury; Hotspur was killed in the fighting; and before long, thanks not least to the efforts of young Henry, Prince of Wales (the future Henry V), the Welsh revolt soon collapsed as well. Nevertheless, there was a prominent Percy element in a further rebellion of 1405 (as a result of which Richard Scrope Archbishop of York, one of its leaders, was executed) and, again in 1408 (when Henry Percy Earl of Northumberland was killed). By then, however, Henry IV's growing ill health had made it impossible for him to rule effectively and power was increasingly being exercised on his behalf by Thomas Arundel Archbishop of Canterbury (another of his very earliest supporters).

Once he had 'crushed those who rebelled against him', reported the chronicler Adam of Usk, Henry IV 'fell sick' and, for the next five years until his death, was tormented 'by a rotting of the flesh, a drying up of the eyes and a rupture of the intestines'. By May 1410 he had withdrawn from London to the midlands and power had largely passed into the hands of Henry, Prince of Wales and a small coterie of aristocratic supporters. Towards the end of 1411, however, Henry IV reasserted himself, as recorded by Thomas Walsingham:

> Prince Henry, the king's eldest son, and almost all the other lords of England, agreed to ask the king to lay down the crown of England and allow his eldest son to be crowned, because he was so horribly disfigured with leprosy. But when this was put to him twice by various lords in council, King Henry refused to give way and immediately set out on horseback over much of England, notwithstanding his leprosy.

Prince Henry, in fact, submitted to his father and, before Henry IV's death on 20 March 1413, the two were fully reconciled. The manner of the king's end is dramatically, if fancifully, reconstructed by the Burgundian chronicler Enguerrand de Monstrelet. Henry IV, he tells us, was so:

> ...sorely pressed at the end of his sickness that those who attended him, not perceiving him to breathe, concluded he was dead and covered his face with a cloth. It was the custom in England, whenever the king was ill, to place the royal crown on a cushion beside his bed, and for his successor to take it on his death. The Prince of Wales, being

informed by the attendants that his father was dead, had carried away the crown. Shortly after, however, the king uttered a groan and his face was uncovered. Looking then for the crown, he asked what had become of it. His attendants replied that 'my lord the prince has taken it away'. He bade them send for the prince and, on his entrance, asked him why he had carried away the crown. 'My lord', answered the prince, 'your attendants, here present, affirmed to me that you were dead and, as your crown and kingdom belong to me as your eldest son after your decease, I had it taken away'. The king gave a deep sigh and said, 'My fair son, what right have you to it, for you know well I had none'. 'My lord', replied the prince, 'as you have held it by right of your sword, it is my intention to hold and defend it in similar manner during my life'... Shortly after, [the king] departed this life.

3

Henry V, Henry VI and the Hundred Years War

Henry V, England and the Establishment of the Lancastrian Empire in France 1413-1422

Henry V's character, life and achievements are unusually well reported in contemporary and near-contemporary biographies and chronicles and, even before the king's untimely death in 1422, the heroic portrayal later immortalised by William Shakespeare was beginning to take shape. Perhaps at the king's own urging, a royal chaplain compiled a life of Henry V in about 1417, presenting him as a model Christian prince, clearly carrying out God's wishes both at home and abroad:

> When young in years but old in experience, he began his reign, like the true elect of God savouring the things that are above, he applied his mind with all devotion to encompass what could promote the honour of God, the extension of the Church, the deliverance of his country, and the peace and tranquillity of kingdoms.

This early biographer was particularly impressed by Henry V's successful Agincourt campaign of 1415:

> [Our] older men [do not] remember any prince ever having commanded his people on the march with more effort, bravery or consideration, or having, with his own hand, performed greater feats of strength in the field. Nor, indeed, is evidence to be found in the chronicles or annals that any king of England ever achieved so much in so short a time and returned home with so glorious a triumph.

The chronicler Thomas Walsingham, writing very soon after the king's death, brought in an entirely positive verdict:

> King Henry V left no one like him among Christian kings or princes. His death, not only by his subjects in England and France but in the whole of Christendom, was deservedly mourned. He was pious in soul, taciturn and discreet in his speech, far-seeing in counsel, prudent in judgement, modest in appearance, magnanimous in his actions, firm in business, persistent in pilgrimages and generous in alms, devoted to God and supportive and respectful of the prelates and ministers of the church. War-like, distinguished and fortunate, he had won victories in all his military engagements.

'Thinking of his memorable deeds', Walsingham concluded, 'people felt awe at his sudden and terrible death', and 'mourned inexpressibly'. A few years later, in about 1437, Tito Livio, an Italian enjoying the patronage of Henry V's brother Humphrey Duke of Gloucester, can surely be regarded as an official biographer of the king. At his accession, Livio tells us, the young Henry V was:

> ...taller than most men, his face fair and set on a longish neck, his body graceful, his limbs slender and marvellously strong. Indeed, he was miraculously fleet of foot, faster than any dog or arrow. Often he would run with two of his companions in pursuit of the swiftest of does and he himself would always be the one to catch the creature. He had a great liking for music and found enjoyment in hunting, military pursuits and the other pleasures that are customarily allowed to young knights.

Once crowned and anointed, and after all the nobility had sworn an oath of loyalty to him, he:

> ...appointed men whom he considered to be honest and fair to be judges throughout his kingdom and selected other necessary officials for posts in all his lands. Then, when affairs had been properly settled in Ireland, Scotland and Wales, Henry decided to win back the kingdom of France which belonged to him by birthright.

Most contemporary and near-contemporary writers, in fact, tended to concentrate on Henry V's successes in France and, of course, his exploits across the English Channel have always formed the basis of the popular view of the king. Even continental commentators were inclined to admire Henry V's determination of purpose, strict discipline and valiant deeds, particularly chivalric chroniclers who had personal experience of military campaigning. The Burgundian Enguerrand de Monstrelet, for instance, believed Henry V was:

> …very wise and capable in everything he undertook and he had an iron will. When he ruled in France, he made greater conquests than any before him for many years past. He was so feared by his nobles and captains that there was no one, however close or dear to him, who was not afraid to go against his orders, especially those of his own kingdom of England. Everyone under his rule, in France and England alike, whatever his rank, was reduced to this same state of obedience. The chief reason for this was that anyone who thwarted his will and disobeyed his orders was most cruelly punished and received no mercy.

Certainly, Henry V could be autocratic, inflexible and ruthless, even cruel and tyrannical, but, for his contemporaries, he was also the very epitome of energetic, just and warlike kingship. Before his accession to the throne, so an anonymous English chronicler tells us, Henry V 'inclined greatly to riot and drew to wild company' but, in all probability, stories of the king's wild and irresponsible youth are more the stuff of legend than history. While still only a teenager he played a major role in suppressing Owen Glendower's Welsh rebellion and his political career began early as well; indeed, in 1410 and 1411 he virtually ruled the country. He was unusually well educated for a king's son, able to read and write English (his first language), French and Latin, deeply if traditionally pious, and the founder of notably austere religious houses. As Tito Livio later recorded, early in his reign he:

> …had two religious houses built on the River Thames, one for the Carthusian order, to which he gave the name of Bethleham, and the other, which is known as Syon, for the nuns of St Brigit. He sought and obtained indulgences for both these religious houses from the pope and endowed them with many privileges and a great income.

Henry V's narrow, strict and unflinching orthodoxy is best illustrated by his determined efforts to stamp out heresy and, especially, his reaction to Sir John Oldcastle's Lollard uprising in the winter of 1413/14. Tito Livio certainly approved. The king, he tells us:

> …summoned a large number of men-at-arms who made an assault on the heretics and overcame them almost without a struggle. The rebels were seized and put to death. The king's men crucified their captives,

except for the leaders who were kept in chains for many days and afflicted with the torture they deserved. Thus the first great victory of the king was gained for Christ and God's Church against evil heretics.

Henry V responded no less vigorously to an aristocratic conspiracy against him, betrayed on the very eve of his departure for France in 1415. Richard Earl of Cambridge, Henry Lord Scrope and Sir Thomas Grey, so the king's first anonymous biographer reported, 'conspired not only to prevent the intended expedition' to France but also 'to inflict disaster by killing the king'. When news of the assassination plot reached Henry V's ears, he promptly had all three of them beheaded. Clearly, much of the king's energy in the years to come was devoted to campaigning across the English Channel. Indeed, relative to the length of his reign, he spent more time absent from England than any king since Richard the Lionheart. Yet, since he needed the support of both nobility and people, he also made every effort to ensure peace was preserved and justice enforced by his agents at home.

Henry V was probably the greatest English general before Marlborough in the early eighteenth century; his great success at Agincourt, even if not of the king's own making, thoroughly humiliated the French; and, as a result, the English gained a reputation for invincibility in the field that was to last until the catastrophic defeat of Henry VI's forces at Formigny in 1450. Perhaps, even as early as 1415, Henry V's driving ambition was not only to conquer territory in France but secure the French throne for himself and unite France and England in a dual monarchy. More probably, his initial aim was the recovery of lands his predecessors had lost, particularly Normandy. Only in his last years, when he realised it was within his grasp, did he firmly set his sights on the French crown and kingdom as a whole. Certainly, the diplomatic situation favoured him from the very beginning. The Valois king Charles VI had suffered intermittent bouts of insanity since 1392 and, by 1415, he was so often out of action that his rare periods of lucidity seemed more worthy of comment than his prolonged periods of madness. Political vacuum at the centre had helped spawn great rivalry between powerful French baronial factions: the Armagnacs (eventually coming under the leadership of the French dauphin, Charles VI's son, the future Charles VII) and the Burgundians led by John the Fearless Duke of Burgundy. Indeed, since about 1410, civil war had raged. Henry V was just the man to take advantage of such a state of affairs and, when diplomacy failed, he could invade France confident of at least Burgundian neutrality and the real possibility of an Anglo-Burgundian alliance. Once the latter became a reality in

1419 (following the murder of John the Fearless) the French crown, too, came within Henry V's grasp, and he was not the man to shun such a prize.

Henry V's first campaign began with the king's landing in Normandy in August 1415. For over five weeks he besieged the town of Harfleur and, after its capitulation, marched northwards towards Calais. En route, he was forced into battle at Agincourt on 25 October by a much larger French army. Repeating their mistakes at Crécy and Poitiers, however, the French chose to mount a cavalry charge across unfavourable terrain on dismounted English men-at-arms supported by longbowmen and infantry, and the result was a spectacular English victory. Tito Livio particularly stressed Henry V's personal bravery in action:

A great many princes, lords and noblemen and the noble King Henry himself did not cease from the labour of battle, nor did the king fail his men by seeking to avoid dangers to his own life but, like an unvanquished lion, he fought against the enemy with great ardour, receiving many blows on his helmet and armour.

Back home, the campaign was triumphantly celebrated in a contemporary ballad:

Our king went forth to Normandy,
With grace and might of chivalry;
There God for him wrought marvellously,
Wherefore England may call and cry,
Deo gracias!

He set a siege, the sooth for to say,
To Harfleur town with royal array;
That town he won and made affray;
That France shall rue till Domèsday,
Deo gracias!

Then went our king with all his host
Through France, for all the hostile host,
He spared no dread of least or most,
Until he came to Agincourt coast,
Deo gracias!

Then forsooth that knight comely
In Agincourt field he fought manly;

> Through grace of God most mighty
> He hath both the field and the victory,
> *Deo gracias!*
>
> There dukes and earls, lord and baron
> Were taken and slain, and that well soon;
> And some were led into London
> With joy and mirth and great renown,
> *Deo Gracias!*
>
> May gracious God now save our king
> His people and his well-willing;
> Give him good life and good ending,
> That we with mirth may safely sing,
> *Deo gracias!*

Henry V's second invasion, in 1417, was primarily directed towards the systematic conquest of Normandy and, hopefully, adjoining provinces. In the long, slow, grim war of sieges that ensued, the quality of his generalship became only too apparent, as he methodically reduced castles, fortresses and hostile towns, and then organised the rule of conquered territory from these self-same strongholds. Such an endeavour needed fighting troops that were both loyal and disciplined and here, too, Henry V very much proved his mettle as a commander. The assassination of John the Fearless Duke of Burgundy by his Armagnac enemies in 1419 so angered the new duke, Philip the Good, that he promptly allied with the English and this, together with the successful occupation of Normandy, opened the way for the Treaty of Troyes in 1420. Under the terms of this not only did the English king secure Charles VI's daughter Catherine of Valois as his wife but it was agreed that, on the French king's death, his crown should pass to Henry V and his heirs (with Henry acting as regent, in the meantime, for the hopelessly insane Charles). Perhaps, had he lived, Henry V might have made the dual monarchy of France and England a permanent reality; or, perhaps, it was fortunate for the king's future reputation that he died prematurely. Certainly, the St Albans' chronicler Thomas Walsingham was much moved by the manner of Henry V's death:

> In the course of a lengthy illness, which he had contracted as a result of long and excessive labours, the king suffered from an acute fever, with violent dysentery, which so consumed his strength that the doctors dared not give him internal medicine and despaired of his life. Seeing that his death was approaching, the

king called together his dukes and others who were able to be present, to represent the kingdoms of England and France and the duchy of Normandy. He made wise arrangements, wrote his will and provided for his debts to be paid from his treasuries and numerous jewels. After taking holy communion and the other sacraments that were the duty of a Christian, in true penitence, proper faith, certain hope, perfect charity and right remembrance, he gave up his soul to his creator on the last day of August [1422] after he had reigned for nine years, five months and fourteen days.

THE MINORITY OF HENRY VI 1422 – 1437

Born at Windsor castle on 6 December 1421, the only son of Henry V and Catherine of Valois, Henry VI became the youngest English prince ever to succeed to the throne when, on 31 August 1422, his father died of dysentery while campaigning in France. Evidence for the young king's upbringing and education is sparse but illuminating. His early care was entrusted to women, notably Alice Butler, an expert in 'courtesy and nurture', who was even given licence 'to chastise us from time to time'; in November 1423 he made a public appearance in parliament although, en route to London, he had apparently so 'shrieked, cried and sprang' that his journey had had to be delayed; and, in April 1425, he was 'led upon his feet' to the choir of St Paul's 'whence he was borne to the high altar', after which he was 'set upon a fair courser and so conveyed through Cheap and other streets of the city'. In 1428 Richard Beauchamp Earl of Warwick became his tutor, with instructions to:

...remain about the king's person, to do his utmost in teaching him good manners, literature, languages, nurture and courtesy and other studies necessary for so great a prince; to exhort him to love, honour and fear the Creator; and to draw himself to virtues and eschew vice; to chastise him reasonably from time to time, as occasion shall require; [and to lay before him] mirrors and examples of times passed of the good grace, prosperity and well-being that have attended virtuous kings.

During the next few years he learned to speak French fluently and read Latin, became well versed in the scriptures and history and, presumably, proficient enough in horsemanship, hunting and similar royal/aristo-cratic pursuits. On 6 November 1429 he was crowned in Westminster Abbey where, apparently, he sat 'beholding his people all about sadly and wisely', and listening to the service with 'great humility and devotion'; while, at Notre Dame in Paris on 16 December 1431, he became the only English monarch ever to be crowned king of France. By 1432, however, warning bells about his shortcomings were beginning to be sounded:

> Considering how the king is grown in years, in the stature of his person and in knowledge of his high and royal authority, causing him more and more to begrudge and loath chastisement, [the Earl of Warwick requests the council] to assist him in the exercise of his authority over the king's person. [Moreover, since the king] has been distracted by some from his learning, and spoken to about unsuitable matters, the earl, fearing the harm that may befall the king if such contacts be allowed, desires that, in all conversation men may have with the king, he [or his assignees] be present and privy to it.

According to the contemporary chronicler John Harding, Warwick had so despaired of the king by 1436 that he sought release from his role as guardian:

> ...of his simplehead
> He could little within his breast conceive,
> For good from evil he could scarce perceive...
> The Earl of Warwick then conceived
> Of the simpleness and great innocence
> Of King Henry, as he it well perceived,
> Desired to be discharged of his diligence
> About the king...

Clearly, the young Henry VI soon displayed his lack of aptitude for, or interest in, military – and, perhaps, political – matters; he proved prone, from an early age, to give credence to ill-judged, unsuitable advice and counsel; and, by the time he declared his majority at an end in 1437 (perhaps at the urging of those around him), he had probably already become the obsessively religious and morally censorious cleric-in-king's-clothing he was to remain for the rest of his life. Certainly, if we are to believe a foreign envoy writing in November 1437, by the age of sixteen Henry VI:

> ...avoided the sight and conversation of women, affirming these to be the work of the devil and quoting from the Gospel, 'He who casts his eyes on a woman so as to lust after her has already committed adultery with her in his heart'. Those who knew him intimately said that he

had preserved his virginity of mind and body to this present time, and that he was firmly resolved to have intercourse with no woman unless within the bonds of matrimony.

Royal minorities were always potentially difficult times in the Middle Ages and that of Henry VI was no exception. In particular, there developed a bitter feud between the young king's uncle Humphrey Duke of Gloucester and his great rival Henry Beaufort, Bishop of Winchester (who was raised to the status of cardinal by the pope in 1427). The two had little in common except ambition. Gloucester, Henry V's younger brother, had been designated regent in England by Henry V before his death but, once the king was no more, his claims to the regency were rejected by the nobility in council. Instead, he was allowed only the title of protector (with very limited responsibilities), while real power was vested in the council itself. Gloucester, no doubt, found some consolation in his activities as a patron of learning and enthusiastic book collector, but much of his energy was directed into the feud with Beaufort and, increasingly, criticising the conduct of the ongoing war in France. Cardinal Beaufort was a man of considerable political ability who often showed statesmanlike qualities; however, he was also inflexible and, on occasion, notably mercenary. The Beaufort/Gloucester feud certainly gave the council a good deal of trouble during the minority, even, for a time, threatening to thrust England into out-and-out civil strife. At the end of September 1425, so a contemporary London chronicle tells us, 'my lord of Gloucester and the bishop at Winchester were not good friends', so much so that:

> ...certain men kept the gates of the bridge of London by the command of the lord of Gloucester and the mayor. Then, between nine and ten of the bell, there came certain men of the bishop of Winchester and drew the chains of the posts at the bridge end of the Southwark side. These men included both knights and squires, with a great many archers, and they made ready for battle, and barricaded windows and set up casks [as barriers], as if it had been in a land of war, as though they would have fought against the king's people and broken the peace. When the people of the city heard of this, they shut their shops in haste and came down to the gates of the bridge, [for the keeping and] salvation of the city against the king's enemies.

Moreover, although the situation was resolved by negotiation and no harm came to the city, these events were clearly perceived as highly threatening at the time. Similarly, there developed a private feud between John Mowbray Duke of Norfolk and Thomas Holland Earl of Huntingdon which resulted in much disruption and lawlessness in East Anglia (particularly in 1428). Yet, although the Beaufort/Gloucester feud rumbled on into the 1430s, the minority of Henry VI was, for the most part, comparatively free of serious disorder. Throughout, in fact, the council showed considerable determination to function in a businesslike and impartial manner, even when confronted by major problems such as preserving law and order, keeping the government solvent and defending Henry V's legacy in France.

Whether Henry V could ever have translated the Treaty of Troyes into a permanent settlement is a moot point. As it was, both he and the French king Charles VI died in 1422. The infant Henry VI was promptly declared king of England and France and, before long, machinery for operating a dual monarchy of the two realms was established. In reality, however, there were what amounted to three states in France and the Low Countries: a Burgundian state (ruled by Duke Philip the Good); a northern Lancastrian Anglo-French state (under the control of John Duke of Bedford, Henry V's brother, as regent for Henry VI); and a southern Valois French state (ruled by Charles VI's son Charles VII, generally styled the dauphin until his coronation in 1429). Nevertheless, there was no immediate decline in England's military fortunes in France. John Duke of Bedford had many of the qualities of his late brother: an able general and a statesman of some distinction, he was clearly the ideal man to serve as regent for his young nephew. Under Bedford's leadership English expansion across northern France continued and when, in 1424, Charles VII's generals offered battle at Verneuil, he won a victory in the field almost as impressive as Agincourt. The Burgundian chronicler Jean de Waurin, an eyewitness of the battle, remarked:

> I saw the assembly at Agincourt, where there were many more princes and people, and also that of Cravant [a battle won by the English in 1423], which was a very pretty affair; but the assembly at Verneuil was certainly the most formidable of all and the best fought of them all… The battle lasted about three quarters of an hour, very terrible and bloody…

By the autumn of 1428 almost the whole of northern France and the Low Countries was governed by England or Burgundy, so the English now turned south to besiege Orleans, the key to opening up Valois-held territory in southern France. At this point, however, Joan of Arc appeared on the scene.

Historians will never agree on the precise importance of Joan of Arc and, in this, they reflect the disagreements in contemporary and near-contemporary chronicles. According to an anonymous Burgundian chronicler of the time, Joan (a simple peasant girl) did make a tremendous impact on the court of Charles VII and, indeed, played a major role both in inspiring the Valois king personally and forcing the English to raise the siege of Orleans:

> With the Maid in arms and always near [to help] him with a great number of men under her command, the Dauphin acquired new courage. He began to conquer fortified places and regions through the exploits and the prowess of the Maid whose fame was spreading everywhere. A mere word or summons from her was sufficient to determine a fortress to surrender. Her marvellous deeds [inspired] the belief and hope that here was something divine. She did astonishing feats of arms with her bodily strength [and] admonished her troops in the name of Jesus.

Yet, according to another contemporary Burgundian commentator Enguerrand de Monstrelet, for a long time neither the king nor his counsellors put much faith in this young maiden who 'dressed just like a man'. Indeed, they 'considered her to be out of her right mind'. Moreover, although he tells us that the English 'had never been so much afraid of any captain or commander in war as they were of the Maid', he also warns us not to forget that, at Orleans, Joan 'had with her all or most of the noble knights and captains who had been in the city throughout the siege'. As for English chronicles, they tend to pass over Joan of Arc as quickly as possible. An anonymous London chronicler, for instance, was notably economical when reporting Joan's capture in May 1430:

> …before the town of Compiègne, there was a woman taken armed in the field, with many other captains, who was called La Pucelle de Dieu, a false witch, for through her power the dauphin and all our adversaries trusted wholly to have conquered again all France, [for they regarded her] as a prophetess and a worthy goddess.

Clearly, Joan of Arc's martyrdom (she eventually fell into English hands and was burnt at the stake as a heretic) was very important in establishing her posthumous reputation as the saviour of France. Nevertheless, she did play a major role in raising the siege of Orleans and, indeed, defeating the retreating English army at the battle of Patay soon afterwards. Clearly, too, not only were the English now forced on to the defensive but it is possible to detect a new spirit amongst the French, not least Charles VII (who promptly captured much of

Champagne and the upper Seine valley, got himself crowned at Rheims, and even began to threaten Paris). During the early 1430s, Bedford did manage to stabilise the English position but, in 1435/36, came three major blows in rapid succession: Bedford's death, Burgundy's defection to the Valois and the final loss of Paris to Charles VII. Perhaps, if England had had an adult monarch capable of military leadership, such setbacks might not have proved fatal. Unfortunately, Henry VI was still only a teenager and, anyway, entirely lacked the martial ambitions and abilities of his father.

HENRY VI, ENGLISH POLITICS & THE END OF THE LANCASTRIAN EMPIRE IN FRANCE 1437–1453

The personality of Henry VI, his political agenda (if he had one) and the character of the court clique which increasingly came to envelop him are crucial to understanding both Lancastrian domestic politics 1437-1453 and the ignominious collapse of English hegemony in France. Unfortunately, it is far from easy to establish convincingly just what Henry VI was like or exactly what his role was during these years.

The most intimate surviving portrait is provided by John Blacman, a Carthusian monk who served as the king's chaplain and confessor for a while and probably put pen to paper towards the end of the Yorkist period. Here we have Henry as both 'upright and just' and a man 'more given to God and to devout prayer than to handling worldly and temporal things'; he enthusiastically embraced the virtues of humility, even off-setting the pomp of crown-wearing by donning 'a rough hair shirt next to his skin'; and not only was he personally 'chaste and pure from the beginning of his days' but also took great precautions to secure the chastity of his servants. Thus, Blacman tells us, he so disapproved of female nudity that when:

> ...at Christmas time a certain great lord brought before him a dance or show of young ladies with bared bosoms who were to dance in that mode before him, [he] very angrily averted his eyes, turned his back upon them, and went out to his chamber, saying 'Fy, fy, for shame'... At another time, riding by Bath, [the] king, looking into the baths [there], saw in them men wholly naked, at which he was displeased, and went away quickly, abhorring such nudity as a great offence. [Also] he would keep careful watch through hidden windows of his chamber lest any foolish impertinence of women [should] cause the downfall of any in his household...

In Blacman, too, we have the suggestion that Henry VI much preferred reading religious and devotional tracts to the day-to-day business of government:

> [The] king himself once complained heavily to me in his chamber at Eltham, when I was alone there with him studying his holy books, and giving ear to his wholesome advice and the sighs of his most deep devotion, [concerning] a knock on his door by a certain mighty duke of the realm. The king said, 'They so interrupt me that, whether by day or night, I can hardly snatch a moment for reading holy scriptures without disturbance'.

And, although not a physical coward, Blacman's Henry VI was a man who never resorted to violence or cruelty himself and became distressed when others did so in his name:

> Once, when he was journeying from St Albans to London via Cripplegate, he saw over the gate there the quarter of a man on a tall stake, and asked what it was. When his lords answered that if was the quarter of a traitor, who had been false to the king's majesty, he said: 'Take it away. I will not have any Christian man so cruelly handled for my sake'. And the quarter was removed immediately... Again, four nobles of high birth were convicted of treason [and] condemned by the judges to a shameful death, [but] he compassionately released and delivered them...

Could such a king ever have been actively involved in politics? Or was he, as another contemporary cleric John Capgrave strongly implied, entirely and exclusively a royal personification of religious piety:

> With what reverence he adores the sign of the cross when his priests meet him. For I know how many men of more robust life, who did not have the cross in great reverence, were turned by the example of our most devoted king to a greater fervour of faith and to a most faithful embracing of the most glorious sign of our Lord. It would be most pleasing to our lord [the king] if his subjects should be reformed by his good example.

In all probability, Henry VI did play a real role in politics (at any rate until 1453) but a truly inept and disastrous one. Perhaps the Burgundian chronicler Jean de Waurin got to the heart of the matter when he remarked that the king was:

> ...neither intelligent enough nor experienced enough to manage a kingdom such as England... For it is a true proverb which says, 'Very

afflicted is the land whose prince is a child or rules like one'... For, because the king, Henry VI, has not in his time been such a man as is needful to govern such a realm, each one who has had power with him has wished to strengthen himself by getting control over the king.

Once Henry VI declared his minority at an end in 1437 the way certainly now lay open for him to make his personal mark and, when his interest was engaged, he probably did so. His pivotal role in the foundation of Eton in 1440 and King's College, Cambridge, in 1441 is well documented. He managed, on occasion, to fulfil the courtly duties required of him and he supported, even if he did not initiate, efforts to bring about a permanent peace between England and France. Jean de Waurin was not alone, however, in noting his fatal susceptibility to management and manipulation by those around him. As late as 1450 a Prussian agent in London remarked that Henry VI (although now the same age as his father had been at Agincourt) 'is very young and inexperienced and watched over as a Carthusian', while, according to a contemporary English commentator:

Lord Saye, with other persons around Henry VI, would not permit anybody to preach before the king unless they had first seen the sermon in writing, or unless the preacher would swear and promise that he would not preach anything against those who were around the king, or against the actions of his privy – or more truly his evil – council.

Much was made, too, of the harsh treatment of men whose loyal service to the crown over many years should have rendered them unassailable. When envy reared its head in courtly circles in the mid-1440s, remarked Jean de Waurin, it was particularly directed at the admirable Richard Duke of York. Above all, he declared:

...envy prompted the Duke of Somerset, who despised the Duke of York, and who found a way to harm him. He [Somerset] was well liked by the queen of England, Margaret of Anjou, [who] worked on King Henry, her husband, on the advice of the Duke of Somerset and his following, so that the Duke of York was recalled from France to England. Then he was totally stripped of his authority to govern Normandy.

Even more passion was aroused by the fate of Humphrey Duke of Gloucester, found dead in mysterious circumstances the morning after he had been arrested at Bury St Edmunds in 1447. 'The certainty of how he died, and in what manner, is not known to me', recorded one anonymous English chronicler; however, he added:

> Some said he died of sorrow; some said he was murdered between two
> feather beds; and others said that a hot spit was put in his fundament...
> When he was dead he was exposed, so that all men might see him, [but
> no one] could see any wound or evidence of how he died... This duke
> was a noble man and a great scholar, and had honourably ruled this
> realm to the king's advantage. No fault could ever be found in him.

Humphrey Duke of Gloucester's death, remarked another contemporary commentator, was:

> ...everywhere regretted and mourned by the English people, who
> voiced their discontent against the Earl of Suffolk, William Aiscough
> Bishop of Salisbury and James Fiennes Lord Saye, men known to enjoy
> the king's particular favour.

And, when both parliamentary and popular unrest surfaced with a
vengeance in 1450, all three of them were murdered.

For many contemporaries, the most serious indictment against
Henry VI and his government by the summer of 1453 was the collapse
of English power in France. Was this inevitable even as early as 1437?
The death of John Duke of Bedford, and the end of the Anglo-
Burgundian alliance, probably did finally consign the Treaty of Troyes
to the dustbin of history but England remained in control of
Normandy, Maine and parts of Anjou; the English still had Gascony
and Calais; and the Lancastrian regime should have been able to sustain
a prolonged defensive war, not least since the reputation of English
armies for invincibility in the field remained virtually intact. Disaster
was indeed averted for several years, thanks not least to the efforts of
Richard Duke of York during his two spells as commander-in-chief in
France (in 1436/37 and, again, from 1440 to 1445). Certainly, if we are
to believe Jean de Waurin, York:

> ...governed admirably and had many honourable and notable successes
> against the French... Everything he did was highly commendable not
> only for himself but also for the honour and furtherance of the crown
> of England, and for the exaltation of his master the king, whom he
> served with due reverence and loyalty.

Waurin was writing some years after York's death, and may well reflect
later Yorkist propaganda about the duke's achievements, but he did at

least maintain England's authority in its French provinces and probably deserved reappointment when his commission came to an end. Instead, Waurin continues, Edmund Beaufort Duke of Somerset replaced him 'due to the solicitation and exhortation of the queen and some of the barons who, at that time, were in positions of power in the kingdom', while York himself became lieutenant in Ireland (perhaps as part of a deliberate stratagem to marginalise him). Final defeat in France, in fact, resulted not from Richard of York's mistakes while commander-in-chief there in the early 1440s but the misguided policies pursued by Henry VI's government and the determination of Charles VII to win control of the entire French kingdom.

There has been much debate about how much blame can be attached to Henry VI personally or whether responsibility lies primarily with those around him. It is impossible to come to any definitive conclusions on this, but the king does seem to have been firmly committed, perhaps on principle, to policies designed to promote a permanent Anglo-French settlement, as demonstrated by his acceptance, in 1444, of an Angevin marriage in return for a truce and his promise, in 1445, to surrender the strategically vital county of Maine. The king's marriage to Charles VII's niece Margaret of Anjou duly took place in April 1445 and, early in 1448, Maine was indeed ceded to the French in order to ensure an extension of the truce. Meanwhile, Charles VII took full advantage of the prevailing truce to crush internal resistance to his rule and carry out financial and military reforms in France. Clearly, it was essential that the English government maintain its forces across the Channel at full strength and in a state of readiness. This it singularly failed to do. Instead, partly as a result of political divisions and mounting financial problems at home, defences of fortresses were neglected, garrisons dwindled, insufficient stores were sent out and the field army was allowed to disintegrate. The Lancastrian regime was certainly in no position to provoke the French yet, in March 1449, it sanctioned a foolhardy attack on the Breton fortress of Fougères. Brittany appealed to Charles VII and, in August 1449, he launched an invasion of Normandy. Since English garrisons in Normandy were both below strength and demoralised, and the local population offered little support either, the province was rapidly lost, a loss that became virtually inevitable as a result of the battle of Formigny in April 1450. According to a contemporary French commentator Jacques le Bouvier, at Formigny:

> ...there were killed, by the report of the heralds who were there, and of the priests and good people who buried them, 3774 English, [who]

were buried in fourteen trenches. On this day only five or six of the French were slain. They behaved themselves exceedingly well, for there were not in all, by the report of the heralds [above 3000 French fighting men, whereas the English had between 5000 and 6000.] And therefore wise men say that the grace of God was the cause of the victory of the French.

Although much of the blame for English failure in Normandy could be placed firmly on the shoulders of Edmund Beaufort Duke of Somerset, Henry VI (much to the chagrin of Richard Duke of York) responded by promoting him in the autumn of 1450. In the spring of 1451, moreover, Charles VII followed up his success in Normandy by invading Gascony (an English province since the mid-twelfth century) and, at the end of June 1451, Bordeaux (its chief city) surrendered. Even Henry VI's government could not stomach this. The veteran John Talbot Earl of Shrewsbury was despatched to Gascony and, before the year was out, Bordeaux and its surrounding area were once more in English hands. It proved only a temporary reprieve for, on 17 July 1453, Talbot was defeated and killed at the battle of Castillon and, some three months after that, Bordeaux finally succumbed to Valois control. Jean Chartier, another French commentator of the time, reported both the battle of Castillon and the fate of John Talbot ('a very old man mounted on a little hackney') in graphic terms:

There began a great and terrible assault, with acts of great bravery on both sides, hand-to-hand fighting, and marvellous struggles with lances and many valiant blows. The struggle lasted for more than an hour, for the English kept on returning to the attack with great ardour and the French were not slow to receive them with courage… When Breton reinforcements arrived, however, they did so well, with the aid of God and by their prowess, that the English eventually turned their backs, and were put to flight and defeated… All their banners were thrown down and many left dead on the field. In particular, Talbot's hackney was struck by a shot from a culverine, so that it fell at once to the ground quite dead; Talbot was thrown under it; and, at once, he was killed by some archers. Thus died the famous and renowned English leader, who for so long had been reputed one of the most formidable scourges of the French and one of their most sworn enemies, and who had seemed to be the dread and terror of France.

Formigny and Castillon were the only two occasions in the entire Hundred Years War when the English lost major pitched battles in

France: yet, as a result of these defeats, the Lancastrian empire on the continent was reduced to just one town (Calais) and, within two years, England itself had dissolved into civil war.

4

HENRY VI, RICHARD OF YORK AND THE WARS OF THE ROSES

THE ORIGINS OF THE WARS OF THE ROSES

William Shakespeare, and the Tudor chroniclers on which he drew so heavily, must bear prime responsibility for the enduring notion of the Wars of the Roses as dynastic wars, originating in the tragic circumstances surrounding Richard II's deposition and Henry IV's seizure of the throne in 1399. Yet, in fact, such an interpretation is already to be found in Yorkist propaganda in the later fifteenth century, with the house of Lancaster (in the person of Henry VI) represented as rightly deprived of the throne by the Yorkist king Edward IV in 1461: the civil wars are dramatically portrayed by Yorkist apologists as God's punishment on England for the unnatural usurpation of Henry IV and the sinful murder of Richard II. The Burgundian chronicler Jean de Waurin certainly reflected just such a pro-Yorkist stance that 'ill-gotten gains cannot last' when he pictured Henry VI losing the crown which his grandfather Henry IV had 'violently usurped and taken from King Richard II' and whom he had then 'caused to be shamelessly murdered'. Lancastrian propagandists in the 1450s, by contrast, had gone out of their way to stress the legitimacy of Henry VI's occupation of the throne and the right of his son Prince Edward of Lancaster to succeed him. And, according to John Blacman, when Henry VI was asked (during his imprisonment in the Tower of London by Edward IV in the later 1460s):

…why he had unjustly claimed and possessed the crown of England for so many years, he would answer: 'My father was King of England and peaceably possessed the crown of England for the whole of his reign. And his father and my grandfather were kings of the same realm. And I, a child in the cradle, was peaceably and without any protest crowned and approved as king by the whole realm, and wore the crown of England some forty years, and each and all of my lords did me royal homage and plighted me their faith, as was also done to my predecessors'.

The personality of Henry VI and his regal shortcomings have always been central to historical debate about the origins of the Wars of the Roses. Contemporaries were reluctant to criticise the king personally but even John Blacman, by implication at least, had distinct reservations about his capacity to rule, while Yorkist partisans deliberately highlighted his faults and failings. In around 1460, for instance, Richard Neville Earl of Warwick declared, in a letter to a Papal legate, that 'our king is stupid and out of his mind, he does not rule but is ruled'; Warwick's brother George Neville wrote in similar vein, in April 1461, of 'that puppet of a king, that statue of a king'; and an anonymous but firmly Yorkist chronicler recorded, under the year 1459, that 'the realm of England was out of all good governance, as it had been many days before, for the king was simple and led by covetous counsel and owed more than he was worth'. The St Albans' chronicler John Whethamsted, again notably sympathetic to the Yorkists, applauded the king as 'honest and upright' but nevertheless considered him 'his mother's stupid offspring', a son 'greatly degenerated from the father who did not cultivate the art of war', a 'pious king' admittedly but 'half-witted in affairs of state'. And, according to yet another pro-Yorkist commentator, Henry VI was 'deposed from the crowns of England and France' in 1461 because 'he had ruled tyrannously like his father and grandfather'.

Contemporary chroniclers clearly believed there was a link between the loss of English possessions in France in the early 1450s and the onset of civil strife at home. As a result of Henry VI's breaking his promises, remarked one anonymous commentator, and because of his marriage to Margaret of Anjou:

…what losses has the realm of England had, by losing Normandy and Gascony, by division of the realm, and the rebelling by the commons against their princes and lords. What division among the lords, what murder and slaying of them! In conclusion, so many that many a man has lost his life. And, in the end, the king deposed…

Richard of York was certainly inclined to make much of this, stressing, in particular, Edmund Beaufort Duke of Somerset's dismal record in

Normandy compared with his own period of service there in the early 1440s. In a manifesto directed to the citizens of Shrewsbury in February 1452, he remarked on the 'derogation, loss of merchandise, damaging of honour and villainy' resulting from the loss of Normandy, placing the blame firmly on Somerset's shoulders. York's early ally John Mowbray Duke of Norfolk, in 1453, castigated Somerset no less vigorously for 'the great dishonour' suffered by the realm as a result of 'the loss of two so noble duchies as Normandy and Gascony'. And, in a manifesto issued from Calais in 1460, York's aristocratic allies were still attacking those 'enemies of the common weal' who 'have allowed all the old possessions which the king had in France' to be 'shamefully lost and sold'.

Another area of failure by Henry VI's government often commented on by contemporaries in the context of the slide towards civil war was the chronic condition of the royal finances in the 1440s and 1450s. The cost of defending the Lancastrian empire in France in the 1440s, the disruption of English shipping once Anglo-French warfare resumed in 1449 and the eventual loss of all the king's continental possessions (apart from Calais) by the autumn of 1453 obviously had serious implications for government income and expenditure. The mid-fifteenth century, moreover, saw a major economic recession and this certainly had a real impact on the crown's revenue. For the government's critics, however, the sheer wastefulness of Henry VI's regime and its apparent inability to manage its financial affairs effectively was the heart of the problem. As early as June 1450, a manifesto circulating during Jack Cade's rebellion declared that the king was 'so placed that he cannot pay for his meat and drink'; a Yorkist manifesto of 1459 asserted that the crown had been 'immeasurably and outrageously spoiled of its livelihood and possessions'; and another, in 1460, remarked pointedly on 'the poverty in which the king finds himself'. An anonymous pro-Yorkist chronicler, too, recorded that by the end of the 1450s the king's debts:

> ...increased daily but payment there was none. All the possessions and lordships that pertained to the crown the king bad given away [so] that he had almost nothing to live on. And of the impositions that were imposed on the people, such as taxes, tallages and fifteenths, all that came from them was spent in vain, for he maintained no household and waged no wars.

Even Sir John Fortescue, an eminent contemporary judge, Lancastrian partisan and author of several political treatises, believed regal poverty was indeed a fundamental weakness of Henry VI's government: if a king be poor, he declared, this can only be highly prejudicial to his prestige;

worse still, it is 'most to his insecurity' since 'his subjects will rather go with a lord that is rich and may pay their wages and expenses' than a king who 'has nought in his purse'.

Clearly, the perceived personal inadequacies of Henry VI lie behind the stress in several contemporary sources on the importance during the 1440s and 1450s of growing resentment at the power, wealth and influence of those around the king. The St Albans' chronicler John Whethamsted, for instance, portrayed the Yorkist lords in 1459 as 'stiffening their necks in order to chastise with rods of iron those familiars of the king who daily called those lords false and betrayers of the king', while an anonymous monk writing at Crowland Abbey in Lincolnshire similarly highlighted:

> ...certain persons enjoying the royal intimacy, who were rivals [of Richard Duke of York], and who brought serious accusations of treason against him, and made him to stink in the king's nostrils. [Eventually] many of the nobles of the realm, who held the duke in some degree of honour, [determined] to watch for an opportunity to inflict due vengeance for their malice upon their malignant rivals, in case they could find any means of removing them from the side of the king, in whose presence they were in continual attendance.

Perhaps, as they frequently stressed in proclamations, manifestos and letters, the Yorkist lords were genuinely concerned about the public good and the well being of the commonweal: in 1459, for instance, they claimed to be motivated by 'the tender love that we bear to the commonwealth and prosperity of this realm and pride in the king's estate', while, in 1460, they again professed to be true liegemen of the king, devoted to 'the prosperity and welfare of his most noble estate, and to the commonweal of all this land'. Lancastrian apologists were inclined to defend Henry VI's regime in similar terms. A tract of 1459, for instance, vigorously argued that the common good could only be served by maintaining obedience to the king and his laws, while the pure malice and long premeditated wickedness of the Yorkists (only too evident in their willingness to resort to violence and treachery) proved the falseness of their professed concern for the commonwealth. How far high-minded principles like these, rather than perceived self-interest, really did inspire the mid-fifteenth century English nobility is difficult to determine but, certainly, such ideas were indeed much debated during these turbulent years.

Private aristocratic feuds and escalating lawlessness were vigorously highlighted by contemporary commentators. The chronicler John Harding, for instance, contrasted the ineffectual leadership of Henry VI with that of his father Henry V, resulting, so he believed, in increasing misrule and lawlessness in the shires (especially the development of feuds between neighbouring magnates) and a notable failure of the legal processes to cope:

> The peace at home and law so well maintained
> Were root and head of all his [Henry V's] great conquest,
> Which exiled is away and foully now disdained…
> In every shire with jack [ets] and salets [helmets] clean,
> Misrule does rise, and makes the neighbours war.
> The weaker goes beneath, as oft is seen,
> The mightiest his quarrel will prefer
> That poor men's causes are set back too far,
> Which if the peace and law were well conserved
> Might be amended, and thanks of God deserved.

A Yorkist manifesto of 1459 declared that 'abominable murders, robberies, perjuries and extortions' are 'openly used and practised in this realm, while great violence is not punished but favoured and cherished'; another, in 1460, made much of the notion that 'all righteousness and justice are exiled from the land and no man is afraid to offend the laws'; and Sir John Fortescue deliberately emphasised 'the perils that may come to the king by overmighty subjects'. Richard of York in his own propaganda, and chroniclers of a pro-Yorkist bent, frequently headlined the bitter personal feud between himself and Edmund Beaufort Duke of Somerset. York certainly blamed Somerset for the collapse of English power in France, while an anonymous English chronicler, reviewing the political situation on the eve of the first battle of St Albans in 1455, remarked that Somerset, by whom 'the king was principally guided and governed', invariably 'kept near to the king, and dared not depart from his presence, dreading always the power' of York and his Neville allies. Nor was the York/Somerset feud the only aristocratic confrontation seen as feeding into burgeoning civil war. In the west country, for instance, the rivalry between Thomas Courtenay Earl of Devon and William Lord Bonville clearly did much to influence their response to national developments in the 1450s. Even more importantly, bitter dispute raged between the great northern families of Neville and Percy from at least 1453, resulting in the Middleham Nevilles forging an alliance with York in the winter of 1453/54, while the Percies threw in their lot with the Lancastrian regime. Indeed, according to one annalist, the onset of private war between Percies and Nevilles at Heworth Moor in August 1453 marked 'the beginning of the greatest sorrows in England'.

Clearly, the origins of the Wars of the Roses are nothing if not complex. Dynastic considerations cannot be ignored. There was an enormous reluctance to remove Henry VI from the throne in the 1450s (for all his shortcomings as a ruler) on the grounds that he was England's rightful and anointed king; yet there is evidence, as well, that the house of Lancaster was only too conscious of the shadow of 1399 still hanging over the dynasty even after half a century of rule. Even if Lancastrians and Yorkists were not, in practice, out-and-out devotees of principle, the political crises of the 1440s and 1450s certainly did spawn considerable ideological argument and controversy. Neither can economic considerations be set on one side. The Lancastrian government's financial situation was chronically weak by the early 1450s, while Henry VI's exercise of political patronage, partisan and divisive as it was, did help foster jealousy and rivalry between great men. Aristocratic feuds, often both personal and political in derivation, have their part to play in explaining the wars, as does failure by government adequately to maintain law and order. Equally clearly, apportioning blame for the disasters in France was a major issue in domestic politics in the 1450s, fuelling York's mounting hatred of Somerset in particular. Yet, in the end, all avenues lead back to the king and it is difficult to avoid the conclusion that, if Henry VI had not been the man he was and if his government had not developed along the lines it did, the Wars of the Roses might never have happened.

THE EARLY STAGES OF THE
WARS OF THE ROSES 1450–1459

Whether or not the events of 1450 can be regarded as the real beginning of the Wars of the Roses, it was certainly a traumatic year for Henry VI and his government. Early in the year there is evidence of seditious bills, anti-government propaganda and rioting in London, as well as a minor uprising against the king in Kent. Most dramatically, Adam Moleyns, Bishop of Chichester, a prominent member of Henry VI's inner circle, was lynched by an enraged mob of unpaid soldiers and sailors at Portsmouth. Mounting discontent at failure in France and misgovernment at home resulted, in February 1450, in parliament's impeachment for treason of the king's chief minister, William de la Pole Duke of Suffolk. He was duly condemned and sentenced to banishment and, while in the very act of sailing into exile, so a contemporary letter writer noted:

...in the sight of all his men, he was taken out of a great ship into a boat; there was an axe and a block; one of the most ignorant of the ship's company bade him lay down his head, struck it off with half a dozen strokes of a rusty sword, and laid his body on the sands at Dover; and some say that his head was set on a pole by it.

Most serious of all, Jack Cade's rebellion – a formidable popular uprising – broke out in May 1450. Centred in the south-east of England, and involving gentlemen and yeomen as well as peasants and artisans, this rebellion was clearly a major challenge to Henry VI's government: indeed, the rebels succeeded in getting into London, amidst a good deal of violence, and it was only with the utmost difficulty that the citizens were able to get them out again. Moreover, it is clear that the grievances and objectives of the rebels were highly political. The king's 'false council', declared a surviving rebel manifesto, has 'lost his law, his merchandise is lost, the sea is lost, France is lost, and his common people are destroyed'. The only solution, the rebels asserted, was for the king to 'send away from him all the false progeny and affinity' of the late William de la Pole Duke of Suffolk and 'take about his noble person men of his true blood', especially the 'high and mighty prince' Richard Duke of York.

The Lancastrian regime, although now lacking two of its most prominent members – William Aiscough, Bishop of Salisbury, 'slain by his own parishioners and people at Edington after he had said mass', and James Fiennes Lord Saye and Sele, seized and beheaded by the rebels in London – managed to survive this onslaught but, with the return of Richard of York from Ireland (where he had been in virtual exile) in September 1450, there came a fresh assault on its prestige and authority. Yet, despite the deaths of Moleyns, Suffolk, Aiscough and Saye, despite Cade's rebellion, despite recent disasters on the continent (culminating in the loss of Normandy), and despite powerful criticisms by both York and his supporters in parliament, the old court clique continued to flourish around the king. Moreover, the failure – only too evident in 1451 – of a petition to remove Edmund Beaufort Duke of Somerset – newly returned from France and widely perceived to be Suffolk's political heir – and other 'familiars' from the king's presence probably reflects the continued determination of Henry VI to protect his chosen men. As an anonymous annalist succinctly recorded:

In November [1450] parliament met. During it, a great disagreement arose between the Dukes of York and Somerset and, not long afterwards, Somerset was robbed [and] nearly killed... [After Christmas 1450] the Duke of Somerset became captain of Calais and most familiar with the king, so that he controlled everything, both within the royal household and outside it. In this same parliament [in 1451] the Commons petitioned the king to remove several of his familiars but nothing came of it.

Early in 1452, having failed to make progress by constitutional means and even more bitter than he had been in 1450, Richard of York resorted to armed force. It proved a costly miscalculation. The attempted *coup d'état* of 1452 attracted virtually no support from the nobility – not even the Nevilles had broken rank at this stage – and York was forced to surrender at Dartford, suffer the humiliation of seeing Somerset triumphant and swear a solemn and public oath of allegiance to Henry VI at St Paul's, promising never again to 'make any assembly of your people without your command or licence', even in his own defence. Certainly, Somerset and his friends were now even more firmly entrenched in power around the king and, seemingly, determined to demonstrate the fact, as an anonymous London chronicler colourfully reported:

> [In 1452/53] the king, complying with the counsel of the Duke of Somerset, rode to several of the Duke of York's townships where the tenants were compelled to come naked with choking cords around their necks, in the direst frost and snow, to submit to the king because, previously, they had supported their lord against the Duke of Somerset before his hour had come. Moreover, although the king himself pardoned them, the Duke [of Somerset] ordered them to be hanged.

By the summer of 1453, in fact, the victory of Henry VI and his inner circle seemed complete, while York appeared hopelessly isolated and thoroughly discredited. Despite all his personal shortcomings and the manifest failures of his government over the years, the king had apparently risen phoenix-like from what had, at the beginning of the decade, all the symptoms of a lethal crisis for his regime: if England had been hovering on the brink of civil war in 1450 or 1452, it now appeared firmly off the agenda once more.

Two dramatic, and possibly connected, events in July 1453 changed the situation beyond all recognition. Firstly, news reached England of the defeat and death of John Talbot Earl of Shrewsbury at the battle of Castillon; secondly, Henry VI suffered a complete mental collapse. Even before mid-1453 rumours concerning the king's mental shortcomings had occasionally surfaced: in 1442, for instance, a Kentish yeoman had been accused of saying that 'the king is a lunatic'; a London draper, in 1447, was alleged to have remarked that Henry 'is not as steadfast of wit as other kings have been before'; and, in 1450, two Sussex husbandmen were indicted for declaring that the king was 'a natural fool' who 'would oftimes hold a staff in his hands with a bird on the end, playing therewith as a fool', and that 'another king must be ordained to rule the land'. John Blacman related later how, for a time, the king was 'not conscious of himself, or of those around him, as if he were in a trance', although, for Blacman, this was not so much insanity as spiritual rapture. Even more graphically, the chronicler John Whethamsted described how the king 'lost his wits and memory for a time, and nearly all his body was so unco-ordinated and out of control that he could neither walk, nor hold his head upright, nor easily move from where he sat'. Clearly, Henry VI was utterly incapable of governing the country now, whatever the situation before, and he was destined to remain in this condition until the end of 1454.

To make matters worse, at any rate as far as Richard of York was concerned, in October 1453 Queen Margaret of Anjou gave birth to a son, bringing the queen herself into politics as a ruthless, even fanatical, supporter of Prince Edward of Lancaster's right to succeed to his father's throne. During the next few months, in fact, she attempted, initially, to conceal her husband's condition and, when this inevitably failed, made considerable efforts to prevent the council or, worse still, Richard of York from taking power by securing it for herself: a newsletter of January 1454, indeed, not only described Henry VI's entire lack of response to his recently born son and highlighted the increasingly dangerous political climate but also reported that Margaret of Anjou had 'made a bill of five articles', the first of which is that 'she desires the whole rule of this land'. Richard of York was determined, at all costs, to prevent either the queen or his hated rival Edmund of Somerset obtaining the upper hand during these faction-ridden months and, in November 1453, Somerset found himself a prisoner in the Tower of London. Even more significantly, and certainly ominously for the future, the winter of 1453/54 saw the forging of a political alliance between Richard of York and the Nevilles (Richard Neville Earl of Salisbury and his son Richard Neville Earl of Warwick, two of the most powerful nobles in England and, hitherto, attached to the court), an alliance which could both forward York's ambitions and be of assistance to the Nevilles in their now raging feud with the Percies in the north of England. The sudden death of Cardinal John Kemp, chancellor of England and a powerful opponent of York, on 22 March 1454, finally precipitated matters in favour of the York/Neville alliance, especially once a parliamentary delegation had seen for itself just how incapacitated the king was:

[On 25 March 1454] lords spiritual and temporal were in the king's high presence in the place where he dined. [Articles were put to him expressing] great concern for his health [but from him] they could get no answer or sign. [After dinner] they came to him again [and] urged him for an answer, by all ways and means they could think of, but they received none. From that place [the king] was led, between two men, into the chamber where he slept and the lords pressed him once more, [but] they received no answer, word or sign.

A few days later York became protector of the realm, although with only limited powers, and Salisbury succeeded Kemp as chancellor.

Pro-Yorkist chroniclers tended to paint a glowing picture of Richard of York's months as protector. He 'governed the entire realm of England well and honourably', and 'miraculously pacified all rebels and malefactors in accordance with his oath and without great severity', declared one enthusiastic commentator, while, according to another, he and Salisbury 'honourably ruled and governed'. Perhaps effective measures were taken at last to curb lawlessness and aristocratic feuding, particularly in the north of England, but, although Somerset remained in prison, no formal charges were laid against him and many members of the council may well have been more concerned to prevent Margaret of Anjou securing power than provide York with unequivocal backing for full-scale reform of government and administration. At the end of 1454, moreover, Henry VI recovered at least most of his senses and, although the king never again enjoyed robust health (if he ever had) and, as the years went by, became so withdrawn into himself as to be rendered a mere political cipher, even his partial restoration to mental normality had profound implications. Somerset was released from the Tower early in February 1455 and now, if not before, became a fully committed ally of Margaret of Anjou in her objective of making the house of Lancaster unassailable once and for all. Before the month was out York's protectorate was terminated and, as a result, the Nevilles found themselves excluded from the magic circle of high politics as well. Feeling seriously threatened, and not without justification, York, Salisbury and Warwick retired to their estates, proceeded to arm and, on 22 May 1455, successfully confronted their rivals at St Albans.

The first battle of St Albans, essentially a skirmish in the streets of an English market town between rival lords and their retinues, had more political than military significance. Edmund Beaufort Duke of Somerset, Henry Percy Earl of Northumberland and Thomas Lord Clifford were all killed fighting for the king, and it may well be they had been deliberately targeted by York and the Nevilles: if so, the events at St Albans in May 1455 may have set in motion a series of bloodfeuds that were to resurface with a vengeance at Wakefield in December 1460. Certainly,

Edmund of Somerset was killed and his son Henry Beaufort might well have thirsted for revenge; so too was the second Earl of Northumberland (perhaps deliberately singled out for slaughter by the Nevilles) and this probably gave added venom to the Percy/Neville feud in years to come; and young John Lord Clifford's behaviour at Wakefield (where, perhaps, he deliberately butchered York's second son Edmund Earl of Rutland in cold blood) can best be explained by deep resentment at his father's fate during the fighting at St Albans. More immediately, the balance of political advantage passed to York and the Nevilles. Henry VI, who had apparently been struck in the neck by a stray arrow during the battle: fell into Yorkist hands, and the plums of political office rapidly followed. Even so, the Yorkist lords still lacked any substantial baronial support, hence their anxiety, both at court and in parliament, to present themselves as having behaved loyally to Henry VI throughout recent events. During the autumn of 1455, however, a new and violent flare-up of the Courtenay/Bonville feud in the south-west and the prevalence of disorder elsewhere in the country resulted, on 19 November, in Richard of York once more becoming protector of the realm. Perhaps, too, Henry VI had suffered another mental breakdown: certainly, at the end of October 1455, a contemporary newsletter reported that 'some men are afraid that the king is sick again' and, on 11 November, Richard of York was empowered 'to hold and dissolve parliament' since 'the king cannot appear in person'. As it turned out, however, York's second protectorate lasted only about three months. By early February 1456, according to another contemporary newsletter, although Henry VI (now, apparently, recovered again) was willing enough to let York continue as his 'chief and principal councillor', Margaret of Anjou was not. The queen, declared this commentator, is 'a great and very active woman' who 'spares no pains to pursue her objectives towards an end and conclusion favourable to her power'. Soon afterwards, on 25 February 1456, Henry VI came to parliament in person and formally dispensed with Richard of York's services.

Although, following the end of his second protectorate, Richard of York remained a prominent member of Henry VI's council, for several months he virtually disappeared from the political scene. Margaret of Anjou, if we are to believe Yorkist propaganda, soon took advantage of the situation, as her hostility to the York/Neville connection became ever more implacable: indeed, not only did she engineer the court's withdrawal to the midlands in August 1456 (where she was joined, ominously, by the sons of the nobility killed at St Albans) but, over the next few years, deliberately sought to build up political support for the Lancastrian dynasty there and in the north-west, perhaps with the central aim of eliminating the Yorkist lords altogether. If the contemporary commentator Thomas Gascoigne is to be relied upon, 'almost all the affairs of the realm' at this time 'were conducted according to the queen's will, by fair means or foul'. In October 1456 Richard of York was thoroughly humiliated at a council meeting in Coventry and, in December of the same year, assaulted by young Henry Beaufort Duke of Somerset; in November 1456 Richard Neville Earl of Warwick was almost ambushed while journeying to London; and, in November 1458, there may well have been another attempt on Warwick's life. Why, then, did full-scale civil war not break out until the autumn of 1459? Perhaps Margaret of Anjou and her supporters were neither so powerful nor so malignant as pro-Yorkist chroniclers would have us believe. Perhaps the Yorkist lords, far from seeking to escalate political conflict, actually made every effort to prevent it. Perhaps, even, Henry VI's own endeavours to promote peace and unity among the nobility, culminating in the so-called Loveday of 25 March 1458, should not be too easily discounted. This was certainly celebrated in a contemporary ballad:

> ...Love has put out malicious governance,
> In every place both free and bond,
> In York, in Somerset, as I understand,
> In Warwick also is love and charity.
> In Salisbury too, and in Northumberland,
> That every man may rejoice in concord and unity...
> In every quarter love is thus laid,
> Grace and wisdom have thus the domination...
> At [St] Paul's in London, with great renown,
> On our Lady day in Lent this peace was wrought;
> The king, the queen, with lords many a one,
> To worship that Virgin as they ought,
> Went in procession, and spared right nought,
> In sight of all the commonalty,
> In token that love was in heart and thought,
> Rejoice, England, in concord and unity.

And although, as another contemporary noted, 'peace and concord did not last long', perhaps the king's efforts did at least delay the resumption of hostilities. Even more important in preserving precarious peace, probably, was the reluctance of most of the nobility to take up arms at all. As in 1452 and 1455, the majority of lords clearly remained loath to become involved in a civil war.

THE WARS OF THE ROSES IN EARNEST 1459-1461

During 1459 the political situation deteriorated markedly and responsibility for this probably lies primarily with Margaret at Anjou and her supporters rather than, as asserted at the Coventry parliament later in the year, York, Salisbury and Warwick:

> [Following the Loveday of 1458] your highness trusted that tranquillity and due obedience would have followed on the part of the Duke of York and the Earls of Warwick and Salisbury. And you summoned them at different times to come to your councils. These summonses they disobeyed and they sent feigned and untrue excuses alleging frivolous business which, nevertheless, your highness accepted. Meanwhile, they enriched themselves by your gifts and grants, while continuing in their premeditated, malicious and damnable opinions and false and traitorous desires...

By contrast, if we are to believe one anonymous pro-Yorkist chronicler, the queen and her affinity 'ruled the realm as she liked' and, in particular, 'sought the alliance of all the knights and squires of Cheshire', making her young son Edward of Lancaster 'give a livery of swans to all the gentlemen of the countryside and to many others, trusting through their strength to make her son king'; while, according to another, she firmly threw down the gauntlet in June 1459 at a council meeting in Coventry where, in their absence and 'at the urging of the queen', the Yorkist lords were proclaimed traitors. When news of this reached the ears of York, Warwick and Salisbury, the chronicler continues, they 'resolved to journey to the king'. Certainly, too, they now began to arm with a vengeance and when, in September 1459, royal troops intercepted Richard Neville Earl of Salisbury near Newcastle-under-Lyme in Staffordshire, bloodshed soon followed. The battle of Blore Heath, fought on 23 September, resulted, in fact, from Margaret of Anjou's determination to prevent Salisbury joining his son Warwick and Richard of York at York's castle of Ludlow in Shropshire. Although, so we are told, this was a 'deadly battle' where 'many of the notable knights and squires of Cheshire who had received the livery of the swans' were slain, it proved an indecisive engagement since York, Salisbury and Warwick did indeed rendezvous at Ludlow soon afterwards. Not so events at Ludford Bridge, outside Ludlow, on the night of 12/13 October 1459, when, recognising the impossibility of successfully confronting a much larger royal force, the Yorkist lords simply fled: Richard of York and his second son Edmund Earl of Rutland hastily took ship for Ireland, while Salisbury, Warwick and York's eldest son Edward Earl of March (the future Edward IV) escaped to Calais. When the Coventry parliament – the Parliament of Devils as it was dubbed in Yorkist propaganda – met in November 1459, a detailed recital of Richard of York's alleged offences since 1450 and a vigorous character assassination of both York and his leading supporters formed a prelude to the condemnation of the Yorkist lords as traitors and the confiscation of their estates. Clearly, only force could now serve to restore the Yorkists' position.

During the early months of 1460 the Yorkist earls mounted a vigorous propaganda campaign from Calais, particularly targeting south-eastern England. In March 1460 Richard Neville Earl of Warwick sailed to Ireland to consult with Richard of York and, perhaps, at this time the possibility of deposing Henry VI was first seriously discussed. Three months later the Nevilles and Edward Earl of March embarked from Calais, landing at Sandwich in Kent on 26 June, and, although the Lancastrian government had put defence measures in place in anticipation of an invasion, they proved ineffective. The anti-government sentiment in south-eastern England that had produced Cade's rebellion a decade earlier remained as powerful as ever and, as the Yorkist lords made their way towards London, they attracted a great deal of support. The city authorities, if only after considerable soul-searching, opened the capital's gates to Warwick, Salisbury and March on 2 July and, henceforth, London proved a great asset to the Yorkists. Shortly afterwards, Warwick and March set off in search of Henry VI. At Northampton they ran him to ground and, after prolonged but abortive negotiations, battle was joined outside the town on 10 July. Most battles of the Wars of the Roses tend to be poorly reported, and this is certainly true of Northampton, although an anonymous chronicler does remark, intriguingly, that the 'ordnance of the king's guns availed not, for that day was so great rain that the guns lay deep in the water and were so quenched that they might not be shot'. Victory went to the Yorkists and, most importantly, Henry VI now fell into their hands. At this stage, despite rumours to the contrary, there was no question of removing the king from the throne; rather, as a chronicler writing at Crowland Abbey later learned, 'the victorious earls paid all honours of royalty to King Henry', conducting him to London 'in solemn procession', the Earl of Warwick, 'bare-headed, carrying a sword before the king, in all humility and respect'. Soon, a Yorkist-controlled regime was established in Henry VI's name, albeit a partisan and narrowly based administration very much dominated by the Nevilles, exercising little authority beyond London and south-eastern England.

Strangely absent for several weeks was Richard of York until, perhaps out of the blue, he returned from Ireland early in September 1460. From the moment of his arrival in Cheshire, moreover, he probably made it clear that he had come to claim the throne for himself and, when he entered London early in October, it was like a king: surrounded by a substantial body of retainers, trumpets blaring, banners charged with the arms of England held aloft and with his sword borne before him in truly regal fashion. The St Albans' chronicler John Whethamsted was probably an eyewitness of the dramatic sequence of events that now unfolded:

Entering the palace [of Westminster, Richard of York] marched straight through the great hall until he came to the solemn chamber where the king, with the Commons, was accustomed to hold parliament. When he arrived he made directly for the king's throne, where he laid his hand on the drape or cushion, as if about to take possession of what was his by right, and held his hand there for a brief time. At last, withdrawing it, he turned towards the people and, standing quietly under the cloth of state, looked eagerly at the assembly awaiting acclamation. Whilst he stood there, turning his face to the people and awaiting their applause, Thomas Bourchier Archbishop of Canterbury arose and, after a suitable greeting, enquired whether he wished to see the king. The duke, who seemed irritated by this request, replied curtly: 'I do not recall that I know anyone in the kingdom whom it would not befit to come to me and see my person, rather than I should go and visit him'. When the archbishop heard this reply, he quickly withdrew and told the king of the duke's response. After the archbishop had left, the duke also withdrew, went to the principal chamber of the palace, smashed the locks and threw open the doors, in a regal rather than a ducal manner, and remained there for some time. When news of the duke's high-handedness became known to the people, [everyone] immediately began to grumble fervently against him and assert he had acted rashly…

If we are to believe the Burgundian chronicler Jean de Waurin, even York's friends were dismayed by his actions, particularly Richard Neville Earl of Warwick who:

…went to the palace which he found full of armed men [and] entered the duke's chamber where he found him leaning on a cupboard. When the duke saw him he walked forward and so they greeted each other. There were angry words between the two of them, for the earl disclosed to the duke how the lords and people were unhappy at his desire to strip the king of the crown. During these exchanges the Earl of Rutland arrived and said to the Earl of Warwick: 'Fair cousin, you must not be angry, for you know that it is our right to have the crown, which belongs to my lord my father, and he will keep it as anyone may see'.

When Richard of York submitted a formal claim to the throne, prolonged and probably heated debate took place in parliament until, on 24 October 1460, a compromise was cobbled together in the so-called Act of Accord. Under its terms Henry VI was to retain the crown as long as he lived but, after his death, York and his heirs were to succeed. In practice Henry VI now became, even more than before, a virtual prisoner of the Yorkists.

Clearly, none of this was acceptable to stalwart Lancastrians, most particularly Margaret of Anjou, since the Act of Accord – if ever fully implemented – would have disinherited her beloved son Edward of Lancaster. In response, the Lancastrian leadership assembled a powerful force in northern England and, shortly before Christmas 1460, Richard of York himself (accompanied by Richard Neville Earl of Salisbury and Edmund Earl of Rutland) arrived at his castle of Sandal, near Wakefield, in Yorkshire. A few days later, on 30 December, he made the foolish decision to engage a much larger army than his own at the battle of Wakefield and, perhaps partly as a result of treachery in his own ranks, sustained a major defeat in the field. During the battle, according to an indignant John Whethamsted, York and Salisbury were taken alive and, once it was over, treated 'with great mockery', especially Richard of York:

> They stood him on a little anthill and placed on his head, as if a crown, a vile garland made of reeds, just as the Jews did to the Lord, and bent the knee to him, saying in jest: 'Hail King, without rule. Hail King, without ancestry. Hail leader and prince, with almost no subjects or possessions'. And, having said this and various other shameful and dishonourable things to him, at last they cut off his head... The Lord Salisbury they took to the castle of Pontefract and there, at the impious, shameless and savage instigation of certain perverse men, they beheaded him.

In fact, Richard of York almost certainly lost his life during the fighting, as did Salisbury's son Sir Thomas Neville, but Salisbury himself was indeed executed at nearby Pontefract the following day. Thus, arguably, the deaths of Henry Percy, second Earl of Northumberland at St Albans in 1455 and his son Thomas Lord Egremont at Northampton earlier in 1460 were revenged. Also, if another contemporary commentator is to be relied upon, 'in the flight after the battle [John] Lord Clifford killed Edmund Earl of Rutland, son of the Duke of York, on the bridge at Wakefield', so avenging his own father's death at St Albans. Next day, he continues, the heads of all the leading Yorkists who had lost their lives were despatched to the city of York, placed on various gateways there, and, as a final insult, Richard of York was 'in contempt crowned with a paper crown'.

Fortunately for the Yorkists, Margaret of Anjou and her military advisers entirely failed to reap the benefit of the great Lancastrian success at Wakefield. For a start, the appalling behaviour of the queen's largely northern army as it marched south in January 1461 caused serious alarm in the midlands and south. According to John Whethamsted, in 'every place through which they came' the northerners 'robbed, plundered and devastated'; an anonymous London-based chronicler recorded that, as they came south, the northern men robbed 'all the country and people as they came as if they had been pagans or Saracens and not Christian men'; and, if we are to believe a monk writing at Crowland Abbey, the Lancastrian army:

> ...swept onwards like a whirlwind from the north and, in the impulse of their fury, attempted to overrun the whole of England... Thus did they proceed with impunity, spreading in vast crowds over a region thirty miles in breadth and, covering the whole surface of the earth like so many locusts, made their way almost to the very walls of London, all the movables they could possibly collect in every quarter being placed on beasts of burden and carried off.

Clearly, such sources need to be treated with considerable caution but they cannot be dismissed out of hand as mere retailers of anti-northern prejudice and pro-Yorkist propaganda. Margaret of Anjou's army was, indeed, a notably undisciplined force. Even so, it did score a considerable victory in the field over a force commanded by Richard Neville Earl of Warwick at the second battle of St Albans on 17 February 1461 and, as a result, Henry VI was reunited with his wife. When news of the Lancastrian victory reached London, sheer panic seems to have broken out at the prospect of hosting so notorious a force, as a contemporary newsletter reported:

> When the news of [St Albans] was brought here, the mayor sent to the king and queen, it is supposed to offer obedience, provided they were assured that they would not be plundered or suffer violence. In the meantime they keep a good guard at the gates, which they keep practically closed, [but] nothing is done either by the tradespeople or by the merchants, and men do not stand in the streets or go far away from home. We are all hoping that as the queen and prince [Edward of Lancaster] have not descended in fury with their troops, the gates may be opened to them upon a good composition, and they may be allowed to enter peacefully.

Fortunately for the capital, Margaret of Anjou decided against either entering London by agreement or taking the city by force. Instead, and probably foolishly, she retreated back to the north, taking both her husband and her victorious army with her. Meanwhile, Richard of York's eldest son Edward Earl of March won what seems to have been a largely Welsh battle at Mortimer's Cross near Hereford in Shropshire on 2 February 1461 and, about three weeks later, successfully rendezvoused with Richard Neville Earl of Warwick in the Cotswolds. Together, the two earls journeyed to London, where they were enthusiastically admitted on 26 February, and, on 4 March, the young Edward was proclaimed king as Edward IV.

5

EDWARD IV, WARWICK THE KINGMAKER AND THE WARS OF THE ROSES

EDWARD IV: A PLAYBOY KING?

Many contemporary commentators clearly found Edward IV a far more powerful personality, and an altogether more vigorous and engaged ruler, than the king so slightly portrayed in William Shakespeare's *3 Henry VI*. Yet they are by no means unanimous in their verdicts. 'King Edward has become master and governor of the whole realm', reported a London-based correspondent about a fortnight after the new king's defeat of Margaret of Anjou's northern army at Towton on 29 March 1461; indeed, he continued enthusiastically:

> Words fail me to relate how well the commons love and adore him, as if he were their God. The entire kingdom keeps holiday for the event [Towton] which seems a boon from above. Thus far he appears to be a just prince who intends to amend and organise matters otherwise than has been done hitherto, so all comfort themselves with hopes of future well-being.

For an anonymous contemporary chronicler, too, the young Edward, 'now in the flower of his age, tall of stature, elegant in person, of unblemished character, valiant in arms', was an illustrious defender of the kingdom raised up by God, while a German visitor Gabriel Tetzel described him, in 1466, as 'a handsome upstanding man'. Yet a Northumberland-born cleric John Warkworth, writing in Cambridge towards the end of the king's reign, was notably critical of Edward IV's failure to live up to men's expectations of him in the 1460s:

…when King Edward reigned, the people looked for prosperity and peace but it came not; rather, one battle after another, and much trouble and great loss of goods among the common people, [and] at every battle they had to come out of their counties at their own cost. These, and other causes, brought England right low…

And, if we are to believe this chronicler, when Henry VI was restored to the throne in 1470, 'all his good lovers, and most of the people, were right glad'.

An Italian visitor Dominic Mancini, in England during Edward IV's last year and writing within a few months of the king's death in 1483, was particularly struck by Edward's affability and capacity to project a favourable image of himself while, at the same time, highlighting the paradoxes in his character and behaviour:

Edward was of a gentle nature and cheerful aspect: nevertheless, should he assume an angry countenance, he could appear very terrible to beholders. He was easy of access to his friends and to others, even the least notable. Frequently he called to his side complete strangers, when he thought they had come with the intention of addressing or beholding him more closely. He was wont to show himself to those who wished to watch him and seized any opportunity occasion offered of revealing his fine stature to on-lookers. He was so genial in his greeting that, if he saw a newcomer bewildered at his appearance and royal magnificence, he would give him courage to speak by laying a kindly hand upon his shoulder. To plaintiffs and to those who complained of injustice, he lent a willing ear; charges against himself he contented with an excuse if he did not remove the cause. He was more favourable than other princes to foreigners who visited his realm for trade or any other reason. He very seldom showed munificence and then only in moderation; still he was very grateful to those from whom he received a favour. Though not rapacious for other men's goods he was yet so eager for money that, in pursuing it, he acquired a reputation for avarice…

When it came to the pleasures of the flesh, Edward IV's appetite knew no bounds: 'In food and drink he was most immoderate', reported Mancini, for:

…it was his habit, so I have learned, to take an emetic for the delight of gorging his stomach once more. For this reason, and for the ease that was especially dear to him after his recovery of the crown [in 1471], he had grown fat in the loins whereas, previously, he had been not only tall but rather lean and very active. He was licentious in the extreme: moreover, it was said that he had been most insolent to numerous women after he had seduced them, for, as soon as he grew weary of dalliance, he gave up the ladies much against their will to other courtiers. He pursued with no discrimination the married and unmarried, the noble and lowly...

Moreover, although 'he took none by force', once he had 'conquered them, he dismissed them'.

Unlike Mancini, the Burgundian commentator Philippe de Commines, who probably wrote his influential *Memoirs* in the early 1490s, never visited England. As a servant of both Charles the Bold Duke of Burgundy (1467-1477) and Louis XI of France (1461-1483), however, he was certainly well versed in continental politics and he did meet Edward IV at least twice: once in 1470, when the English king was in exile in Burgundy, and again in 1475, when he led a military expedition to France. Clearly, Commines was not impressed by a king who, he believed, was dominated by Richard Neville Earl of Warwick in his early years and, later on, much preferred the role of playboy to that of politician. Edward IV in 1470, he declared, was 'not an outstanding man' but he was a 'very handsome prince, more handsome in fact than any other I saw at that time', as well as 'very courageous'. Already, however, the king was accustomed to:

...more luxuries and pleasures than any prince of his day because he thought of nothing else but women, far more than is reasonable, hunting and looking after himself. During the hunting season he would have several tents brought along for the ladies. All in all he made a great show of this and had a personality as well suited to such pursuits as any man I have ever seen.

In his final assessment of Edward IV, too, Commines was no less critical, judging him:

...very young and the handsomest of the fine princes of his generation when he achieved a mastery of his affairs. No man ever took more delight in his pleasures than he did, especially in the ladies, feasts, banquets and hunts. [In later years] he pursued his pleasures even more than before, fearing nobody, and growing very fat and gross. And in the prime of his life he reached the limits of his excesses and died suddenly of apoplexy...

The most important contemporary commentator on Edward IV personally, and the best informed narrator of the events of his reign, was an anonymous cleric who, after a long career in the royal service during the 1470s and early 1480s, finally put pen to paper at Crowland Abbey in the spring of 1486. Clearly, this Crowland chronicler not only knew the king well but also believed his achievements were considerable. While not failing to report Edward IV's fondness for 'convivial company, vanity, debauchery, extravagance and sensual enjoyment', he also found a good deal to admire, emphasising, in particular, the attractiveness of the king's person, his remarkable memory, his orthodoxy in religion, the magnificence of his court and his application to the business of government. In his later years, moreover, Edward became 'a very wealthy prince' even if, unfortunately, such riches also brought growing high-handedness and arrogance – most clearly demonstrated by the execution of his own brother George Duke of Clarence in 1478 – as a result of which 'he appeared to be feared by all his subjects while he himself stood in fear of no one'.

Clearly, then, Edward IV received a mixed reception in contemporary sources: admiration for his financial achievements, for instance, was offset by criticism of his avarice; similarly, conventional disapproval of his love of pleasure and taste for debauchery sat side by side with comment on his considerable ability, capacity to get on with people and willingness (despite an evident lack of moderation in his way of life) to devote himself to politics, military matters and government. Edward IV was certainly a startling contrast to his hapless predecessor Henry VI and, for all his faults, much more cut out for the tricky task of ruling England in the fifteenth century.

THE WARS OF THE ROSES CONTINUED 1461-1464

Since contemporaries put so much emphasis on popular support among Londoners in enabling Edward Earl of March to seize the throne, at the age of eighteen, on 4 March 1461, it would be foolish to dismiss this as no more than politically engineered enthusiasm. Nevertheless, it was the young Edward himself, no doubt urged on by his older and more politically experienced cousin Richard Neville Earl of Warwick – later dubbed the Kingmaker – who took the initiative. Indeed, the Yorkist lords had little choice in the matter, arguably, now Henry VI was no longer available to provide a figurehead. Even after Edward IV had taken possession of the crown, however, there remained Margaret of Anjou's as yet undefeated army in the north of England and the new king wasted no time in confronting this most visible threat to the successful establishment of a Yorkist royal dynasty. In a preliminary skirmish at Ferrybridge, near Pontefract in Yorkshire, on 28 March, the Lancastrian John Lord Clifford was killed and, according to one

1, 2 & 3. Badges of the Houses of Lancaster, York and Tudor

4. Richard II from a contemporary portrait, Westminster Abbey.

5. Seal of Richard II.
6. Badge of Richard II.

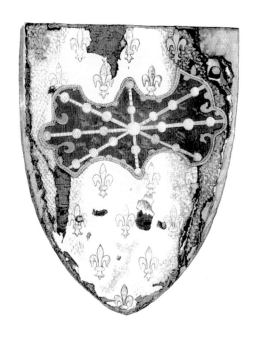

7. Shield of Henry V from his chantry chapel in Westminster Abbey.
8. Badge of Henry V from MS Vincent 152 at the Heralds College.

9. A scene from the *Beauchamp Pageant*, an illustration of the battlefield at Shrewsbury just after the battle, and Prince Henry (the future Henry V), standing to the right with his father on the left.

10. Richard Neville, Earl of Warwick, 'Warwick the Kingmaker'.
Victorian glass, Cardiff Castle.

11. Seal of Richard Neville, Earl of Warwick.

12. Henry VI as depicted on a wooden screen, *c.*1500, of
St Catherine's Church, Ludham, Norfolk.

13. Edward IV and his consort Elizabeth in the north window at Canterbury Cathedral. This was a gift to the church from Edward in *c.*1480.

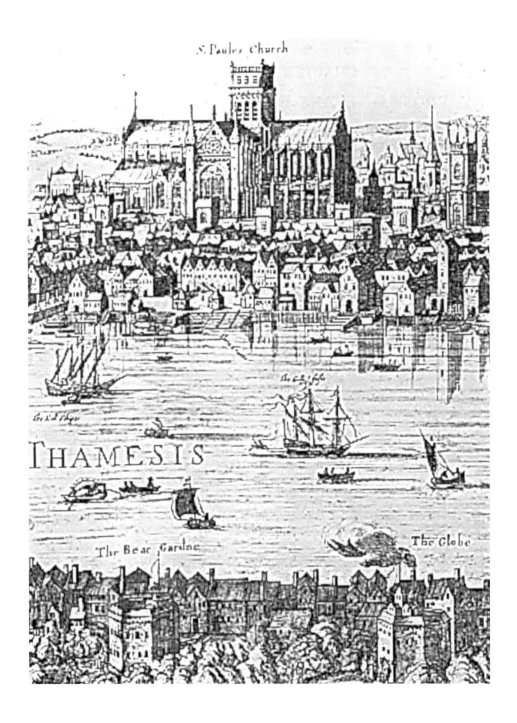

14. Drawing of a stretch of the Thames showing the Globe theatre.

15. The Swan theatre in a similar sketch.
16. Warrant from James I, ordering the issue of letters patent authorising the King's servants, Lawrence Fletcher, William Shakespeare, Richard Burbage and others, to play 'comedies, tragedies, stage plaies', etc, in the usual house.

AD INVICTISSIMVM
ANGLIÆ, FRANCIÆ, HYBERNIÆ-
QVE REGEM
Fidei defenforem ,

HENRICUM VIII.
POLYDORI VIRGILII
URBINATIS

In Anglicam Hiftoriam fuam prooemium.

IAM INDE *ab initio rerum humanarum, cunctis mortalibus ,* HENRICE Rex *maxime , gloriam virtutis , rerumque gestarum memoriam perpetuandi, commune ftudium fuit : hinc fanè urbes conditæ, illisque conditorum nomina impofita : hinc ftatuæ repertæ , hinc pyramidum moles , multaque id genus magnifica opera extructa funt : hinc item fuère femper, qui n.n dubitarint , patriæ tuendæ caufa , etiam immaturam oppetere mortem. Ea tamen omnia cùm temporis curriculo partim corruerent, partim oblivione obfcurarentur , deinde homines coeperunt & ipfa opera & facinora celebrare literis , quæ ufque eò fempiterna reddiderunt omnia, ut poft ea pro fe quifque benefacta pariter imitanda , atq, malefacta multò diligentiſsimè declinanda curarit : quando hiftoria ut hominum laudes*

A 2 *loqui-*

17. Page from an early printed edition of Polydore Vergil's *Anglica Historia*.

18. Badge of Richard III from MS Vincent 152 at the Herald's College.

19. Misericord carving of Richard III at Christchurch Priory.
20. Seal of Henry VII: the king is portrayed seated on a throne with attributes of majesty.

THE
HISTORIE
OF THE PITIFVLL

Life, and unfortunate Death

of *Edward* the fifth , and
the then Duke of *Yorke*
his brother :

With the troublesome and

tyrannical government of Usvr-
ping *Richard* the third, and
his miserable end

Written by the Right Honor-
able Sir *Thomas Moore*

sometimes Lord Chanc-
cellor of England.

LONDON,

Printed by *Thomas Payne* for
the Company of *Stationers*, and
are to be sold by *Mich: Young*,
at his shop in *Bedford-street* in
Covent-Garden, neere the
new Exchange. 1640.

21. Page from Thomas More's *History of Richard III*.

22. Arms of Henry VII.
23. Henry VII.

contemporary chronicler, the 'Earl of Warwick was hurt in his leg by an arrow'. Next day, at Towton, the Lancastrians received a truly devastating blow. No wonder Warwick the Kingmaker's brother George Neville, Bishop of Exeter felt moved to hyperbole when writing of this, the biggest and bloodiest battle of the entire Wars of the Roses, a few days later:

> That day there was a great conflict, which began with the rising of the sun, and lasted until the tenth hour of the night, so great was the pertinacity and boldness of the men, who never heeded the possibility of a miserable death. Of the enemy who fled, great numbers were drowned in the river near the town of Tadcaster, eight miles from York, [a] great part of the rest who got away [were] slain, and so many dead bodies were seen as to cover an area six miles long by [more than] three broad...

The total number of men involved may well have exceeded 50,000 and, undoubtedly, it was a long and hard-fought struggle, hampered by atrocious weather, and producing massive casualties. Chronicle accounts of the battle have pronounced tabloid qualities: '38,000 fell on that day', declared one commentator, bodies were piled in pits and trenches, and the blood of the slain 'ran down in the furrows and ditches, along with melted snow, in a most shocking manner', while, according to another, 'there was the son against the father, the brother against brother, the nephew against nephew'. Many northern Lancastrian lords – most notably Henry Percy, third Earl of Northumberland – were certainly killed in the action and, after the battle was over, Henry VI, Margaret of Anjou, Edward of Lancaster and Henry Beaufort Duke of Somerset, among others, were lucky to escape capture in York and, eventually, to find refuge in Scotland. Once the result of Towton became known, however, most Englishmen – including the majority of baronage and gentry – recognised the reality of the Yorkist triumph and acknowledged Edward IV's authority as king.

Not that Lancastrian resistance was at an end. On the contrary, Edward IV's position on the throne remained far from secure, at any rate until the summer of 1464, and he contrived actually to lose his crown (if only for a few months) as late as 1470/71. Hence the new Yorkist regime's efforts, from the beginning, to consolidate its position by promoting men of proved loyalty (such as Richard Neville Earl of Warwick and his brother John Lord Montagu in the north, William Lord Hastings in the midlands and William Lord Herbert in Wales), attempting to win over former opponents (even, for a time, Henry Beaufort Duke of Somerset), reducing the level of local disorder, countering the threat of foreign invasion (particularly from France and Scotland) and, most importantly, dealing with Lancastrian resistance at home, especially in Wales and the north of England. Yorkist fears of Lancastrian sedition are nicely demonstrated by the speed and vigour of the government's reaction to 'a great conspiracy' headed by John de Vere Earl of Oxford in February 1462, as a result of which, so a contemporary newsletter reported, 'he, his eldest son and many other knights and squires lost their heads'. Moreover, late 1463 saw Henry Beaufort Duke of Somerset and several fellow Lancastrians trying to co-ordinate rebellions in both Wales and England culminating, early in 1464, in an apparent effort to secure Edward IV's overthrow when anti-government disturbances broke out in several English and Welsh counties.

During his early years, without doubt, it was the far north of England – especially the Percy stronghold of Northumberland – that provided the biggest headache for Edward IV and, time and time again, its great fortresses – notably Alnwick, Dunstanburgh and Bamburgh castles – served as highly visible rallying points for Lancastrian resistance, while both Scotland and, intermittently, Louis XI of France sought to exploit the king's northern difficulties to their own advantage. Not until the spring of 1464 – with Lancastrian defeats in the field at Hedgeley Moor in April and Hexham in May – was the far north at last reduced to a semblance of order, largely thanks to the very considerable efforts of the Earl of Warwick and, even more, his brother John Lord Montagu (who, in the process, not only helped Edward IV make his rule a reality there but also, and ominously, consolidated their own power in northern England).

Finally, in July 1465, Henry VI – abandoned by his wife Margaret of Anjou when she and Edward of Lancaster fled to the continent in 1463 – fell into Yorkist hands, as colourfully described by the chronicler John Warkworth:

King Henry was taken near a house of religion in Lancashire. He was betrayed, by means of a black monk of Abingdon, [being] at his dinner at Waddington Hall, and was carried to London on horseback, with his legs bound to the stirrups, and so brought through London to the Tower, where he was kept a long time...

Once incarcerated, according to another commentator:

King Edward ordered all possible humanity to be shown towards him, consistent with his safe custody, and, at the same time, gave directions that he should be supplied with all suitable necessities and treated with becoming respect.

EDWARD IV, WARWICK THE KINGMAKER AND THE WOODVILLES 1464–1469

Whether or not Richard Neville Earl of Warwick was a kingmaker in 1461, he was certainly Edward IV's most prominent and powerful supporter during the early 1460s, and was clearly perceived to be so by contemporaries. Philippe de Commines, for instance, declared unequivocally that:

> …the leading supporter of the house of York was the Earl of Warwick [who] could almost be called the king's father as a result of the service and education he had given him. Indeed, he had made himself a very great man, for in his own right he was already a great lord…

And, for Commines at least, Warwick's kingmaking credentials were not in doubt either:

> [The] Earl of Warwick governed King Edward in his youth and directed his affairs. Indeed, to speak the truth, he made him king and was responsible for deposing King Henry…

The Burgundian chronicler Jean de Waurin, who met Warwick when he visited England in 1467, and again at Calais in 1469, was certainly impressed by him and, even more, his capacity to appeal to ordinary people:

> The Earl of Warwick had in great measure the voice of the people, because he knew how to persuade them with beautiful soft speeches; he was conversable and talked familiarly with them – subtle, as it were, in order to gain his ends. He gave them to understand that he would promote the prosperity of the kingdom and defend the interests of the people with all his power, and that as long as he lived he would never do otherwise. Thus he acquired the goodwill of the people to such an extent that he was the prince whom they held in the highest esteem, and on whom they placed the greatest faith and reliance.

Certainly, Warwick – already a 'super-magnate' even before 1461 – benefited massively from Edward IV's patronage in the 1460s. So did other members of the Neville family, most notably Warwick's brothers John Neville (created Earl of Northumberland in 1464) and George Neville (who became Archbishop of York in 1465). And all provided good service to the king. Yet Edward IV clearly ruled as well as reigned and, when it suited him, he was fully prepared to block the aims and ambitions even of the Kingmaker.

Perhaps the origins of the rift between the king and his greatest subject, and the renewal of the Wars of the Roses that eventually resulted, can be found in Edward IV's marriage to the Lancastrian widow Elizabeth Woodville in May 1464. Contemporary commentators were certainly not impressed by the king's unorthodox choice of a bride. The chronicler John Warkworth, for instance, stressed that the marriage was a clandestine affair, that it took place while Warwick was abroad trying to negotiate a French match for the king, and that the earl was 'greatly displeased' when he found out what Edward had done; another anonymous chronicler reported that the king, 'prompted by the ardour of youth and relying entirely on his own choice, without consulting the nobles of the kingdom, privately married the widow of a certain knight'; and, if we are to believe Dominic Mancini, it was a clear case of Edward IV's sheer inability to control his carnal instincts:

> One of the ways he indulged his appetites was to marry a lady of humble origin, named Elizabeth, despite the antagonism of the magnates of the kingdom, who disdained to show royal honours towards an undistinguished woman promoted to such exalted rank. She was a widow and the mother of two sons by a former husband and, when the king first fell in love with her beauty of person and charm of manner, he could not corrupt her virtue by gifts or menaces. The story runs that when Edward placed a dagger at her throat to make her submit to his passion, she remained unperturbed and determined to die rather than live unchastely with the king. Whereupon Edward coveted her all the more and judged the lady worthy to be a royal spouse since she could not be overcome in her constancy even by an infatuated king.

The marriage on May Day 1464 certainly was a clandestine affair and the fact that it was not made public for several months suggests that Edward IV was only too well aware of the likely reaction of his magnates, especially as it brought no diplomatic advantages. That reaction, when the marriage was eventually announced in the autumn of 1464, does indeed seem to have been one of incredulity: a newsletter of October 1464, for instance, reported that 'the greater part of the lords and the people in general seem very much dissatisfied'; another remarked that the king's marriage had 'greatly offended the people of

England'; and, according to Jean de Waurin, the royal council told Edward in no uncertain terms that 'he must know well that she was no wife for a prince such as himself'. Nevertheless, what was done was done and, in all probability, the shock/horror reaction to the new queen proved no more than a nine days' wonder. Even Warwick the Kingmaker, irritated though he may well have been initially, had no choice but to accept the *fait accompli*, while most of the nobility attended the queen's sumptuous coronation in May 1465.

More galling to Warwick, probably, was the advancement of the Woodville clan that almost inevitably followed the king's marriage, particularly the impact of the queen's kin on the aristocratic marriage market. Certainly, a contemporary annalist reported his 'great and secret displeasure' at the marriages of Catherine Woodville (the queen's sister) to young Henry Stafford Duke of Buckingham (whom he had had his eye on for one of his own daughters), Sir Thomas Grey (one of the queen's sons by her first marriage) to Anne Holland (daughter and heiress of the Duke of Exeter) whom he had confidently expected to marry his nephew George Neville, Mary Woodville (another of the queen's sisters) to William Lord Herbert's son and the 'diabolical marriage' of Sir John Woodville ('the queen's brother, aged twenty years') to Warwick's own elderly aunt Catherine Duchess of Norfolk ('a slip of a girl of about eighty years old'). Perhaps what upset him most, though, were the implications of Woodville match-making for the marriage prospects of his own daughters and co-heiresses, Isabel and Anne (he had no sons), especially once Edward IV made it clear there was no chance of either or both of them marrying either or both of the king's brothers, George Duke of Clarence and Richard Duke of Gloucester. Almost certainly, too, Warwick resented what he saw as growing Woodville political influence and the consequent lessening of his own and that of his family. What particularly rankled was Edward IV's – perhaps partly Woodville-inspired – preference for a Burgundian rather than a French alliance, culminating in the marriage of the king's sister Margaret to Charles the Bold Duke of Burgundy in July 1468. Indeed, according to the well-informed Crowland chronicler:

Richard Neville Earl of Warwick, who for some years had appeared to favour the French as against the Burgundians, was deeply offended [by this marriage]. He would have preferred to arrange a marriage for the Lady Margaret within the kingdom of France so that some kind of favourable understanding might result between the kings of these two realms, instead of assisting the cause of Charles Duke of Burgundy through an English alliance, because the earl bore a bitter hatred for this man. This, in my opinion, was the real cause of dissension between the king and the earl...

Hence, no doubt, Warwick's determined – and ultimately successful – efforts to drive a wedge between Edward IV and his brother Clarence, and his possible involvement in Lancastrian-inspired conspiracies against the king in 1468. Neither Warwick himself, who continued to benefit from Edward's patronage until at least February 1469, nor Clarence, arguably, had any real justification for what was becoming ever more nearly treasonable behaviour. Warwick, however, simply could not stomach either his rivals for the king's ear at court, particularly the Woodvilles, or what he (probably rightly) perceived as his own waning power and influence over Edward. As for Clarence, he probably fell victim to his cousin's legendary charm. When they openly rebelled against the king, in the summer of 1469, it is certainly no coincidence that the Woodvilles and their court connections were a prime target.

THE WARS OF THE ROSES RESUMED 1469-1471

As early as February 1465 Margaret of Anjou, a politically disgruntled and financially embarrassed exile on the continent since the summer of 1463, was lobbying the aid of Louis XI of France to recover the crown of England for her husband Henry VI and, ultimately, her son Edward of Lancaster who, by February 1467, was already showing signs of being far more like his grandfather Henry V than his own father, as a contemporary newsletter from France noted:

> This boy, though only thirteen years of age, already talks of nothing but cutting off heads or making war, as if he had everything in his hands or was the god of battle or the peaceful occupant of [the English] throne.

In May 1467 it was reported that the French king had sent for Margaret and, by October 1468, he had apparently hinted that he would indeed 'help the old Queen of England'. Already, too, the notion of 'treating with the Earl of Warwick to restore King Henry in England' had been canvassed and, certainly, by the later months of 1468 Warwick the Kingmaker was becoming increasingly resentful of Edward IV's policies, the growing prominence of the Woodvilles at court and his own apparently waning influence on events.

During the summer of 1469 Warwick's hand can surely be detected behind the rebellion of Robin of Redesdale in Yorkshire, a rising that culminated in a victory for Edward IV's opponents at the battle of Edgecote near Banbury on 26 July and, indeed, the king's capture and imprisonment soon afterwards. Yet Edward's release, or possible escape, only a few weeks later and the failure of another probably Neville-inspired rebellion in Lincolnshire in March 1470 (resulting in the flight of both Warwick and Clarence to France) seemed to mark the end of all the Kingmaker's hopes. Louis XI, however, regarded Warwick's arrival in France as a golden opportunity to advance his own interests, if only he could now secure reconciliation between the earl and Margaret of Anjou. Clearly, it took all the wily French king's very considerable negotiating skills to pull this one off, not least since the Lancastrian queen's hostility to Warwick (whom she regarded as mainly responsible for her husband losing his throne in the first place) bordered on the fanatical. Louis XI's determination and powers of persuasion are nicely underlined by a newsletter sent from the French court at the end of June 1470:

> His majesty has spent and still spends every day in long discussions with the queen to induce her to make an alliance with Warwick and to let the prince her son go with the earl to the enterprise of England. Up to the present the queen has shown herself very hard and difficult and, although his majesty offers her many assurances, it seems that on no account whatever will she agree to send her son with Warwick, as she mistrusts him. Nevertheless, it is thought that in the end she will let herself be persuaded to do what his majesty wishes.

The reconciliation did indeed take place some three weeks later when, so it was reported:

> With great reverence Warwick went on his knees and asked the queen's pardon for the injuries and wrongs done to her in the past. She graciously forgave him and he eventually did homage and fealty there, swearing to be a faithful and loyal subject of the king [Henry VI], queen and prince…

Soon afterwards it was agreed that a marriage be contracted between Edward of Lancaster and Warwick's daughter Anne (his other daughter Isabel had already married George Duke of Clarence, without Edward IV's permission, the year before), as a prelude to the earl's crossing to England, driving out the Yorkist king and restoring Henry VI to the throne. Once he had accomplished this task, but only then, Margaret of Anjou and her son would themselves leave France for England.

Warwick and Clarence, accompanied by a number of stalwart Lancastrian lords (most notably, John de Vere Earl of Oxford and Jasper Tudor Earl of Pembroke) and supplied with ships by Louis XI, finally set sail for England early in September 1470. On arrival in the West Country they issued a proclamation declaring their commitment to Henry VI, condemning Edward IV as a usurper and calling on all men of fighting age to join them. Moreover, not only did they attract considerable popular support but, within three weeks of their coming, Edward IV (finding himself virtually deserted, apparently) fled the country and sailed for Burgundy. Early in October 1470, following the arrival of Warwick and Clarence in London, Henry VI was restored to the throne. Several years of imprisonment in the Tower had all too obviously left their mark on him: indeed, if we are to believe John Blacman, 'like a true follower of Christ' he had 'patiently endured hunger, thirst, mockings, derisions, abuse and many other hardships'. More mundanely, the chronicler John Warkworth reported that, when freed from incarceration, the king was neither 'honourably arrayed' nor 'so cleanly kept as should be such a prince'. Clearly, Henry VI was even less capable of governing now than he had been a decade earlier and the government established in his name was very much dominated by Richard Neville Earl of Warwick (truly a kingmaker in 1470, whatever his role may have been in 1461). Over the next six months Warwick struggled to reconcile as many Yorkist supporters as he could, as well as trying to ensure continued Lancastrian backing for his fragile regime but, in practice, he found it almost impossible to satisfy one faction without alienating another. The situation was certainly not helped either by the failure of Margaret of Anjou and Edward of Lancaster, whether as a result of caution or adverse weather, to fulfil their promise to cross the Channel. The Crowland chronicler's judgement on the so-called readeption of Henry VI was stark:

> You might [in October 1470] have come across innumerable folk to whom the restoration of the pious King Henry was a miracle and the transformation the work of the All Highest; but how incomprehensible are the judgements of God, how unfathomable his ways; for it is well known that less than six months later no one dared admit to having been his partisan…

Edward IV returned to England in March 1471 and, after a none too enthusiastic reception in Yorkshire, began attracting increasing backing as he marched south. Even the ever-disgruntled Clarence rejoined his brother. Once news of Edward's imminent arrival in London became known, a desperate attempt was made to rally support for Henry VI but, if we are to believe a probable eyewitness, it proved entirely counter-productive:

> [The] king was conveyed from the palace of St Paul's through Cheap and Cornhill, and so on about to his lodging again by Candlewick Street and Watling Street, accompanied by the Archbishop of York,

who held him by the hand all the way, and Lord Zouch, an old and impotent man, [who] bore the king's sword. And so, with a small company of gentlemen going on foot before, one on horseback carrying a pole or long shaft with two fox tails fastened on the end, and a small company of serving men following, this progress was held, more like a play than the showing of a prince to win men's hearts, for by this means he lost many and won none or right few, and ever he was shown in a long blue gown of velvet, as though he had no more to change with.

Certainly, on 11 April 1471, Edward IV entered the capital unopposed, perhaps even for the three reasons put forward by Philippe de Commines: namely, the number of Yorkist sympathisers who now emerged from sanctuary; the king's merchant creditors who hoped, thereby, to recoup money they had lent him in earlier years; and, rather fancifully, 'several noble women and wives of rich citizens, with whom he had been closely and secretly acquainted, who won over their husbands and relatives to his cause'. As for Henry VI, according to a letter written soon afterwards by Edward IV's sister Margaret of Burgundy, the two kings now met, shook hands, and Henry even naively declared 'My cousin of York, you are very welcome and I know that in your hands my life will not be in danger'. The Yorkist king remained in London just two days before marching out to confront Warwick's army as it, too, approached the capital. The extraordinary battle of Barnet was fought, in a thick mist, early on Easter Sunday morning 14 April. Clearly, confusion reigned for much of the time but, in the end, it was a notable Yorkist victory. The turning point probably came when, as John Warkworth relates, the 'star with streams' livery of John de Vere Earl of Oxford's men was mistaken, in the fog, for the Yorkist 'sun with streams' device, and Oxford's force came under attack by fellow Lancastrians. Edward IV himself, so an admittedly official Yorkist account tells us, fought 'manfully, vigorously and valiantly' and, by the time it was all over, both Warwick the Kingmaker and his brother John Neville had lost their lives. Edward IV was allowed no time to enjoy the fruits of victory, however, for on the very same day that Barnet was fought Margaret of Anjou set foot on English soil for the first time since 1463.

The Lancastrian queen, accompanied by her son Edward of Lancaster, landed at Weymouth in Dorset and, when news of her arrival reached London, Edward determined to confront Margaret and her supporters well away from the capital and before her force had grown too large. What is particularly striking in the second half of April 1471, in fact, is the speed with which the king responded to Margaret of Anjou's arrival, culminating in the battle of Tewkesbury fought on 4 May. Once more victory went to Edward IV and, although there is considerable disagreement in the sources, the balance of likelihood is that Edward of Lancaster was killed in the fighting and Margaret of Anjou herself now became a prisoner of the Yorkists. The battle of Tewkesbury, following so quickly on the heels of Barnet, finally put paid to Lancastrian hopes, despite a spirited attempt by Thomas Neville, Bastard of Fauconberg to raise the south-east and seize London. On 21 May 1471 Edward IV entered the capital once more amidst considerable spectacle, apparently displaying Margaret of Anjou as a veritable trophy of his success, and now (at last!) fully secure on the throne. Not that this was a time for sentiment. On the very night of Edward IV's arrival in London, Henry VI's miserable life finally came to an end in the Tower. The official Yorkist version of the event – that he died 'of pure displeasure and melancholy' – can surely be discounted, while any role Edward's brother Richard Duke of Gloucester may have had in Henry's demise is far from clear. Edward IV himself, in all probability, was responsible for ordering both his rival's death and the disposal of his corpse once the deed was done. So ended the Lancastrian dynasty.

THE WARS OF THE ROSES SUSPENDED 1471–1483

'Lancastrianism' was virtually a spent force by mid-1471. Indeed, it was reported from France on 2 June that Edward IV had now become 'the peaceful lord and dominator' of England 'without having any further obstacle whatever'. Both Henry VI and Edward of Lancaster were dead and Margaret of Anjou, although soon ransomed by Louis XI, spent her last decade (she died in 1482) as an impotent political exile in France. The Yorkist king was relieved, too, of the menacing power of the Nevilles and, before long, his brother Richard of Gloucester proved himself a loyal lieutenant in ruling the north of England. The last whimper of Lancastrian resistance in England came with the incorrigible John de Vere Earl of Oxford's seizure of St Michael's Mount in Cornwall for a few months in 1473/74. Inevitably, it failed and Oxford consequently suffered a decade of exile and imprisonment for his pains. As for another exile, Henry Tudor Earl of Richmond (the future Henry VII), he was too young and politically insignificant to pose any kind of threat. Nor, for that matter, did the king's other brother George Duke of Clarence who, despite backing the restoration of Henry VI in 1470, had been forgiven by Edward IV in 1471. Clarence's continued determination to prove himself a thorn in the king's flesh, however, eventually brought him to disaster in 1478 when, so Dominic Mancini learned:

...whether the charge was fabricated or a real plot revealed, the Duke of Clarence was accused of conspiring the king's death by means of spells and magicians. When the charge had been considered before a court, he was condemned and put to death. The mode of execution preferred was that he should die by being plunged into a jar of sweet wine.

Edward IV's 'second reign' – 1471-1483 – was relatively peaceful, in fact, and during these years the Yorkist king not only made real progress in restoring the authority of the crown but also clocked up real achievements in government. As the Crowland chronicler (who served Edward throughout this period) noted, following an English invasion of France in 1475 (when Edward allowed himself to be bought off by the French king Louis XI without a blow being struck!), the English king turned his attention in particular:

> ...to the question of how he might in future collect an amount of treasure worthy of his regal estate from his own resources and by his own effort. Accordingly, [he] resumed possession of nearly all the royal estates, without regard to whom they had been granted, and applied the whole thereof to supporting the expenses of the crown. Throughout all parts of the kingdom he appointed surveyors of the customs... The revenues of vacant prelacies [he] would only let out of his hands for a sum fixed by himself... He also examined the register and rolls of chancery and exacted heavy fines from those who were found to have taken possession of estates without following the procedures required by law... These, and more of a similar nature than can possibly be conceived by anyone inexperienced in such matters, together with the annual tribute of £10,000 due from France and frequent tenths and fifteenths from the church, made him, within a few years, a very wealthy prince; so much so that, in the collection of gold and silver vessels, tapestries and highly precious ornaments, both regal and religious, in the building of castles, colleges and other notable places, and in the acquisition of new lands and possessions, not one of his predecessors could equal his remarkable achievements...

Moreover, according to the same source, 'rigorous justice was put into operation whenever necessary', as a result of which 'public acts of robbery were checked for a long time'. And, by the time of Edward IV's death, the royal finances do seem to have been in a better condition than they had been for decades; England was almost certainly less lawless in 1483 than it had been in 1461; and, although magnate factionalism around the king had by no means been eliminated, his young son Edward V might well have enjoyed a largely untroubled succession but for the antics of his ambitious and ruthless uncle Richard Duke of Gloucester.

6

RICHARD III, HENRY VII AND THE WARS OF THE ROSES

RICHARD III: A TYRANNICAL KING?

William Shakespeare, never more faithful to his Tudor sources, portrayed Richard III as the archetypal villain and, so the king's modern defenders assure us, must be treated with great caution if not discounted altogether by any historian seriously in search of the truth about England's last Plantagenet ruler. Yet even the king's contemporaries were frequently critical. For Dominic Mancini, the Italian visitor to London in 1482/83 who put pen to paper within a few months of Richard III becoming king at the end of June 1483, Richard of Gloucester, in the aftermath of his brother Edward IV's death (in April 1483), proved himself a master of dissimulation, motivated by intense personal ambition and an 'insane lust for power', ruthlessly removing men who stood in his way and, on grounds that were dubious to say the least, callously depriving his nephew Edward V of the throne so that he might take the crown for himself. The sophisticated and well-informed Crowland chronicler, who might have been John Russell, Bishop of Lincoln (Richard III's chancellor June 1483-July 1485) and completed his account of the king's usurpation and reign by early May 1486, was no less damning in his verdict. Indeed, his personal antagonism to Richard III and loathing of his entourage is only too evident: he condemned his arbitrary seizure of the throne; he was positively scathing about the tyrannical, northern-dominated regime which, he believed, the last Yorkist king established in southern England; and he welcomed Henry VII as 'an angel sent from heaven through whom God deigned to visit his people and free them from the evils which had hitherto afflicted them beyond measure'. On the continent, too, the shrewd Burgundian commentator Philippe de Commines' informants at the French court (who may well have included the exiled Henry Tudor himself and certainly some of his followers) convinced him that Richard III was indeed an arrogant, cruel and ruthless man who was justly deprived of the throne by Henry VII, God's chosen agent, at the battle of Bosworth. Neither Mancini, the Crowland chronicler nor Commines sought to portray Richard III as an out-and-out monster but, clearly, they did highlight features of the king's character and behaviour that were to provide solid foundations for Tudor chroniclers and historians later on.

Yet there is also contemporary comment on Richard III that is altogether more positive. Some of it, no doubt, reflects the king's own propaganda. The 1484 statute settling the crown on Richard III and his descendants, for instance, incorporated what purported to be a petition presented to him in June 1483, delivering a blistering attack on his brother Edward IV's regime and urging him to take the throne himself as a man of exemplary character devoted to good government and 'naturally inclined to the prosperity and common weal' of the realm. Nor can Thomas Langton, Bishop of St David's, a northerner who benefited considerably from Richard III's patronage, be regarded as impartial. Nevertheless it is surely significant that, in a private letter to a fellow cleric written in September 1483, he declared that the king:

> ...contents the people wherever he goes better than ever did any prince; for many a poor man that has suffered wrong many days has been relieved and helped by him and his commands in his progress. And in many great cities and towns were great sums of money given to him which he has refused. On my faith, I never liked the qualities of any prince as well as his; God has sent him to us for the welfare of us all.

An Italian visitor Pietro Carmeliano portrayed Richard III, in 1484, as a veritable paragon of virtue:

> If we look [for] religious devotion, what prince is there in our time who shows a more genuine piety? If for justice, who can we reckon above him throughout the world? If we look for prudence and waging war, who shall we judge his equal? If we look for truth of soul, for wisdom, for loftiness of mind united with modesty, who stands before our King Richard? What Christian Emperor or Prince can be compared with him in good works and munificence? To whom are

theft, rebellion, pollution, adultery, manslaughter, usury, heresy and other abominable crimes more hateful than to him? Obviously, no one.

A Scottish envoy Archibald Whitelaw, in an oration to Richard III during an audience in September 1484, flattered the king in no less extravagant terms:

> ...of all the sovereigns I have known, you stand out as the greatest – in the renown of your nobility, in your sway over your people, in your strength of arms, and in the wealth of resources at your command. [Your] most celebrated reputation for the practice of every form of virtue [has] reached into every corner of the world; moreover, there is the excellent and outstanding humanity of your innate benevolence, your clemency, your liberality, your good faith, your supreme justice, and your incredible greatness of heart.

And, when news of Bosworth reached the city, it was put on record in York that the late king had been 'piteously slain and murdered, to the great heaviness of this city'. Perhaps contemporary eulogies of Richard III need to be treated with even more caution than more familiar hostile verdicts on the king but their existence is, at the very least, a warning against too readily accepting the Shakespearian villain.

Certainly, the notion of Richard III as not only an evil tyrant but also a physically deformed monster can safely be rejected. No contemporary commentator suggests any bodily malformation nor, for that matter, do early portraits of the king: the portrait of Richard III in Windsor castle, for instance, painted some thirty years after his death (although probably based on a more nearly contemporary likeness) owes its deformed shoulder only to later alteration. In all probability, the Tudor hunchback does derive from some oddity about the king but it might be no more than the fact that he seems to have been significantly shorter than his two brothers. The riddle of Richard III's personality cannot, in the last analysis, be resolved. Clearly, he did not share Edward IV's exuberant love of pleasure; there is some evidence that his marriage of convenience to Anne Neville was not, on that account, entirely barren of affection; and the death of his only legitimate son in 1484 does appear to have caused him real distress. Yet he did sire at least one, possibly two, bastards; Thomas Langton, when accompanying the king on his post-coronation progress, reported that 'sensual pleasure holds sway to an increasing extent'; and the Crowland chronicler believed that, during Christmas festivities in 1484, 'far too much attention was given to dancing and gaiety'. Evidently, Richard III was personally pious; he advanced a number of learned clergy; and he seems to have had a considerable interest in liturgy and religious music. Yet he also had some of the less endearing characteristics of an early modern Puritan or even a present day born-again Christian; his vituperative denunciation of his brother's regime, his condemnation of the morals of his opponents, and his humiliation of Edward IV's former courtesan Mistress Shore leave a nasty taste in the mouth; and it is difficult to avoid the conclusion, given his own amoral (if not immoral) behaviour on occasion, that there was a streak of hypocrisy in him (as, indeed, there was a capacity for self-deception and a tendency to swallow his own hyperbolical propaganda).

Richard III, both before and after he became king, certainly enjoyed projecting himself as a chivalry-inspired man of action, particularly in military matters, a fact recognised by commentators during his own lifetime: a contemporary ballad refers to him as 'the Duke of Gloucester, that noble prince, young of age and victorious in battle'; Pietro Carmeliano remarked on his 'prudence in fostering peace and waging war'; and, in his flattering oration of September 1484, Archibald Whitelaw praised his 'strength of arms' and 'embodiment of military skill'. As constable of England in the 1470s, an overtly chivalric post, he took his responsibilities very seriously indeed, revelling in military cere-monial and the work of royal heralds, as well as delighting in his own family's martial reputation and playing a major role in his father's reburial at Fotheringhay in 1476. A capable military commander (as he demonstrated during an expedition to Scotland in 1482) and very much at home in the company of soldiers, there seems little doubt either that he was personally courageous, as demonstrated by his behaviour on the battlefields of Barnet, Tewkesbury and Bosworth. As an administrator, too, he was not without ability, as his record both in the north of England between 1471 and 1483 and as king amply demonstrates. Moreover, he possessed a real capacity to inspire loyalty, as best shown by the firm backing he generally received from his powerful northern affinity. Yet, equally clearly, he was inordinately ambitious for power, ruthless in his pursuit of it (even if this involved dissimulation and deception) and capable not only of contemplating but also sanctioning the removal of men (or children!) who stood in his way.

RICHARD OF GLOUCESTER AND THE NORTH 1471-1483

Born at Fotheringhay in Northamptonshire in 1452, and raised to the dukedom of Gloucester by his brother Edward IV soon after he seized the throne in 1461, Richard III enjoyed a conventional aristocratic upbringing. During the later 1460s he spent several years in Warwick the Kingmaker's household when, it is reasonable to assume, he developed a considerable affection for Warwick's Yorkshire castle of Middleham and its surrounding countryside (which he retained for the rest of his life); early in 1469 he was recalled to the royal court by Edward IV and, a few months later, created constable of England (at the age of seventeen); and, during the crisis of 1469-1471 when Warwick challenged the Yorkist king's authority, he proved notably loyal to his brother. Richard fled to Burgundy with Edward in the autumn of 1470; he shared his months in exile there and returned with him to England in the spring of 1471; and he played a prominent role in the battles of Barnet and Tewkesbury. Indeed, Gloucester's alleged involvement in the murder of Prince Edward of Lancaster following Tewkesbury was eventually to figure as the first major incident in later Tudor denigration of Richard III (although, in fact, the prince was almost certainly slain during the battle itself). There is a stronger case for Richard of Gloucester's participation in the murder of Henry VI in the Tower of London shortly afterwards but the balance of likelihood is that Edward IV himself was responsible for the Lancastrian king's death (with Gloucester either playing no part at all or, at most, acting in a supervisory capacity on his brother's behalf). Similarly, although Gloucester probably concurred in the trial and execution of his brother George Duke of Clarence in 1478, there is no reliable evidence that he did so because he already had an eye on the throne for himself.

The Crowland chronicler was of the firm opinion that Richard III gave his greatest confidence to, and placed the most reliance upon, men from the north of England. Historians, too, have firmly stressed both the importance of Richard's northern background and connections by 1483 and the role of northerners during his protectorate and reign from 1483 to 1485. Probably first getting to know the north (especially Yorkshire) during his time in Warwick the Kingmaker's household in the later 1460s, Richard of Gloucester became a veritable northerner in his own right after 1471. Certainly, Gloucester's rule of the north between 1471 and 1483 seems to have been notably successful: his material advancement in the region, both as a result of royal patronage and his own efforts, is well documented; he built up a powerful and loyal affinity there; and there is plenty of evidence that his government of the north won him a considerable degree of popularity. Indeed Dominic Mancini, who probably never got further north than London himself, learned in 1482/83 that:

[Following Clarence's death Richard of Gloucester] kept himself within his own lands and set out to acquire the loyalty of his people through favours and justice. The good reputation of his private life and public activities powerfully attracted the esteem of strangers. Such was his renown in warfare that, whenever a difficult and dangerous policy had to be undertaken, it would be entrusted to his discretion and general-ship. By these skills Richard acquired the favour of the people...

During the 1470s, in fact, Richard of Gloucester established a regional hegemony in the north eclipsing even that enjoyed by Warwick the Kingmaker in the 1460s. In the process he reunited northern society, created a formidable personal following and brought a degree of stability to the region not seen for years. Moreover, his successful campaigning against the Scots in Edward IV's last years – most notably, a major expedition into Scotland in 1482 that resulted in the capture of the border town of Berwick – provided the final flourish to the creation of an admirable reputation.

Not that Richard of Gloucester's interests were ever exclusively northern. As constable and admiral of England and, once Clarence was no more, great chamberlain as well, he held national briefs. He possessed estates in southern as well as northern counties; he attended parliamentary sessions in 1472-1475, 1478 and 1483; he played a high profile role on ceremonial state occasions such as the wedding of his young nephew Richard of York in 1478; and, since his name appears on every royal charter issued between February 1478 and January 1483, he clearly remained in close touch with both the royal court and central government. Certainly, too, he provided the largest private contingent for Edward IV's invasion of France in 1475 and, although Philippe de Commines reported his deep dissatisfaction at the treaty of Pecquigny which brought the expedition to an inglorious end, he soon recognised it as a *fait accompli* and never wavered in his loyalty to the king.

THE PROTECTORATE OF RICHARD OF GLOUCESTER 1483

No one will ever know for certain whether Richard of Gloucester set his sights on the throne immediately he heard of Edward IV's sudden death (on 9 April 1483) or if, at first, he merely intended to obtain firm control of his nephew Edward V so as to prevent the Woodvilles seizing power and ensure his own security. Indeed, if we are to believe Dominic Mancini, Gloucester and his principal ally Henry Stafford Duke of Buckingham sought 'at every turn to arouse hatred against the queen's kin and to estrange public opinion from her relatives'. Edward IV himself, however, cannot be entirely cleared of blame for what happened after his demise; his son and heir was a minor who had long resided at Ludlow in a Woodville dominated environment and the queen and her family could legitimately expect a prominent role in the new regime; his only surviving brother (who, arguably, had the best claim to be protector) was an immensely powerful northern lord who, in part as a result of Edward's generous and sustained patronage, packed a good deal of political clout; and there were certainly divisions in the royal court, most notably between the late king's closest and most loyal supporter William Lord Hastings and the queen's son Thomas Grey, Marquis of Dorset, as the Crowland chronicler noted:

> The more farsighted members of the council thought that the uncles and brothers [of Edward V] on the mother's side should be absolutely forbidden to have control of the person of the young man until he came of age. [William Lord Hastings] was afraid that if supreme power fell into the hands of the queen's relatives they would then sharply avenge the alleged injuries done to them by that lord. Much ill-will, indeed, had long existed between Lord Hastings and them.

Certainly, too, there is evidence that Richard of Gloucester believed himself to be vulnerable in the political climate occasioned by his brother's premature death, not least because of his insecure title to many of his estates (particularly his ex-Neville lands in northern England). Yet it is Gloucester's behaviour, whatever his motivations, that dominated the action packed months April to July 1483.

Even if, as seems likely, the notion of a long-standing feud between Richard of Gloucester and the Woodvilles is no more than the product of hastily concocted propaganda justifying the duke's moves against them, there is no doubt that a massive gulf did rapidly open up between Gloucester and the queen's family once Edward IV was no more. There seems little doubt either that, in April and May 1483, William Lord Hastings gave firm backing to Gloucester as the best means of establishing Edward V on the throne and securing his coronation. Richard of Gloucester, meanwhile, played his own cards with considerable skill, whether from genuine concern to outmanoeuvre the Woodvilles or (more probably) flagrant dissimulation in his own self-interest. Apparently, he despatched letters from the north of England to both queen and council declaring his loyalty to Edward V, presided over a commemoration service for his late brother in York and (in company with many northern nobility and gentry) swore a solemn oath of fealty to the new king, and then marched south with a large retinue. On 29 April Gloucester, and his no doubt predominantly northern entourage, arrived at Northampton. There he joined forces with Henry Stafford Duke of Buckingham (who had his own reasons for disliking the Woodvilles and may, even, have helped poison Richard's mind against them), entertained the queen's brother Anthony, Earl Rivers and her son Sir Richard Grey and, next morning, promptly arrested the pair of them. Proceeding to nearby Stony Stratford, he took possession of his probably indignant royal nephew, arrested his companions and sent them (along with Rivers and Grey) to the northern stronghold of Pontefract. These dramatic events are vigorously recounted by the Crowland chronicler:

> [When Richard of Gloucester] reached Northampton, where the Duke of Buckingham joined him, there arrived to pay their respects Anthony Earl Rivers, the king's maternal uncle, Richard Grey, a very honourable knight [and others]. When first they arrived they were greeted with a particularly cheerful and merry face and, sitting at the duke's table for dinner, they passed the whole time in very pleasant conversation [but, next morning, they were arrested]. Immediately after [Gloucester and Buckingham] rushed into the place where the youthful king was staying [in Stony Stratford] and took prisoner the servants who were attending him, [including] Thomas Vaughan, an aged knight, the prince's chamberlain. The Duke of Gloucester, leader of the conspiracy, did not put off or refuse to offer his nephew, the king, any of the reverence required of a subject, [asserting] that he was only taking precautions to safeguard his own person since he knew for certain there were men close to the king who had sworn to destroy his honour and his life...

News of her brother-in-law's barnstorming initiative soon reached Queen Elizabeth Woodville in London and, no doubt thoroughly alarmed, she hastily took sanctuary in Westminster Abbey, along with her daughters and younger son Richard of York. Soon afterwards Gloucester, Buckingham and the young king themselves arrived in the capital and, on 10 May, Gloucester was formally appointed protector of the realm by the council.

Once formally established as protector, if we are to believe Dominic Mancini, Richard of Gloucester 'set his thoughts on removing, or at least undermining, everything that might stand in the way of his mastering the throne'. Certainly, he lost no time in beginning to exercise the extensive powers of political patronage now at his disposal and Henry Stafford Duke of Buckingham, in particular, received spectacular rewards, becoming virtually a viceroy in Wales. Richard of Gloucester's prime objective in May 1483, however, may well have been to secure continuity with Edward IV's regime. Most of his brother's former householdmen and servants remained in post, probably a pointer to the continuing political influence and steadying hand of William Lord Hastings, and there were very few changes in the personnel of government (either at national or local level). Even so, by early June 1483, moves might well have been afoot, probably involving the Woodvilles and perhaps Hastings too, to curb Richard of Gloucester's power and contain his ambitions. Indeed, when the protector wrote to the city of York on 10 June requesting military assistance (and, significantly, elicited a notably positive response a few days later), he cited a Woodville conspiracy to 'murder and utterly destroy' himself and Buckingham as urgent justification. Moreover, if fears were already growing about Gloucester's real intentions early in June, they must certainly have been given a massive further boost by the dramatic events at the Tower of London on 13 June, when the protector not only rid himself of Hastings (the man most likely to resist any moves to displace Edward V) but also removed a pair of staunch ecclesiastical loyalists as well – Thomas Rotherham Archbishop of York and John Morton Bishop of Ely. 'Without justice or judgement', declared the Crowland chronicler, 'the three strongest supporters of the new king were removed'. As for the protector's justification for his behaviour – a rapidly disseminated story alleging the complicity of Hastings in a conspiracy with the Woodvilles to overthrow him – it was widely dismissed as malicious propaganda even at the time. According to Dominic Mancini's vivid account, Richard of Gloucester:

> …considered that his prospects were not sufficiently secure without the removal or imprisonment of those who had been the closest friends of his brother and were expected to be loyal to his brother's offspring. In this class he thought to include Hastings, the king's chamberlain, Thomas Rotherham, whom shortly before he had relieved of his office, and the Bishop of Ely. Therefore the protector rushed headlong into crime, for fear that the ability and authority of these men might be detrimental to him; for he had sounded their loyalty through the Duke of Buckingham, and learnt that sometimes they foregathered in each other's houses. One day these three and several others came to the Tower about ten o'clock to salute the protector, as was their custom. When they had been admitted to the innermost quarters, the protector, as prearranged, cried out that an ambush had been prepared for him, and they had come with hidden arms, that they might be the first to open the attack. Thereupon the soldiers, who had been stationed there by their lord, rushed in with the Duke of Buckingham, and cut down Hastings on the false pretext of treason; they arrested the others, whose life, it was presumed, was spared out of respect for religion and holy orders. Thus fell Hastings, killed not

by those enemies he had always feared but by a friend whom he had never doubted. But whom will insane lust for power spare, if it dares violate the ties of kin and friendship? After this execution had been done in the citadel, the townsmen, who had heard the uproar but were uncertain of the cause, became panic-stricken, and each seized his weapons. But, to calm the multitude, the duke instantly sent a herald to proclaim that a plot had been detected and Hastings, the originator of the plot, had paid the penalty... At first the ignorant crowd believed, although the real truth was on the lips of many, namely that the plot had been feigned so as to escape the odium of such a crime...

Even if Hastings, portrayed almost invariably as an honourable and upright magnate whose only fault was an unbending commitment to Edward V and his brother, was not nearly so guileless as the Crowland chronicler, for one, would have us believe, his remark that Gloucester and Buckingham, in the days following Hastings' execution, 'did whatever they wanted' seems amply borne out by the facts. Most notably, on 16 June, Elizabeth Woodville was persuaded by a probably very reluctant Cardinal Thomas Bourchier, Archbishop of Canterbury to allow her younger son Richard of York to leave sanctuary. Indeed, according to the Crowland chronicler, Gloucester and Buckingham themselves:

> ...came by boat to Westminster with a great crowd, with swords and clubs, and compelled the lord cardinal of Canterbury to enter the sanctuary, with many others, to call upon the queen, in her kindness, to allow her son Richard Duke of York to leave and come to the Tower for the comfort of the king his brother. She willingly agreed to his proposal, sent the boy out, and he was then taken by the lord cardinal to the king [Edward V] in the Tower of London.

'From that day', the chronicler added, 'both these dukes showed their intentions not in private but openly'.

THE USURPATION AND REIGN OF RICHARD III 1483-1485

The precise circumstances surrounding Richard of Gloucester's seizure of the throne remain somewhat mysterious but the thrust of events, once Hastings was dead and both Edward IV's sons firmly under the protector's control, seems clear enough. On Sunday 22 June 1483, iron-ically enough the day on which Edward V's coronation should have taken place, sermons were preached at St Paul's and elsewhere in

London calling into question Edward IV's right to rule (and his son's after him) on the grounds that he (Edward IV) was a bastard and urging the validity of Richard of Gloucester's claim to the throne as Richard of York's only legitimate and rightful successor. These may well have received a notably cool reception, as did a flamboyant speech delivered by the Duke of Buckingham to leading men of London in the Guildhall on 24 June. Perhaps it was in this speech that the story of Edward IV's pre-contracted marriage to Eleanor Butler, invalidating his later marriage to Elizabeth Woodville and bastardising his children by her, received its first public hearing. Just such a case for the protector becoming king may well have been advanced in an elaborate petition presented to Richard of Gloucester on 26 June and the pre-contract (as well as the invalidity by reason of his father's treachery of any claim by George Duke of Clarence's son Edward to the succession) certainly formed the mainstay of an act of parliament in January 1484 confirming the new king's title (although, on balance, it is likely that the whole story was a fabrication). Responding to the petition (the very production of which may well have reflected fears in London of Gloucester's ruthlessness if checked and the anticipated arrival in the capital of formidable forces from the north of England and elsewhere), the protector now formally accepted the crown.

Once established on the throne Richard III made hasty preparations for the coronation of himself and his wife Anne, preparations clearly involving a prominent role for his provincial (especially northern) supporters. Indeed, en route to London, northerners supervised on the king's behalf the elimination of Rivers, Grey and Vaughan at Pontefract, perhaps, as the Crowland chronicler reported, 'without any form of trial'. Early in July Richard himself visited his newly arrived forces in their camp to the north of the city of London and they certainly seem to have been powerfully present during the magnificent coronation celebrations on 6 July. Soon after this Dominic Mancini left England for France but, already, rumours had reached his ears in London that Edward V was dead:

> ...after Hastings was removed, all the attendants who had waited upon the king were debarred access to him. He and his brother were withdrawn into the inner apartments of the Tower proper, and day by day began to be seen more rarely behind the bars and windows, till at length they ceased to appear altogether. The physician Argentime, the last of his attendants whose services the king enjoyed, reported that the young king, like a victim prepared for sacrifice, sought remission of his sins by daily confession and penance, because he believed that death

was facing him… I have seen many men burst into tears and lamenta-
tions when mention was made of him after his removal from men's
sight; and already there was a suspicion that he had been done away
with. Whether, however, he has been done away with, and by what
manner of death, so far I have not at all discovered.

The Crowland chronicler, too, reported a rumour circulating by the
autumn of 1483 that 'King Edward's sons, by some unknown manner
of violent destruction, had met their fate', as well as citing the words
of 'a certain poet' that Richard III could not be content until he had
'suppressed his brother's progeny'. On the continent, a contemporary
German chronicler recorded that the king had 'had his brother's
children killed'; the French chancellor, in January 1484, declared that
Edward IV's sons had been 'put to death with impunity and the royal
crown transferred to their murderer'; and Philippe de Commines,
similarly, reported a few years later that Richard III 'had his two
nephews murdered and made himself king'. Clearly, no one will ever
know for certain when, or even whether, Richard III had his nephews
murdered in the Tower of London. They had certainly disappeared
from view by early July 1483 and there seems to have been a stillborn
plot to liberate them before the month was out. Yet, even during
Buckingham's rebellion, when producing them could have scotched
widespread rumours in southern England that they were dead, they
remained firmly hidden from view. Also, significantly, their mother
Elizabeth Woodville ended up supporting a movement designed to put
Henry Tudor Earl of Richmond on the throne, suggesting that, by
October 1483, she had given up all hope that her sons were alive. The
presumption must be that the Princes in the Tower had indeed met a
violent end by early October 1483, an end sanctioned by their uncle as
the culminating act of several months spent in a ruthless pursuit of
personal security and political power.

Richard III's seizure of the throne did not arouse much enthusiasm in
London nor, seemingly, in southern England generally, and northerners,
notably prominent during the coronation celebrations, soon began to
enjoy the fruits of his patronage. So too did close associates and backers
such as Henry Stafford Duke of Buckingham, John Howard, newly
created Duke of Norfolk, and Francis, Viscount Lovell. Even many
former servants of Edward IV continued to enjoy the king's favour for
the time being (although they may simply have been awaiting the
opportunity to rise against him). A fortnight after the coronation,
Richard embarked on a major progress, no doubt designed both to
consolidate his support – especially in the north – and widen the appeal

of his new regime, culminating in a three-and-a-half week visit to the city of York. As he made his way back to London, however, he learned at Lincoln in mid-October that rebellion had broken out in the south and west. Clearly, this was a rebellion of major proportions, showing the extent of resentment and mistrust felt by many towards the new regime. Perhaps it reflected, in part at least, jealousy and suspicion in southern and western parts of Richard III's powerful and influential northern affinity. Fears regarding the fate of the Princes in the Tower played a significant role as well. And then, of course, there is the extraordinary defection of Henry Stafford Duke of Buckingham, hitherto Richard's closest and most spectacularly rewarded supporter. Ominously, Henry Tudor Earl of Richmond emerged, at the same time, as a potentially serious rival, especially once his marriage to Edward IV's eldest daughter Elizabeth of York was mooted. Although most of the country (particularly the north of England) remained loyal to the king, Wales responded unenthusiastically to Buckingham's treachery, and the various strands of unrest were unco-ordinated, the rebellion was certainly a major threat to Richard III and one to which he responded vigorously. The constituent uprisings either collapsed or were put down, while Buckingham himself, whose desertion obviously shook the king considerably, was peremptorily executed. Yet, given the extent of southern defection and the numbers who now fled the country, he was forced more and more into dependence on his former ducal affinity. This meant, in particular, men from the north of England, and their advancement in the royal household, and plantation not only in southern and western counties but in the midlands as well, is striking, as the Crowland chronicler dramatically highlighted. Northerners, he declared, were 'planted in every part of the kingdom, to the shame of all the southern people who murmured ceaselessly and longed more each day for the return of their own lords in place of the tyranny of the present ones'. Moreover, although the newcomers never completely dominated central or local government under Richard III, their pivotal position in the king's regime in 1484/85 cannot seriously be doubted.

Since he reigned for so short a time, it is difficult either to judge Richard III's potential and qualities as a ruler or draw meaningful conclusions about his government as king. Also, what looks like good kingship and firm government may, in reality, be nothing more than Richard trying to widen and deepen the basis of his support. Nevertheless, he does seem to compare not unfavourably with Edward IV and Henry VII, neither of whom would have much of a reputation as rulers if they had to be assessed merely on their early years in power. Richard III's only parliament – perhaps with the king's personal encouragement – passed measures clearly benefiting the people; his determination to promote justice and secure law and order is evident from government records; and, although the cost of defending the realm eventually compelled him to resort to clearly unpopular financial devices, he did make some effort to improve royal financial administration as well. Even so, with the threat of Henry Tudor looming ever larger in 1484/85, his reliance on his own affinity (especially northerners) always remained paramount. Indeed, his attempt to consolidate his position during the last months of the reign, not least his abortive project, following the almost certainly natural death of his wife Anne, to marry his own niece Elizabeth of York, may, in the end, have proved counter-productive since it perhaps weakened his northern support and helped determine the outcome of the battle of Bosworth. Certainly, when he at last faced his rival on the battlefield early on the morning of 22 August 1485, he was largely backed by the same men who had helped bring him to power two years earlier. Many, though by no means all, of his supporters probably fought for him with vigour but the king's own death in the midst of the action and, according to the Crowland chronicler, striving to the end 'like a spirited and most courageous prince', made the fall of the Yorkist dynasty inevitable.

HENRY VII AND THE END OF THE WARS OF THE ROSES

For William Shakespeare, the defeat and death of Richard III at Bosworth, and the inauguration of over a century of Tudor rule by Elizabeth I's grandfather Henry VII, marked the end of dynastic conflict and civil strife. Yet, even after the victory was won, the virtually unknown Henry VII was by no means secure on the throne and, obviously, he now had to prove his capacity to rule effectively. Moreover, he had neither the background nor training for kingship. An exile on the continent since 1471, he had only recently returned to a country he hardly knew and, indeed, in the summer of 1485 he was to some extent at least being used as a pawn by the French king Charles VIII. Luck, rather than good judgement, enabled him to win the battle of Bosworth, particularly Richard III's foolhardy behaviour in the field (which resulted in his death), the treachery of Sir William Stanley, (who changed sides during the course of the action), and the equivocal behaviour of Henry Percy Earl of Northumberland (whose powerful northern force never became engaged). After the battle was over, so it was reported on the continent, a Welshman put the king's body:

> ...on his horse and carried it, hair hanging, as one would bear a sheep. And so he who had miserably killed numerous people ended his days iniq-

uitously and filthily in the dirt and mire, and he who had despoiled churches was displayed to the people naked and without any clothing, and without royal solemnity was buried at the entrance to a village church.

Even then, Henry VII's position was by no means assured: indeed, his prospects in the years following 1485 were not dissimilar to those of Henry IV after the usurpation of 1399 and Edward IV in the 1460s. Hardly surprisingly, therefore, sheer survival, coupled with the need for dynastic security, proved necessary obsessions as far as Henry VII was concerned: in fact, they provide the main keys to his reign. They explain, for instance, the king's firm measures to counter pretenders to the throne and rebellions, his concern to develop the machinery of strong government (especially his efforts to give the monarchy a sound financial base), his determination to control the nobility and gentry, and his efforts to get to grips with local lawlessness. They also explain his concern, in foreign policy, to get recognition for his dynasty on the continent and neutralise foreign support for insurrection at home.

Henry VII's title to the throne was not strong. He was a usurper and there were rival claimants to the crown, notably Elizabeth of York and the other daughters of Edward IV. Indeed, he soon married Elizabeth – a sensible move, not least since it could be presented in Tudor propaganda as the uniting of two warring dynasties. Then there was Edward Earl of Warwick, son of Edward IV's brother George Duke of Clarence, whom Henry put in the Tower of London (where he remained until 1499 when he was finally executed, allegedly for plotting with the pretender Perkin Warbeck). In addition, there was John de la Pole Earl of Lincoln, nephew of Edward IV and Richard III's designated successor: he was killed at the battle of Stoke in 1487, fighting against Henry VII. And, of course, there were the Princes in the Tower: if Edward IV's sons were still alive in 1485, very unlikely as that is, we need have little doubt that Henry VII rapidly disposed of them.

Perhaps the greatest problem facing Henry VII in his early years was the north of England. Although most northerners who had formerly been prominent in Richard III's entourage accepted the change of dynasty in 1485 (many of them, indeed, soon entered Henry VII's service), a minority played a significant role in resisting the new king and promoting disorder in the late 1480s: in Francis Lord Lovell's abortive rising in the spring of 1486 and, again, in a major rebellion fronted by the pretender Lambert Simnel (purporting to be Edward Earl of Warwick) in the summer of 1487, culminating in the battle of Stoke on 16 June, arguably a victory even more decisive than Bosworth in establishing Henry VII on the throne.

In the 1490s came the longest and potentially most dangerous challenge the first Tudor king had to face: indeed, Perkin Warbeck – masquerading as Edward IV's younger son Richard of York – enjoyed backing, at one time or another, in Ireland, Scotland, France and from Edward IV's sister Margaret, Duchess of Burgundy. Nevertheless, in the end, Henry VII was successful. By the time of his death in 1509 he had settled a new dynasty on the throne, he had survived those rivals he did not actually dispose of; he had gained recognition from his fellow princes on the continent; and he had brought peace and a measure of stability to his country.

7

TUDOR HISTORIANS AND THE WARS OF THE ROSES

EARLY TUDOR CHRONICLERS: JOHN ROUS AND ROBERT FABIAN

William Shakespeare's cycle of Plantagenet history plays has firm foundations in the early Tudor propaganda and prejudice about later medieval England he found so vividly preserved in the accounts of sixteenth-century chroniclers. Clearly, during the reigns of the first two Tudor kings Henry VII (1485-1509) and Henry VIII (1509-1547) there did develop a powerful tradition of the Tudor dynasty as the saviour of England from the chaos and confusion of the Wars of the Roses. Since Henry VII's claim to the throne required recognition of the legitimacy of Lancastrian rule, however, Henry VI obviously posed a real problem. The new king needed an immediate ancestor worthy to have carried the precious blood of Lancaster but even he could hardly claim Henry VI had been a successful ruler: hence why early Tudor writers put so much stress on Henry VI's saintliness, while Henry VII himself made determined (if, in the end, unsuccessful) efforts to secure his canonisation by the pope. Richard III, by contrast, provided an excellent target for denigration. Even before his invasion of England in August 1485, Henry Tudor Earl of Richmond is on record as describing the last Yorkist king as 'that homicide and unnatural tyrant'; soon after he took the throne, he condemned his predecessor as 'the enemy of nature' and, in his first parliament, as responsible for the 'shedding of infants' blood'; and Bernard André, Henry VII's contemporary biographer, deliberately contrasted his splendidly upright patron with the monstrous and evil tyrant he so justifiably deprived of the crown. As for Henry VII himself, he became, courtesy of his perceptive spin doctors, the agent of divine retribution at Bosworth, the man who rescued England from dynastic conflict after decades of bloodshed, and the king who, by his marriage to Elizabeth of York, at last united the warring houses of Lancaster and York.

Even as early as April 1486 the anonymous Crowland chronicler's perspective on pre-Tudor personalities and politics was coloured by what happened at Bosworth but the real founder of Tudor tradition about the Wars of the Roses in general, and Richard III in particular, was the Warwickshire antiquary John Rous. For over forty years Rous was a chaplain of the earls of Warwick and his prime concern in the so-called *Rous Roll* (a history of the earls), written during Richard III's reign, was to please the then lord of Warwick – the king himself! Richard Neville Earl of Warwick (the 'Kingmaker'), whom he had also served, he judged a 'famous knight' who not only 'had all England at his leading' but was also 'feared and respected through many lands'; moreover, 'although fortune deceived him at his end', nevertheless 'his knightly acts had been so excellent that his noble and famous name could never be put out of laudable memory'. George Duke of Clarence (Edward IV's brother), who held the earldom of Warwick for several years in the 1470s, Rous praised as 'a mighty prince, seemly of person and right witty and well visaged, a great alms giver and a great builder'. As for Richard III himself, he was:

> ...a mighty prince in his days, a special good lord to the town and lordship of Warwick where, in the castle, he bore great cost of building. [As king], all avarice set aside, [he] ruled his subjects in his realm full commendably, punishing offenders of his laws, especially extortioners and oppressors of his commons, and cherishing those that were virtuous, by the which discreet guiding he got great thanks of God and love of all his subjects, rich and poor, and great praise of the people of all other lands about him.

Following Henry VII's accession, however, not only did Rous make strenuous efforts to suppress his earlier commendation of Richard III but also, in his *History of the Kings of England* (written shortly before his death in 1491), penned a vociferously hostile portrait of the king. Whereas Henry VI had been 'a most holy man' who had been 'shamefully expelled from his kingdom', he declared, Richard III was:

> ...retained within his mother's womb for two years, [eventually] emerging with teeth and hair to his shoulders... At his nativity Scorpio was in the ascendant [and], like a scorpion, he combined a smooth front with a stinging tail... He was small of stature, with a short face and unequal shoulders, the right higher and the left lower. He received his lord King Edward V blandly, with embraces and kisses, and within about three

months or a little more he killed him together with his brother. And Lady Anne, his queen, daughter of the Earl of Warwick, he poisoned... And what was most detestable to God and all Englishmen, and indeed to all nations to whom it became known, he caused others to kill the holy man King Henry VI or, as many think, did so by his own hands...

Clearly, then, by 1491 many elements of the familiar Tudor portrait of Richard III were already in place. So, too, was Tudor spin on the battle of Bosworth and its significance:

This King Richard, who was excessively cruel in his days, reigned for three years and a little more [sic], in the way that Antichrist is to reign. And like the Antichrist to come, he was confounded at his moment of greatest pride. For having with him the crown itself, together with great quantities of treasure, he was unexpectedly cut down in the midst of his army by an invading army small by comparison but furious in impetus, like a wretched creature, [shouting] again and again that he was betrayed, and crying 'Treason, Treason!'. So, tasting what he had often administered to others, he ended his life most miserably [and], although his days were short, they were ended with no lamentation from his groaning subjects.

During the Wars of the Roses London chroniclers had been very much to the forefront in recording events not only in the capital but also in the country at large and, although fading by early Tudor times, the tradition of historical writing in London was capably maintained by Robert Fabian. A prominent draper, alderman and sheriff of the city in 1493/94, Fabian, who died in 1513, probably wrote both the *New Chronicles of England and of France* (published in 1516) and the considerably more detailed *Great Chronicle of London* during the first decade of the sixteenth century. Certainly, the two frequently convey the same information, seem to share a common style and, at any rate when dealing with the Wars of the Roses and Richard III, have a distinctly early Tudor tone (as in the depiction of the battle of Towton as 'a sore and long and unkindly fight' where 'there was the son against the father, the brother against brother, the nephew against nephew'). Not surprisingly, Fabian was particularly interested in London itself and the political dramas so often played out there and, for the Yorkist era, he could clearly draw on personal experience and knowledge of events in the capital he himself had lived through.

Interestingly, Robert Fabian tended to be sympathetic towards the 'noble and victorious prince' Edward IV and his evocative anecdotes about the king's behaviour on occasion are splendid. For instance, he tells us that, when Edward secretly married Elizabeth Woodville at Grafton, near Stony Stratford, early in the morning of 1 May 1464, there were:

> ...no persons present but the spouse, the spoussess, the Duchess of Bedford [Elizabeth's mother], the priest, two gentlewomen, and a young man to help the priest sing. After the espousals ended, he went to bed, and so tarried three or four hours, and afterwards departed and rode again to Stony Stratford, and came as though he had been hunting, and there went to bed again. And within a day or two, he sent to Grafton to Lord Rivers, his wife's father, telling him that he would come and stay with him for a time, where he was received with all honour, and so tarried there for four days. During this time she was brought nightly to his bed in so secret a manner that almost no one but her mother knew...

In 1474/75, when Edward IV became personally involved in raising cash to finance a projected expedition to France, he:

> ...rode into Essex, Suffolk, Norfolk and other counties, where he handled the people so graciously that he got more money by these means than he would have got from two fifteenths [parliamentary taxes]. It was reported that as he passed through a town in Suffolk he called a rich widow before him, amongst others, and asked her what her goodwill would be towards his great expenses. She liberally granted him £10. He thanked her and drew her to him and kissed her; which kiss pleased her so much that, for his great bounty and kind deed, he should have £20 for £10.

And, perhaps, Fabian himself was one of the Londoners whom Edward IV summoned to join him in Waltham Forest in July 1482:

> [When] the mayor and his company were come, goodly sport was provided for them, [after which] certain knights [conducted them] to a strong and pleasant lodge made of green boughs and other pleasant things. Within the lodge were laid tables, where the mayor and his company were seated, and served right plenteously with all manner of dainties, [especially] venison and all kinds of Gascon wines. Twice during the dinner the lord chamberlain and other honourable persons were sent to them from the king to ensure their welcome, and the king tarried his own dinner till he saw that they were served. [Afterwards] they were again brought into the king's presence in a pavilion not far off where [the king] gave them plenty [of recently slain deer]. And so, taking their leave, they departed, [the king] giving unto the mayor good words and unto them all favourable and cheerful countenance.

Richard III, in sharp contrast to his brother Edward IV, received short shrift indeed from Robert Fabian. Although there were several tales circulating in early Tudor times about Henry VI's death in 1471, he tells us, 'the most common fame went that he was stabbed with a dagger by the hands of the Duke of Gloucester' in the Tower of London. En route to the throne in 1483, he murdered William Lord Hastings for his 'truth and fidelity' to Edward V, secured possession of young Edward's brother Richard of York by means of 'manifold dissimulated fair promises' and, before long, there arose 'much whispering among the people' that he had 'put the children of King Edward [IV] to death'. Equally ruthless was his treatment of a certain William Collingbourne, cast into prison:

...for sundry treasons and for a rhyme in derision of the king and his council, as follows:

> *The cat, the rat and Lovell our dog*
> *Ruleth all England under a hog.*

By which was meant that Catesby, Ratcliffe and Lord Lovell ruled the land under the king who bore the white boar... For this and other offences, he was put to the most cruel death on Tower Hill where, for him, a new pair of gallows was made upon which, after he had hanged a short time, he was cut down, being alive, and his bowels ripped out of his belly and cast into the fire there by him, yet he lived till the butcher put his hand into the bulk of his body; insomuch that he said in the same instant, 'O Lord Jesu, yet more trouble', and so died, to the great compassion of many people.

Certainly, as far as Robert Fabian was concerned, Richard III, deserted by many of his men, fully deserved his defeat and death at Bosworth. Moreover, whereas the 'noble prince' Henry VII was now 'received with all honour and gladness' at nearby Leicester:

Richard, the late king, his body despoiled to the skin and nought left about him so much as would cover his privy member, was trussed behind a pursuivant called Norroy as a hog or other vile beast, and so, all bespattered with mire and filth, was brought to a church in Leicester for all men to wonder upon, and there irreverently buried.

EARLY TUDOR HUMANIST HISTORIANS: POLYDORE VERGIL AND THOMAS MORE

During the fifteenth and early sixteenth centuries the study and writing of history came to play a central role in the humanist programme of education for life and citizenship in Renaissance Italy. In particular, Italian humanists believed that ancient historians such as Sallust and Tacitus, men who played an active role in Roman political and social life themselves as well as writing history, should be read not only as models of Latin prose style but also as an invaluable treasury of political, moral and ethical behaviour. Later medieval English chronicles, by contrast, tended to be written by men, often clerics, whose experience of the wider world of secular politics and society was limited. Often beginning with the Creation and pretending to universal scope, such chroniclers frequently gave credence to myths and legends about the past (for instance, the notion that Brutus was the founder of an ancient British state); they almost invariably saw history as God-driven and tended to favour a narrative chronological approach; they had little sense of periods in history (displaying political, social and cultural characteristics peculiar to themselves) or that the past was often very different from the present; they tended to be insufficiently critical of their sources; and, by and large, they showed no great inclination to grapple with the causes and significance of events. Italian Renaissance historians such as Leonardo Bruni, Poggio Bracciolini, Flavio Biondo, Francesco Guicciardini and Niccolò Machiavelli gave history an altogether more secular setting and content; they were much more interested in non-divine forces and, especially, individuals in causing events; they had a much greater appreciation that the past was different from the present, subscribed to notions of development, even progress, over time; and they certainly regarded history as didactic, as providing, in particular, examples of heroes and villains to be emulated or rejected. Clearly, too, humanists' immersion in the literature of ancient Greece and Rome (especially ancient history) gave them a sense of historical perspective most medieval chroniclers lacked. The historian's prime objective, they believed, should be to discover the truth about the past and, in order to do so, they drew upon and subjected to critical evaluation a range of historical evidence, not only literary sources, where they often weighed one account against another and made a judgement as to which was the more convincing, but also record material, topography and physical remnants such as buildings and coins. All in all, Renaissance historical writing became altogether more analytical, more politically and psychologically sophisticated, than most medieval chroniclers' accounts of past men and events had been.

Polydore Vergil (c.1470-1555), an Italian humanist and fully-fledged Renaissance historian of real quality, was born and brought up in Urbino. Even before he came to England in 1502 he had a considerable scholarly reputation and, soon after his arrival, he commenced his researches into English history, as well as probably keeping a diary of contemporary events. Clearly, too, he soon obtained the favour of Henry VII, obtained a number of ecclesiastical preferments and, by 1507, had received a commission from the king to write a comprehensive narrative survey of England's history from ancient times to the present. He completed the first version of his *Anglica Historia*, written in classical Latin, in 1531 and dedicated it to Henry VIII. A first printed edition (carrying the story down to 1509) appeared in 1534, a second in 1546, and, in 1555, a third edition was published, this time including a continuation of the narrative to 1537. The *Anglica Historia* clearly demonstrates Vergil's humanist credentials as an Italian scholar who had received a thorough classical education. He gave his narrative a coherent structure and even, to a certain extent, a unitary theme; he employed, on occasion, the humanist device of putting rhetorical speeches into the mouths of historical figures; and his classical training is very evident, too, in the language, style and content of the book. In his dedication of the work to Henry VIII, moreover, Vergil clearly stated his objectives. Since most of the monastic chronicles of England were 'bald, uncouth, chaotic and deceitful', he declared, there was an urgent need to remedy their defects in a narrative that was true, edifying and sought always to 'display to the living those events which should be an example and those which should be a warning'. Clearly, he consulted a considerable body of written material and, for events within living memory, many men at the early Tudor court who could supply information, as well as taking on board evidence provided by geography, topography, ancient monuments and archaeology: his handling of his sources, moreover, was remarkably scholarly and sophisticated by early sixteenth century standards. He showed himself nicely aware of the existence of conflicting interpretations and even occasionally (when discussing contentious matters such as the fall of George Duke of Clarence) not only supplies us with a variety of opinions but also attempts to evaluate and, if possible, reconcile them in a common sense manner. Notably critical of myths and legends, he genuinely sought to distinguish fact from fiction; he attempted to probe motive and establish the relationship between cause and effect; and he was even prepared to admit, now and then, that he might not be free from error. Since he was encouraged to write his history by Henry VII, however, perhaps it is hardly surprising that he brought in a largely favourable verdict on the first Tudor king as a man whose spirit was 'distinguished, wise and prudent' and who had a 'brave and resolute mind'. In government, moreover, Henry VII was:

> ...shrewd and prudent, so that no one dared to get the better of him through deceit or guile... He well knew how to maintain his royal majesty and all which appertains to kingship... He cherished justice above all things, vigorously punished violence, manslaughter and every kind of violence, and enabled his subjects to conduct their lives peaceably...

As for the young Henry VIII, whose patronage Vergil also enjoyed, 'everybody loved him', not least on account of his 'handsome bearing', his 'comely and manly features', his 'outstanding physical strength', his 'remarkable memory', his 'skill at arms and on horseback' and his 'scholarship of no mean order'. Yet, although Vergil must have been powerfully motivated (at any rate when dealing with events after 1399) to interpret English history in favour of the Tudors, he cannot be dismissed as a mere dynastic apologist pandering to whatever his royal masters demanded of him. Indeed, he criticised the increasingly avaricious and oppressive rule of Henry VII's last years, made no attempt to disguise his loathing for Cardinal Wolsey and obviously had deep reservations as well about Henry VIII's policies and behaviour during the early 1530s.

In Polydore Vergil's *Anglica Historia* Lancastrian tradition concerning the origins and nature of the Wars of the Roses certainly found a spokesman of distinction, not least since it so evidently appeared to justify early Tudor portrayals of Henry VII and Henry VIII as the restorers of peace and stability after years of horrific civil war. The original cause of intestinal conflict, Vergil believed, lay in Richard II's deposition and Henry IV's usurpation in 1399. The wars as such began when 'King Henry [VI], who derived his pedigree from the house of Lancaster, and Richard of York, who conveyed himself by his mother's side from Lionel, son of Edward III, contended mutually for the kingdom'. As early as 1450, according to Vergil, York 'aspired to the sovereignty', conceiving an 'outrageous lust for principality' and never ceasing thereafter 'to plan how and by what means he might accomplish it'. As for the wars themselves, they resulted not only in the deaths of many men but also, since they continued to rage when Richard of York's sons, successively, seized the throne as Edward IV and Richard III, the ruin of the whole realm. Indeed, he declared, so great was hatred and division among the nobility, that the condition of England became:

> ...most miserable, for churches and houses were everywhere spoiled, sword and fire raged all over, the realm was wholly replenished with armour and weapons, and slaughter, blood and lamentation. The fields were wasted, town and city starved for hunger, and many other mischiefs happened, which proceed commonly from the rage of wars.

Polydore Vergil clearly believed that the personalities, motives and behaviour of individuals were crucially important in determining the course of history, not least during the Wars of the Roses. Moreover, when it came to Henry VI, his manifest failings as a ruler could hardly be denied'! So Vergil chose to highlight instead his admirable qualities as a man. 'There was not in this world a more pure, more honest and more holy creature', he declared; indeed, here was a king positively crying out for canonisation:

There was in him honest reproachfulness, modesty, innocence and perfect patience, taking all human chances, miseries and all afflictions of this life in so good part as though he had justly by some offence deserved the same… He hungered not after riches, nor thirsted for honour and worldly estimation, but was careful only for his soul's health… He did of his own natural inclination abhor all vices both of body and mind, by reason whereof he was of honest conversation even from a child, pure and clean, partaking of no evil, ready to conceive all that was good… [And for his] actions and offices of perfect holiness, [God] showed many miracles in his lifetime.

By contrast, although Vergil judged Margaret of Anjou 'a young lady exceeding others of her time' in beauty and wisdom, he clearly did not approve of this woman 'very desirous of renown' who displayed 'all manly qualities' and determined to 'take upon herself' the rule of the realm. Edward IV was altogether more to his liking, as a king who was:

…very tall of personage, exceeding the stature almost of all others, of comely visage, pleasant looks, broad breasted, diligent in doing his affairs, ready in perils, earnest and horrible to the enemy, bountiful to his friends [but] given to bodily lust… A little before the end of his life he began to slide little by little into avarice [but], after all intestine division appeased, he left a most wealthy realm abounding in all things, which by reason of civil war he had received almost utterly void as well of able men as money, [and] so bound the people's goodwill to him that they mourned for him long after his death.

When it came to Richard III, however, Vergil unleashed his venom with a vengeance and he must certainly be regarded as the first major architect of later Tudor tradition about the king. 'While thinking of any matter', he declared, Richard III 'did continually bite his nether lip, as though that cruel nature of his did rage against itself in that little carcass'. Indeed, 'he was wont to be ever with his right hand pulling out of the sheath to the midst, and putting in again, the dagger which he did always wear'. As soon as he heard of Edward IV's death in 1483, moreover, Richard 'began to be kindled with an ardent desire of sovereignty' and determined thereafter 'to accomplish his purposed spiteful practice by subtlety and sleight'. Subsequently, 'being blind with covetousness of reigning whom no foul fact could now hold back', he seized the throne 'without assent of the commonalty' and did so 'contrary to the law of God and man', and, given the fact that Richard 'thought of nothing but tyranny and cruelty', at the finish God gave victory at Bosworth to Henry VII.

Perhaps the greatest, and certainly the most famous, early sixteenth-century English humanist was Sir Thomas More (1478-1535). A brilliant scholar who became very familiar with both classical Greek and Latin, trained as a lawyer and enjoyed a successful career in the service of Henry VIII, he is best remembered for his *Utopia,* a penetrating critique of contemporary Tudor society, probably written in 1516 (where he successfully combined firm Christian principles and deep knowledge of ancient ethics) and also, of course, for the manner of his death (he was executed by Henry VIII for his implacable resistance to the Reformation). Thomas More, moreover, has been even more influential than Rous, Fabian and Vergil in establishing Richard III's modern reputation as an evil tyrant. His *History of King Richard the Third*, written in English and Latin concurrently during the second decade of the sixteenth century but mysteriously abandoned unfinished and unrevised by its author, was not, in fact, published until after More's death. He may not have seen himself as writing history at all; he can have had no first hand knowledge of Edward IV, Richard III or Yorkist politics and is frequently inaccurate, often prepared to embellish his narrative for dramatic effect (about a third of it consists of invented speeches), and overwhelmingly concerned to portray Richard III as a grand villain. The *History* clearly is very dramatic and More undoubtedly was preoccupied with tyranny (which he detested) when writing it; Richard III as a usurping tyrant dominates his narrative and many of the leading elements in Tudor tradition about the last Plantagenet king – including the king's monstrous appearance, his murder of Henry VI, his engineering the death of Clarence, his plotting for the crown long before Edward IV's death, his master-minding the murder of the Princes in the Tower and the invariable infamy of his motives – either first appear or are first fully developed here. Yet it must also be remembered that there was no shortage of men in the political circles in which More moved who could provide him with inside information. His reliance on classical models like Tacitus and Sallust may go far to explain many of his dramatic devices (his comparison of the 'good' King Edward IV and the 'bad' King Richard III, for instance, is strongly reminiscent of Tacitus' contrast of the Roman emperors Augustus and Tiberius). He probably had access to London chronicles and the manuscript of his fellow Renaissance scholar Polydore Vergil; he was not writing to please any particular patron; and, despite the all too obvious loading of the dice against his villain, More did on occasion attempt to distinguish between rumour and fact. Indeed, a strong case can be made for saying that

More's basic characterisations and storyline (once shorn of its dramatic elaborations) already mapped out to a significant extent in earlier narratives (including Dominic Mancini's contemporary account and the Crowland chronicle) are not only plausible but even convincing.

Sir Thomas More's *History* concentrates firmly on Richard III's character, behaviour and the sequence of events from April 1483 (the death of Edward IV) to October 1483 (the outbreak of Buckingham's rebellion). However, he certainly took on board as well the notion that the Wars of the Roses were truly horrific: in the recent 'inward war among ourselves', he declared, there has been 'so great effusion of the ancient noble blood of this realm' that scarcely half the nobility remained; indeed, the 'long continued dissensions' and the many battles 'so cruel and so deadly fought' have 'cost more English blood than had twice the winning of France'. Certainly, too, More has bequeathed us a compelling pen-portrait of Edward IV as:

...a goodly personage and very princely to behold: of heart courageous, politic in counsel, in adversity nothing abashed, in prosperity rather joyful than proud, in peace just and merciful, in war sharp and fierce, in the field bold and hardy... He was of visage lovely, of body mighty, strong and clean made; howbeit, in his latter days, with over liberal diet, somewhat corpulent and burly...

More was notably forthright, however, on the subject of the king's 'fleshly wantonness':

[The] king's greedy appetite was insatiable and, everywhere all over the realm, intolerable. For no woman was there anywhere, young or old, rich or poor, whom he set his eyes upon [but he would] have her, to the great destruction of many a good woman...

And he particularly dwelt on the qualities of Edward's courtesan Mistress Shore, who may well have been one of More's informants:

[The] king would say that he had three concubines who, in three diverse properties, diversely excelled: one the merriest, another the wiliest, and the third the holiest harlot in the realm, as one whom no man could get out of the church lightly but it were to his bed. [The] merriest was Shore's wife, in whom the king took special pleasure. For many he had but her he loved... Proper she was and fair: nothing in her body that you would have changed, unless you might have wished her somewhat taller.

'Thus say they who knew her in her youth', More added, for now:

…she is old, lean, withered and dried up, nothing left but shrivelled skin and hard bone. And yet being even such, whosoever regards her visage might guess and imagine what parts, now filled, would make it a fair face.

Although strikingly similar to the verdicts of Rous and Vergil, not least in its wording, Sir Thomas More's dramatic hyperbole when describing Richard III scaled even greater heights:

…little of stature, ill-featured of limbs, his left shoulder much higher than the right, hard favoured of visage… He was malicious, wrathful, envious and, from before his birth, ever forward. It is for truth reported that the duchess his mother had so much a do in her labour that she could not be delivered of him uncut, and he came into the world with the feet forward [and] also not untoothed. He was close and secret, a deep dissembler, lowly of countenance, arrogant of heart, outwardly companionable where he inwardly hated, not hesitating to kiss whom he thought to kill, pitiless and cruel… Friend and foe were to him indifferent; where his advantage grew, he spared no man's death whose life withstood his purpose…

When dealing with the murder of the Princes in the Tower, More frankly acknowledged the difficulties confronting him:

I shall rehearse to you the dolorous end of these babes, not after every way that I have heard, but after that way that I have so heard by such men and by such means as methinks it were hard but it should be true.

His own version of the tale is certainly a gripping one. Sir James Tyrell, he tells us, arranged that Edward IV's sons:

…should be murdered in their beds [in the Tower of London]. For this purpose he appointed Miles Forest, one of the four that kept them, a fellow fleshed in murder beforetime. To him he joined one John Dighton, his own horsekeeper, a big square strong knave. Then, all the others being removed from them, this Miles Forest and John Dighton, about midnight, the innocent children lying in their beds, came into the chamber and suddenly lapped them up among the clothes, so bewrapped them and entangled them, keeping down by force the featherbed and pillows hard unto their mouths, that within a while smothered and stifled, their breath failing, they gave up to God their innocent souls into the joys of heaven, leaving to the tormentors their bodies dead in the bed. After the wretches perceived them, first by the struggling with the pains of death, and after long lying still, to be thoroughly dead, they laid their bodies naked out upon the bed and fetched Sir James to see them. Who, upon sight of them, caused those murderers to bury them at the stair foot, deep in the ground under a great heap of stones.

And More could hardly contain his repugnance at so callous and wicked a deed:

> …thus, as I have learned from them that much knew and little cause had to lie, were these two noble princes, these innocent tender children, born of most royal blood, brought up in great wealth, likely long to live to reign and rule in the realm, by traitorous tyranny taken, deprived of their estate, shortly shut up in prison, and privily slain and murdered, their bodies cast God knows where, by the cruel ambition of their unnatural uncle and his pitiless tormentors.

Edward Hall and the Triumph of Tudor Tradition

Edward Hall, a Cambridge graduate and lawyer who died in 1547, was very much a man of the Tudor age; he sat in the Reformation Parliament in the 1530s, strongly supporting the political and religious measures of his patron Henry VIII; and, certainly, he rejoiced in the fact that the dynastic wars of the fifteenth century were brought to an end by Henry VII and his son. The very title page of his massive chronicle, first published in 1548 and covering English history reign by reign from Henry IV to Henry VIII makes his intentions abundantly clear from the start: *The Union of the Two Noble and Illustrious Families of Lancaster and York, being long in continual dissension for the crown of this noble realm, with all the acts done in both the times of the princes, both of the one lineage and the other, beginning at the time of King Henry the Fourth, the first author of this division, and so successfully proceeding to the reign of the high and prudent prince King Henry the Eighth, the indubitable flower and very heir of the said lineages.* The climactic event of this long stretch of history, for Hall, was the marriage of Henry VII and Edward IV's daughter Elizabeth of York since, 'as King Henry the Fourth was the beginning and root of the great discord and division, so was the godly matrimony the final end of all dissensions, titles and debates'. That he saw history very much in dramatic terms, almost akin to the unfolding of a play indeed, is also evident in Hall's chapter headings:

> The Unquiet Times of King Henry the Fourth
> The Victorious Acts of King Henry the Fifth
> The Troublous Season of King Henry the Sixth
> The Prosperous Reign of King Edward the Fourth
> The Pitiful Life of King Edward the Fifth
> The Tragical Doings of King Richard the Third
> The Politic Governance of King Henry the Seventh

The final product of this great moral drama, of course, was his own patron, and telling the story of 'The Triumphant Reign of King Henry the Eighth' in the last chapter occupies half the pages of Hall's narrative.

Although no humanist himself, Hall certainly drew very heavily indeed on Vergil's *English History* and, for his account of Richard III's usurpation, happily plagiarised Thomas More as well. Like them, he saw fifteenth-century political history as very much driven by the personalities, motives and behaviour of kings. He highlighted, too, the role of powerful magnates – Warwick the Kingmaker, for instance, 'whom the common people judged able to do all things' – and he certainly invented and put into the mouths of historical figures lengthy rhetorical speeches. Yet, since he was so over-whelmingly concerned to justify Tudor rule (his chronicle has been described, not without justification, as a 'masterpiece of Tudor propaganda'), tell a good story and bring out the moral lessons to be learned from the past, he had no qualms at all about embellishing, even twisting and suppressing, what he found in his sources.

Certainly, despite its excessive verbosity and repetitiveness, Hall's vast narrative soon proved very popular and helped ensure, in particular, wide-spread acceptance of Tudor propaganda about the nature of the Wars of the Roses. 'What misery, what murder and what execrable plagues this famous region has suffered by the division and dissension of the renowned houses of Lancaster and York', Hall declared:

> ...my wit cannot comprehend nor my tongue declare, neither yet my pen fully set forth. For what noble man lives at this day, or what gentleman of any ancient stock or progeny is there, whose lineage has not been infested with this unnatural division, [until] by the union celebrated between the high and mighty prince Henry the Seventh and the Lady Elizabeth [it] was suspended [in] the person of their most noble, puissant and mighty heir, King Henry the Eighth, and by him clearly buried and perpetually extinct.

What fascinated Edward Hall most of all were the colourful personalities he found in his sources, especially Polydore Vergil, and he is at his most compelling when recounting their behaviour and impact on their times. Although Richard II's downfall in 1399 owed more to frailty of youth than malice of heart, he concluded, his inability to prevent Henry IV's usurpation set the scene for all that was to follow. Henry IV himself not only committed awful crimes when he seized the throne and sanctioned the murder of his predecessor but also, as a result, could never enjoy either peace of mind as a man or any real success as a ruler. Since Henry V deliberately sought to expiate his father's sin by having Richard II reburied at Westminster, however, and then proved a very model of chivalric kingship himself, God's full vengeance on the Lancastrian dynasty was postponed for a generation. Fortunately for Henry VI, he long enjoyed the services of that wise and patriotic statesman 'Good Duke Humphrey' of Gloucester but the proud, covetous and crafty Cardinal Beaufort, still more the 'queen's darling' and evil genius William Duke of Suffolk, brought all Gloucester's efforts to nought and, eventually, he met a most unnatural death. When writing of the last Lancastrian king himself, Hall made little attempt to improve on Vergil or even tamper much with the Italian's phraseology. Vergil's portrait of Margaret of Anjou, too, firmly underpinned Hall's treatment of the queen. She was, he declared, a 'manly woman used to rule and not to be ruled', a woman 'desirous of glory and covetous of honour' and a queen 'whose countenance was so fearful and her look so terrible that, for all men against whom she took a small displeasure, her frowning was their undoing and her indignation their death'. Indeed, 'although she joined her husband with her in name' in ruling the country, in fact 'she did all, she said all, and she bore the whole swing, as the strong ox does when he is yoked in the plough with a poor silly ass'. And once Richard of York's pride led him to claim the crown for himself – even though, in response to a lengthy oration put into his mouth by Hall, 'the lords sat still like graven images in the wall or dumb gods, neither whispering nor speaking, as if their mouths had been sewn up' – the long shadow cast by 1399 reached its inevitable conclusion in bloody civil war. When he came to Edward IV, Hall once more chose to follow Vergil (and, indeed, More) in presenting a generally balanced view of the king as a man who managed to combine a liking for lechery with a capacity for ruling. Similarly, he was only too happy to take on board the hostile portraits of Richard III so vividly penned by his humanist mentors. Never is his venom against England's last Plantagenet king better expressed than in a speech put into Henry Tudor's mouth on the very eve of Bosworth:

> Behold yonder Richard, [a] tyrant worse than Nero, for he has not only murdered his nephew, bastardized his noble brothers and defamed the womb of his virtuous mother, but also employed all the means he could invent to carnally know his own niece under the pretence of a cloaked matrimony, the lady I have sworn and promised to make my wife. If this cause is not just, and this quarrel not godly, let God the giver of victory judge and determine.

For Hall, God did indeed pass judgement, Richard III met a well deserved defeat and death, and the accession of Henry VII (a man 'so formed and decorated with all gifts and lineaments of nature that he seemed more an angelical creature than a terrestrial personage') at last brought the Wars of the Roses to an end.

LATER TUDOR MORALISTS, ANNALISTS AND CHRONICLERS

Polydore Vergil, Thomas More and Edward Hall all believed the past provided a rich repository of political, social and moral lessons for the present; the history of Lancastrian and Yorkist England, in particular, furnished ample and stark evidence of the dire consequences of Plantagenet dynastic rivalry, magnate factionalism and bloody civil war; and such notions certainly inspired the publication in 1559 of the *Mirror for Magistrates*, a curious compilation of imaginary monologues by various authors, where prominent players in fifteenth-century politics deliberately analyse their faults and failings in all too frequently excruciating verse. Since it went through several editions in Elizabeth I's reign, and drew most of its historical content from Hall, the importance of the *Mirror for Magistrates* in popularising Tudor tradition about the Wars of the Roses was clearly considerable. The work's didactic purpose is only too evident, moreover, from its dedication to 'the nobility and all others in office' and its declared intention to demonstrate how God:

> ...has dealt with some of our countrymen, your ancestors, for sundry vices... For here, as in a looking glass, you shall see (if any vice is in you) how the like has been punished [in the past, and] provide a good occasion to move you to the sooner amendment.

Henry VI, for instance, is made to declare:

> The solace of the soul my chiefest pleasure was,
> Of worldly pomp, of fame, or game, I did not pass;
> My kingdoms nor my crown I prized not a crumb:
> In heaven were my riches heaped, to which I sought to come...
> Our kingdoms are but cares, our state devoid of stay,
> Our riches ready snares, to hasten our decay:
> Our pleasures privy pricks our vices to provoke,
> Our pomp a pump, our fame a flame, our power a smouldering smoke...
> [At Tewkesbury] my only son, not thirteen years of age,
> Was slain and murdered strait, by Edward in his rage;
> And shortly I myself to stint all further strife
> Stabbed with my brother's bloody blade in prison lost my life...
> God grant my woeful ills too grievous to rehearse,
> May teach all states to know how deeply dangers pierce:
> How frail all honours are, how brittle worldly bliss,
> That warned through my fearful fate, they fear to do amiss.

Richard Duke of York, for plotting to 'get the crown and kingdom in my hands' and confronting the 'silly king and queen' in the field, was 'slain, being overmatched by might'; Edward IV, as a result of 'his surfeiting and intemperate life, suddenly died in the midst of his prosperity'; and as for Richard III, he certainly met a well-earned fate at Bosworth:

> Lo, here you may behold the due and just reward
> Of tyranny and treason which God doth most detest,
> For if unto my duty I had taken regard,
> I might have lived still in honour with the best.

Sir Thomas Smith, in a pamphlet published in 1561 and purporting to speak for the English realm, urged Elizabeth I to marry so as to perpetuate 'the race of the mixed rose, which brought again the amicable peace long exiled from among my children by the striving of the two roses'. Indeed, he declared:

> From the time that King Richard II was deposed [until] the death of King Richard III, [by] reason of titles, this poor realm had never long rest… Now this king prevailed, now the other… These two blades of Lionel and John of Gaunt never rested pursuing the one the other, till the red rose was almost razed out and the white made all bloody… They set the father against the son, the brother against the brother, the uncle slew the nephew, and was slain himself. So blood pursued and ensued blood, till all the realm was brought to great confusion.

These sentiments were echoed by John Lyly, in his *Euphues and his England*, published in 1580:

> There were for a long time civil wars in this country, by reason of several claims to the crown, between the two famous and noble houses of Lancaster and York, either of them pretending to be of the royal blood, which caused them both to spend their vital blood. These wars continued long, not without great loss both to the nobility and commonalty, [and] turned the realm to great ruin…

Peace was only restored, Lyly continued, as a result of 'a marriage solemnised by God's special providence, between Henry Earl of Richmond heir of the house of Lancaster, and Elizabeth daughter to Edward IV, the undoubted issue and heir to the house of York, whereby (as they term it) the red rose and the white rose were united and joined together'. Much the same line was also taken by later Tudor chroniclers and annalists such as Richard Grafton, John Stow and, of course, William Shakespeare's principal authority, the *Chronicle of Raphael Holinshed*.

Holinshed's Chronicle was, in fact, written by a syndicate of writers of whom Raphael Holinshed – a Cheshire man who came to London early in Elizabeth I's reign where he worked for several years as a translator and print editor – was the co-ordinator and chief. The resulting narrative, first published in 1578 (two years before Holinshed's death) and available to Shakespeare in its second edition of 1587, has no great distinction, not least since its authors so happily, and so extensively, plagiarised the work of others, particularly the huge chronicle of Edward Hall. 'My speech is plain', Holinshed himself wrote, 'without any rhetorical show of eloquence', but his compilation did, at least, condense and simplify Hall's narrative and, as a result, it is altogether more readable. No wonder it proved so handy a quarry of information for the hard-pressed William Shakespeare.

8

THE WARS OF THE ROSES IN STUART AND HANOVERIAN TIMES

SEVENTEENTH-CENTURY PERSPECTIVES

None of William Shakespeare's Plantagenet history plays were performed much in the seventeenth century, at any rate not after the deaths of the playwright himself in 1616 and the actor Richard Burbage in 1619. Even in the eighteenth and early nineteenth centuries, only *Richard III* enjoyed regular revivals and, even then, in an appallingly mangled version first cobbled together by the actor-manager Colley Cibber in 1700. Once the First Folio edition of the entire Shakespearian canon (apart from *Pericles*) had been published in 1623, however, authoritative texts of all the history plays were easily available and, since new editions regularly appeared thereafter, their portrayal of the Wars of the Roses, and Tudor tradition about the wars of which they were the dramatic culmination, certainly exercised a profound influence on subsequent historical writing. So, too, did later Tudor and early Stuart antiquarians. The mania for searching out and preserving medieval manuscripts, stimulated in part by the Dissolution of the Monasteries in the 1530s, eventually led to the foundation of the Society of Antiquaries in 1596 and, among its leading lights, were William Camden, John Stow and Sir Robert Cotton. Camden, a schoolmaster who devoted his holidays to antiquarian trips around England, published his monumental *Britannia* (which incorporated the fruits of several such expeditions) in 1586, various later historical tracts, and even founded a chair of history at Oxford University in 1622. Stow, a former London merchant, devoted over forty years of his life to collecting and transcribing manuscripts as well as producing historical and topographical works of his own, notably the *Annals of England* and *A Survey of London*. Cotton, who was both a prominent man of affairs and a dedicated antiquary, built up an exceptionally large and well-catalogued library of manuscripts and books and, indeed, it was he who rescued the *Crowland Chronicle* from oblivion. Not surprisingly, as a result of the endeavours of such men, the seventeenth century not only saw a proliferation of narrative histories but also real efforts to draw on both original records and the more familiar chronicles of medieval England.

Nevertheless, the origins of the Wars of the Roses continued to be traced back to Richard II's reign and the wars themselves portrayed as sanguinary struggles between warring dynasties. Samuel Daniel, in the 1609 preface to a new edition of his long narrative poem *The History of the Civil Wars between the Houses of York and Lancaster*, first published in 1595, described his purpose as being:

> ...to show the deformities of civil dissension, and the miserable events of rebellions, conspiracies and bloody revengements, which followed (as in a circle) upon that breach of the due course of succession by the usurpation of Henry IV; and thereby to make the blessings of peace and the happiness of an established government in a direct line the better to appear.

The onset of the English Civil War in the 1640s clearly stimulated a renewed interest in earlier internal conflicts and, indeed, between 1641 and 1643 several – perhaps as many as fifteen – narratives of the Wars of the Roses found their way into print. Later in the century the succession of James II to the English throne in 1685 coincided with the publication of *England's Happiness in a Lineal Succession; And the Deplorable Miseries Which ever attended Doubtful Titles to the Crown, Historically Demonstrated, By the Bloody Wars Between the Two Houses of York and Lancaster*. Covering the history of 'that bloody, unnatural and fatal war' between York and Lancaster which 'lasted about 106 years' from Richard II's reign to the execution of Edward Earl of Warwick 'about 1504' (actually 1499), it certainly did not pull its punches:

> ...it is almost incredible to believe how many bloody battles were fought, what multitudes of men were slaughtered, how many treasons and horrid conspiracies were carried on and perpetrated, how much noble blood was spilt, how many families were ruined, how many barbarous executions, how many unreasonable fines, and perpetual banishments happened, during this unfortunate war.

Clearly, such mayhem contained an important lesson, at least as far as this author was concerned, for anyone inclined to disrupt the peaceful accession of Catholic James:

> The many miseries which attended that unfortunate quarrel may serve, at once, to show us their misery and our own happiness under the influence of the most auspicious and promising reign of our present sovereign James the Second.

The personalities of the Wars of the Roses, most notably Edward IV, Warwick the Kingmaker and Richard III, obviously appealed to Stuart no less than Tudor historians. Edward IV's reputation remained high, as is evident from a life of the king by William Habington, published in 1640. 'The king', he declared, 'was, if we compare him with the lives of princes in general, worthy to be numbered among the best.' Moreover, although Edward had to contend with dynastic challenge and political faction, such problems were 'but short tempests or rather small overcastings during the glorious calm of his government'. Warwick the Kingmaker, too, attracted an admiring early seventeenth-century biographer when Thomas Gainford penned his *Unmatchable Life and Death of Richard Neville Earl of Warwick, in his time the Darling and Favourite of Kings*. Warwick, he concluded, was truly great:

> ...by reason of his hospitality, riches, possessions, popular love, comeliness of gesture, gracefulness of person, industrious valour, indefatigable painstaking, and all the signatures of a royal mind and generous spirit.

As far as Richard III was concerned, however, Tudor tradition and Shakespeare's treatment of the king cast a long shadow. Michael Drayton, in 1613, described him as 'this viper, this most vile devourer of his kind'; Sir Walter Raleigh, the following year, judged him not only 'this cruel king' but also 'the greatest monster in mischief of all that forewent him'; and Sir Francis Bacon, in his *History of the Reign of Henry the Seventh* (published in 1622), inevitably drew unfavourable comparisons between the first Tudor king and his Yorkist predecessor. For Bacon, Henry VII was a merciful prince who administered justice fairly and, indeed, proved himself 'a wonder for wise men'; Richard III, although 'jealous of the honour of the English nation', a 'good law-maker for the ease and solace of the common people' and a king who certainly won the devotion of the north of England, nevertheless proved himself a tyrant whose:

> ...cruelties and parricides, in the opinion of all men, weighed down his virtues and merits; and, in the opinion of wise men, even those virtues themselves were conceived to be rather feigned and affected things to serve his ambition rather than true qualities inherent in his judgement.

Bacon's was a decidedly mixed verdict, in fact, as had been the judgements of William Camden and John Stow before him. Camden, while believing that Richard III 'inhumanly murdered his nephews' and usurped the throne, also reported that 'in the opinion of the wise he is reckoned in the number of bad men but of good princes'. Even more positively, Stow not only remarked that Richard's responsibility for the murder of his nephews was unproven but also that old men (who had seen the king) had told him that, although low in stature, the king was not deformed. The first full-scale defence of the last Plantagenet, however, came from the pen of Sir George Buck, Master of the Revels to the first Stuart king James I, in his *History of King Richard the Third*. Convinced that 'all King Richard's guilt is but suspicion' and determined 'to rescue him entirely from these wrongs', Buck, a conscientious antiquarian-cum-historian who consulted a range of manuscripts (including the *Crowland Chronicle)*, produced the first comprehensive assault on Tudor tradition and concluded that the king's 'good name and noble memory' had, indeed, been foully maligned. Certainly, Buck not only praised Richard III's courage, fortitude, magnanimity, justice and piety but also pointed out that 'even his adversaries and calumniators confess that he was a very wise and a prudent and politic and an heroical prince'. William Winstanley, in similar vein, declared in 1684 that:

> …as honour is always attended on by envy, so has this worthy prince been blasted by malicious traducers who, like Shakespeare in his play on him, render him dreadfully black in his actions, a monster by nature, rather than a man of admirable parts.

Yet William Nicholson, when writing of the Yorkist period in the 1690s, came to the bleak conclusion that historians had frequently found themselves too perplexed 'to form a regular history out of such a vast heap of rubbish and confusion'!

EIGHTEENTH-CENTURY VERDICTS

During the seventeenth, and still more the eighteenth, centuries history came to be regarded as a valuable component in the education of an English gentleman and possession of a substantial library a necessary symbol of high social status. Catering for this market, multi-volumed and often expensively bound histories of England proliferated. Frequently covering a long chrono-logical time-span and narrating English political history reign by reign (with a distinct tendency to judge medieval kings by anachronistic eighteenth-century standards), the best of them tended to draw heavily on a narrow range of available sources, the worst derive almost exclusively from earlier histories. A few did rise above the mediocre, however, most notably, in the early eighteenth century, Rapin's fifteen volume *History of England* (published, in French, between 1723 and 1725 and, in English translation, between 1728 and 1732). A French lawyer and Huguenot refugee, Paul Rapin de Thoyras' narrative treatment of the Wars of the Roses era certainly marked a considerable advance on earlier histories: it was well researched by the standards of the time and, indeed, Rapin was able to establish for the first time a reasonably accurate chronology for later fifteenth-century England. Nevertheless, although frequently citing the *Crowland Chronicle*, he tended to prefer later Tudor tradition about the events of the Wars of the Roses and, as far as Edward IV was concerned, placed too much reliance on Philippe de Commines' portrayal of the first Yorkist as a lazy, debauched, cruel and avaricious king who only roused himself from his accustomed lethargy in times of crisis. On Richard III he was critical of certain aspects of the Tudor saga: he believed, for instance, that sixteenth-century chroniclers too readily overlooked the king's good qualities such as courage and concern for impartial justice; he discounted the traditional story of Richard of Gloucester's participation in the murder of Prince Edward of Lancaster, and expressed reservations about his role in Henry VI's death in 1471; and he felt that, although 'some accuse the Duke of Gloucester of poisoning' Edward IV, such a charge 'ought not to be too readily credited'. Even so he concluded that, in the end, 'it would be a hard matter to find in history a prince bad enough to match' Richard III. Between 1747 and 1755 there appeared a *General History of England* by 'Thomas Carte, an Englishman' (a dig at Rapin's French origins, perhaps) and this marked a further advance in historical writing. Unlike Rapin, Carte consulted unpublished original documents and deliberately set out to apply stricter criteria when handling 'ancient writers', sought to classify them in terms of reliability and, among them, regarded the *Crowland Chronicle* as exceptionally valuable for the Wars of the Roses epoch. Not only did he consider Warwick the Kingmaker 'the greatest subject in England for power and estate' and 'the most popular man of the age' who fully deserved all the esteem showered upon him by contemporaries but also, partly on the basis of Sir George Buck (whom he clearly rated highly), lavished praise on Richard III as well. Carte, indeed, exonerated Richard of all blame for the deaths of Edward of Lancaster and Henry VI, believed Edward V might well have died of ill health in the Tower of London and even speculated that his brother Richard of York may not only have survived into Henry VII's reign but later reappeared as Perkin Warbeck. Richard III himself he commended for boldness in war, wisdom in council, impartial justice and the maintenance of law and order: it was the 'much more cruel' Henry VII who truly lacked humanity.

In the 1760s David Hume and Horace Walpole certainly came to very different conclusions about Richard III. The Scottish philosopher David Hume, best remembered for his *Treatise on Human Nature* in 1739, also published a *History of England from the Invasion of Julius Caesar to the Accession of Henry VII* in 1762 as a companion to earlier volumes covering the Tudors and Stuarts. Although claiming to write history merely as 'a resource against idleness', he did express strong views about its value as a means of discovering 'the constant and universal principles of human nature, by showing men in all varieties of circumstances and situations, and furnishing us with materials, from which we may form our observations, and become acquainted with the regular springs of human action and behaviour'. Hume's prime interest lay in the analysis of character, motivation and the causes of events but, at the same time, he strove to be 'entertaining and instructive' and, above all, impartial: 'I may be liable to the reproach of ignorance', he once wrote, 'but I am certain to escape that of partiality'. Sadly, when covering the Wars of the Roses era, he fell far short of this ideal; he rarely dipped into original sources and, if he did, tended to be uncritical; and his narrative only rarely questioned the validity of Tudor tradition. The 'wars of the two roses', he concluded, resulted primarily from aristocratic factiousness and, although he commended Richard of York's moderation as a political leader, he regarded Warwick the Kingmaker as 'the greatest, as well as the last, of those mighty barons who formerly overawed the crown, and rendered the people incapable of any regular system of civil government'. When it came to Richard III, Hume saw no reason to question either the 'singular magnanimity, probity and judgement' of Sir Thomas More or the even more hostile verdicts of Edward Hall and Raphael Holinshed. The king, he concluded, had 'a fierce and savage nature'; he was 'hump-backed and had a very disagreeable visage' (his body being 'in every particular no less deformed than his mind'); and 'never was there a usurpation in any country more flagrant than that of Richard, nor more repugnant to every principle of justice and public interest'. Whereas David Hume was a scholar, Horace Walpole, youngest son of England's first acknowledged prime minister Sir Robert, was very much a gentleman amateur. Clearly, as such, he had a notably low opinion of both English history and its historians, 'If we take a survey of our history and examine it with any attention', he declared:

> …what an unsatisfactory picture does it present to us! How dry, how superficial, how void of information! How little is recorded besides battles, plagues and religious foundations! [And] how incompetent has been the generality of historians for the province they have undertaken.

Walpole was particularly critical of Thomas More and Francis Bacon:

> …let me lament that two of the greatest men in our annals have prostituted their admirable pens, the one to blacken a great prince, the other to varnish a pitiable tyrant. I mean the two chancellors, Sir Thomas More and Lord Bacon. The most senseless stories of the mob are converted to history by the former; the latter is still more culpable.

In his own *Historic Doubts on the Life and Reign of Richard III* (published in 1768), the best known and most influential of all defences of the last Plantagenet king, Walpole combined a lively style and superficially plausible line of argument, firmly pointed out fundamental weaknesses in sixteenth-century portrayals of Richard, and concluded that many of the crimes attributed to the king were not only improbable but contrary to his own interests and clearly at odds with what can definitely be deduced about his character. Walpole's remarks on the Wars of the Roses, however, and his loathing for Henry VII, hardly inspire confidence:

> On neither side [during the wars] do there seem to have been any scruples: Yorkists and Lancastrians, Edward IV and Margaret of Anjou, entered into any engagements, took any oaths, violated them, and indulged their revenge, as often as they were depressed or victorious... Henry VII's character, as we have received it from his own apologists, is so much worse and more hurtful than Richard III's that we may well believe Henry invented and propagated by far the greater part of the slanders against Richard...

Moreover, in 1793, he even retracted his earlier doubts about Richard III, declaring:

> I must now [in the context of the excesses of the French Revolution, presumably] believe that any atrocity may have been attempted or practised by an ambitious prince of the blood aiming at the crown in the fifteenth century.

Altogether more even-handed than Horace Walpole was the verdict on Richard III penned by William Hutton in a study of *The Battle of Bosworth Field* published in 1788. Hutton, who had read widely in the sources available to him, clearly recognised the difficulties confronting any historian of the king:

> Richard the Third, of all the English monarchs, bears the greatest contrariety of character... Some few have conferred on him almost angelic excellence, have clouded his errors, and blazoned every virtue that could adorn a man. Others, as if only extremes could prevail, present him in the blackest dye; his thoughts were evil, and that continually, and his actions diabolical; the most degraded mind inhabited the most deformed body...

In fact, Hutton concluded, 'Richard's character, like every man's, had two sides; he was, at one and the same time, 'a faithful servant, a brave soldier, an admirable legislator, yet one of the vilest of men'; and perhaps, he added:

> ...history cannot produce an instance of such an assemblage of virtues and defects in one person. In him were united as many excellencies as would furnish several shining characters and as many faults as would damn a troop.

Three years after the publication of Hutton's book the fifteen-year-old Jane Austen, a self-confessed 'partial, prejudiced and ignorant historian', certainly expressed her youthful opinions of Lancastrians, Yorkists and the Wars of the Roses in a splendidly forthright manner:

> I cannot say much for [Henry VI's] sense. Nor would I if I could, for he was a Lancastrian... This king married Margaret of Anjou, a woman whose distresses and misfortunes were so great as almost to make me, who hate her, pity her... There were several battles between the Yorkists and Lancastrians, in which the former (as they ought) usually conquered. At length they were entirely overcome. The king was murdered, the queen was sent home and Edward IV ascended the throne.

Edward IV himself, however, was 'famous only for his beauty and his courage'; the 'unfortunate prince' Edward V 'lived so little a while that nobody had time to draw his picture' since he was 'murdered by his uncle's contrivance'; as for Richard III himself:

> The character of this prince has been in general very severely treated by historians, but as he was a York I am rather inclined to suppose him a very respectable man. It has been confidently asserted that he killed his two nephews, which I am inclined to believe true... Whether innocent or guilty, he did not reign long in peace, for Henry Tudor Earl of Richmond, as great a villain as ever lived, made a great fuss about getting the crown and, having killed the king at the battle of Bosworth, succeeded to it.

EARLY NINETEENTH-CENTURY JUDGEMENTS

The romantic movement of the early nineteenth century brought with it both a penchant and admiration for the Middle Ages and a more consistently critical approach to historical evidence. The medieval past need never become arid and dull, moreover, providing its historians combined historical and literary skills and, above all, sought to recapture the authentic atmosphere and spirit of earlier centuries in an imaginative fashion: hence the enthusiasm for chivalry and the heroics of warfare, so well demonstrated in the massive literary output of Sir Walter Scott. Although now best remembered for his historical novels, Scott did venture into more serious history as well and, almost always, managed to balance imaginative reconstruction of the past and real respect for historical authenticity. The era of Lancaster and York, however, did not have the romantic appeal of the eleventh, twelfth and thirteenth centuries. Indeed, it seemed a decayed, debased and decadent age by comparison, and even Sir Walter Scott saw the 'wars of the White and Red Roses' as a series of 'civil discords dreadfully prosecuted'. Nevertheless, the fifteenth century was by no means ignored.

Among early nineteenth-century historians who did cover Lancastrians, Yorkists and the Wars of the Roses, John Lingard and Sharon Turner stand out, not least as a result of their contrasting conclusions on Richard III. The Roman Catholic John Lingard published the third volume of his *History of England*, covering the period 1327 to 1509, in 1819. Firmly wedded to Tudor tradition on the Wars of the Roses, and highly critical of Horace Walpole's efforts to rehabilitate Richard III, Lingard was particularly anxious to reinstate Sir Thomas More (who was, after all, a most admirable Roman Catholic martyr) as a genuine seeker after truth. Inevitably, he ended up condemning that 'monster in human shape' Richard III. Edward IV, since he 'desired to live to the best advantage of his pleasure', was clearly flawed but his younger brother, 'a prince of insatiable ambition who could conceal the most bloody prospects under the mask of affection and loyalty', even more clearly deserved all the criticism so lavishly heaped upon him in Tudor times. Sharon Turner, a careful scholar and historian of distinction who consulted an impressive range of original sources, published his multi-volumed *History of England during the Middle Ages* in the 1820s. His proclaimed objective was to write truly dispassionate history in line with the best practice of his own time:

> Modern criticism, averse alike to fable and rhetoric, wishes history neither to defame nor to blazon, but to explore and narrate the simple truth, wherever it is penetrable, or attainable, unvarnished and untwisted.

The three Yorkist kings to whom he devoted almost three hundred pages of his printed text certainly presented a real challenge, particularly Richard III:

> From an eagerness in the Tudor princes and their partisans to destroy all public sympathy for Richard III and the line of York, which he had headed, and which others after him survived to represent, no part of our history has been more disfigured by passion, prejudice, injustice and inaccuracy than the two reigns of Edward V and Richard III.

Nevertheless, Turner himself succeeded in penning a notably moderate and evenly balanced portrayal of Richard III as very much the 'creature and mirror' of his own violent age. Richard of Gloucester, he believed, 'proceeded to the usurpation of the crown with the approbation of most of the great men, both of the church and state, then in London'. Thereafter, as king, he was 'too liberal to be personally rapacious', his statutes were 'wise and useful' and, indeed, his eventual unpopularity with the 'higher orders' resulted from the fact that 'he was becoming too good a king to suit their interests'. Even so, although 'brave to the utmost edge of peril' in war, he was an 'intellectual coward' who 'preferred to prevent danger by crime' and, on occasion, did 'debase himself into wickedness which Edward IV would have disclaimed.' Most notably, he murdered the Princes in the Tower, an action that 'can neither be vindicated nor denied'. In the end, moreover, he himself was betrayed on the battlefield of Bosworth:

> Thus fell Richard, the victim of treachery unparalleled; for there seems to have been no national movement in favour of Richmond… The nation had no share in the conflict, notwithstanding all that is said of the king's unpopularity. It was an ambush of a few perfidious and disaffected noblemen, against the crown, which succeeded by their hypocrisy; and Richard perished by one of those factions in his aristocracy, from which, by taking the crown, it seemed likely that he had rescued himself. He had suppressed violently what he thought dangerous, and he was over-whelmed by the explosion of a new mine, which he had not suspected to be forming beneath him, because it was prepared and fired by those whom gratitude, honour and conscience ought to have made faithful and attached. Whatever had been his conduct towards his nephew, he had done nothing to them, to deserve that they should have destroyed him.

In Caroline Halsted's two-volume biography of *Richard III as Duke of Gloucester and King of England* (published in 1844) the age of romanticism spawned the most substantial defence of Richard III since Sir George Buck's pioneering onslaught on Tudor tradition in early Stuart times. Aptly enough, Halsted herself was married to a rector of Middleham (Richard III's favourite northern castle); she drew on a wide range of record material (and, indeed, printed some of it); and her severity when dealing with Edward IV and Clarence could hardly provide a starker contrast to her treatment of their younger brother. Unfortunately, as well as possessing a flowery style of writing that frequently makes her work virtually unreadable, Halsted became a victim of her own determined revisionism and her characterisation of Richard III borders on hagiography. For her, the king's 'shining abilities, his cultivated mind, his legislative wisdom, his generosity and his clemency' were beyond question; his seizure of the throne could clearly be justified by his rare talents and ability for government; and he did not murder his nephews. Indeed, Halsted concluded:

> A close examination into the earliest records connected with his career will prove that, among all the heavy and fearful charges which are brought against him, few, if any, originate with his contemporaries… Time [and] the publication of contemporary documents have made known many redeeming qualities, have furnished proof of eminent virtue, and certified to such notable exemplary deeds as already suffice to rescue King Richard's memory from at least a portion of the aggravated crimes which have so long rendered his name odious, and inspired great doubts as to the truth of other accusations which rest on no more stable authority.

9

THE VICTORIANS AND THE WARS OF THE ROSES

LORD MACAULAY, THE WHIG INTERPRETATION AND THE BEGINNINGS OF MODERN HISTORICAL RESEARCH

The Whig interpretation of English history had its genesis in the seventeenth century as men sought to explain the origins and nature of first the English Civil War, then the Glorious Revolution of 1688. It flowered in the eighteenth century, and reached its zenith in Victorian times. Whig historians such as Lord Macaulay in his four volume *History of England* published between 1848 and 1855 and William Stubbs whose three volume *Constitutional History of England* appeared between 1874 and 1878, aware of the dramatic impact of industrialisation on English society, were strongly inclined to see history in terms of progress (a tendency reinforced, from the early 1860s, by the evolutionary theories of Charles Darwin). Their pride in this progress, bound up as it was with powerful nationalistic sentiments, led both to a revelling in the glories of the past and a concentration on those aspects of it which could be portrayed as contributing to present strengths. Pride in their political heritage, moreover, inclined Victorian historians to the study of political and constitutional history. The evolution of parliament, in particular, was a central concern, very much reflecting on-going contemporary debate about democracy and the need for electoral reform. Progress, Victorians believed, owed much to the role of great men, so the identification of constitutional heroes was clearly desirable: thus medieval kings who championed progress (as Victorians defined it) were to be singled out for praise, while those who did not might reasonably be criticised. Religious and moral considerations, likewise, influenced their judgements.

The strong strain of puritanism in Victorian society, in particular, produced in historians a conviction that an important part of their job was to pass moral judgement and use history as a store-house of moral lessons for the present. All this resulted in a strong tendency to study the medieval past very much in terms of the nineteenth-century present, to search the records of earlier times for material relevant to the Victorian era, and in the process to ignore much that was actually vital to a proper understanding of the Middle Ages. And, arguably, no period suffered more from the predilections and prejudices of nineteenth-century Whig historians than the age of Lancaster and York.

No Victorian historian made a greater impact in his own time than Thomas Babington Macaulay. A Whig member of parliament for many years, he began writing his *History of England* (designed, primarily, to chronicle the years 1688 to 1830) in 1839 and, once published, it soon proved immensely popular. This was precisely what Macaulay had planned and anticipated for he firmly believed history should be accessible to the general reader, entertaining and very much a branch of literature (admirable sentiments which were, sadly, to be often forgotten once the age of the professional university historian dawned). What he lacked in subtlety, accuracy and depth of research, moreover, Macaulay more than made up for in style, lucidity, imagination and, above all, confidence in his own judgements of men and events. Not surprisingly, given his own impeccable Whig credentials, Macaulay chose to begin his detailed narrative in 1688 but, in a short opening survey of England's earlier history, he certainly penned a characteristically Whig verdict on the Wars of the Roses. For him, clearly, the end of the Hundred Years War in France and the outbreak of civil war in England were closely connected:

> Cooped up once more within the limits of the island, the warlike people employed in civil strife those arms which had been the terror of Europe. The means of profuse expenditure had long been drawn by the English barons from the oppressed provinces of France. That source of supply was gone; but the ostentatious and luxurious habits which prosperity had engendered still remained; and the great lords, unable to gratify their tastes by plundering the French, were eager to plunder each other.

The wars, in fact, were very much a series of bloody and entirely reprehensible aristocratic conflicts that seriously disturbed England's smooth evolutionary progress:

> Two aristocratic factions, headed by two branches of the royal family, engaged in a long and fierce struggle for supremacy. As the animosity of those factions did not really arise from the dispute about the succession, it

lasted long after all ground of dispute about the succession was removed. The party of the Red Rose survived the last prince who claimed the crown in right of Henry the Fourth. The party of the White Rose survived the marriage of Richmond and Elizabeth. Left without chiefs who had any decent show of right, the adherents of Lancaster rallied round a line of bastards, and the adherents of York set up a succession of imposters. When, at length, many aspiring nobles had perished on the field of battle or by the hands of the executioner, when many illustrious houses had disappeared forever from history, when those great families which remained had been exhausted and sobered by calamities, it was universally acknowledged that the claims of all the contending Plantagenets were united in the House of Tudor.

Lord Macaulay was very much in the tradition of the gifted English amateur historian. Yet, paradoxically, even during his lifetime (he died in 1859) scholarly foundations were beginning to be laid for the massive structure of twentieth-century medieval studies. Crucial, clearly, was the establishment of the Public Record Office in 1838 (where a young James Gairdner learned his trade) and, over the years that followed, many local record offices. The Camden Society was also founded in the 1830s and, in 1857, the Rolls series began, both dedicated to the publication of historical (especially medieval) texts. And, in 1886, the *English Historical Review* became the first serious historical journal to appear in England.

In the early nineteenth century, too, the German historian Leopold von Ranke and his acolytes firmly laid down the academic ground rules for critical 'scientific' historical writing. In 1850 the first university school of history in England was established at Oxford and, in 1866, William Stubbs became the first professional historian to hold the post when he was appointed Regius Professor of Modern History at the university. For good or ill, history was about to become a recognised discipline in its own right and, indeed, achieve real intellectual respectability for the first time.

WILLIAM STUBBS, JAMES GAIRDNER AND THE PROGRESS OF HISTORICAL RESEARCH

When the Conservative Prime Minister Edward Stanley Earl of Derby appointed William Stubbs to the Regius Chair of Modern History at Oxford, he did so on the assurance that this scholarly cleric was a true blue Tory as well as a high Anglican and, certainly, Stubbs made no secret of the fact that he was 'steeped in clerical and conservative principles'. Indeed, he eventually resigned his professorship in 1884 to become Bishop of Chester and, from 1889 until his death in 1901, he was Bishop of Oxford. His credentials as a dedicated academic historian cannot seriously be doubted, not least since he edited with distinction no fewer than nineteen volumes in the Rolls series and, indeed, became convinced that 'the time cannot be far off when all the records of the medieval world which are in existence will be in print in full or in such abundant abstractions as will be thoroughly trustworthy representations of their contents'. Nor should Stubbs' profound influence on the future development of historical studies in England be underestimated: his *Select Charters*, published in 1870, dominated the study of medieval history at Oxford for almost a century, while his *Constitutional History of England* (which appeared, in three volumes, between 1874 and 1878) underpinned most medieval syllabuses at English provincial universities until the 1950s. Yet Stubbs, for all his commendable qualities as a historian, clearly reflected the attitudes and prejudices of his times and, although a political conservative, he very much subscribed intellectually to the Whig interpretation of history (as well as being much influenced by the methodology of Ranke and his disciples). His profound and widely admired political conservatism, his firm belief in the virtues of strong rule and the lessons to be learned from studying England's political and institutional history, and his patriotic pride in the English constitution certainly found frequent expression in his scholarly work. So too did his staunch commitment to traditional standards of religious and moral behaviour, perhaps most clearly evident in his treatment of medieval kings. And perhaps he summed himself and his work up best when he wrote that 'the true field of historic study is the history of those nations and institutions in which the real growth of humanity is to be traced'.

For Stubbs, the fifteenth century, covered in Volume 3 of his *Constitutional History*, brought a depressing halt to all the political and constitutional progress of earlier times (charted in Volumes 1 and 2). When studying fifteenth-century England, he declared, the historian:

> ...turns his back on the Middle Ages... The most enthusiastic admirer of medieval life must grant that all that was good and great in it was languishing even to death; and the firmest believer in progress must admit that as yet there were few signs of returning health. The sun of the Plantagenets went down in clouds and thick darkness; the coming of the Tudors gave as yet no promise of light; it was 'as the morning spread upon the mountains', darkest before dawn.

It was all particularly unfortunate, he thought, since everything seemed set to progress admirably when Henry IV, early in the century, embarked on his Lancastrian constitutional experiment. The reign of the first Lancastrian king, Stubbs believed, saw a premature period of parliamentary kingship, as Henry IV deliberately sought to become a pseudo-constitutional monarch almost three centuries before the Glorious Revolution of 1688.

Unfortunately, it all came to nothing and, instead, England dissolved into civil war under the hapless Henry VI. For Stubbs, in fact, the Wars of the Roses presented the spectacle of 'a civil war between two factions, both of which preserve certain constitutional formalities without being at all guided by constitutional principles'; no events were more futile, more bloody or more immoral than these intestinal conflicts when self-seeking magnates happily embraced 'constitutional' principles when they were out of power, only to practise 'despotism' if, and when, they obtained control of the reins of government; and, indeed, the period 1399–1485 saw the playing out of 'a drama of dynastic history', ended only by the battle of Bosworth, 'the last act of a long tragedy or series of tragedies' whose only unity had been provided by 'the struggle of the great houses for the crown'.

When judging medieval kings William Stubbs, employing a moral measuring rod, tended to categorise them as 'good' or 'bad'; indeed, the future bishop not infrequently prevailed over the present historian!. This certainly seems to have been the case with Henry VI, 'perhaps the most unfortunate king who ever reigned'. Of course, he 'never seems to have looked upon his royal character as involving the responsibility of leadership', yielded under every pressure, 'trusted implicitly in every pretended reconciliation' and 'behaved as if his position as a constitutional monarch involved his acting as the puppet of each temporary majority'. Nevertheless, as a man of exemplary devotion and unquestionable sincerity, he was 'most innocent of all the evils that befell England because of him'. Margaret of Anjou clearly did not square at all well with Stubbs' political and moral conservatism. From the very moment of her arrival in England, he concluded, she came to epitomise:

>...the weakness and strength of the dynastic cause; its strength in her indomitable will, her steady faithfulness, her heroic defence of the rights of her husband and child; its weakness in her political position, her policy and her ministers. To the nation she symbolised the loss of Henry V's conquests, an inglorious peace, the humiliation of the popular Gloucester, the promotion of the unpopular Beauforts... Men began to believe that she was an adulteress or her son a changeling...

Predictably, Stubbs had little time for mid-fifteenth century English aristocrats: Richard of York he regarded as cynical and self-interested; Edmund Beaufort Duke of Somerset possessed little political skill; and, as for Warwick the Kingmaker, his main claim to distinction was that he proved 'the last great feudal nobleman who ever made himself dangerous to the reigning king'. Perhaps inevitably, Edward IV was condemned in no uncertain terms for his cruelty and immorality. Indeed, Stubbs concluded, 'even those writers who have laboured hardest to rehabilitate him have failed to discover any conspicuous merits', for Edward was:

> ...a man vicious beyond any king that England had seen since the days of John and more cruel and bloodthirsty than any king she had ever known... The death of Clarence was but the summing up and crowning act of an unparalleled list of judicial and extra-judicial cruelties which those of the next reign supplement but do not surpass.

Even so, although Richard III was a man of great ability, popular in the north of England prior to his accession, brave, resolute, clear-sighted and often badly served by hostile sources, he was also cunning, unscrupulous, 'amenable to no instincts of mercy or kindness', and never able to rid himself of 'the entanglements under which he began to reign' or clear his conscience from 'the stain which his usurpation and its accompanying cruelties brought upon him'.

James Gairdner, a distinguished archivist, an indefatigable editor of records, letters and chronicles, and the most prolific of all Victorian historians of fifteenth and early sixteenth century England, spent his entire professional career at the recently established Public Record Office. How, then, did he view Henry VI, Edward IV and the Wars of the Roses? He certainly had little time for England's third Lancastrian monarch since, despite possessing a 'pious, humane and Christian character' and a well-intentioned disposition, Henry VI proved himself 'a weak-minded king who was continually in the hands of others'. Nor was Gairdner impressed by Henry's administration in the 1440s and 1450s. As for Richard of York, 'he protested by every loyal means against misgovernment, and exhausted every form of peaceable remonstrance, before he advanced his title to the throne'. The Wars of the Roses, moreover, were not of his making. Indeed, for Gairdner, there was no doubt where the blame for the outbreak of civil war lay:

> At no time in England's history was there a stronger feeling of the needful subordination of the different parts of society to each other; but under a king incapable of governing, this feeling bred a curse, and not a blessing. The great lords, who should have preserved order under the king, fell out among themselves, and in spite of the fervid loyalty of the age, the greatest subject became a kingmaker.

James Gairdner's admiration for Richard of York did not extend to his son Edward IV. Indeed, not only did civil war remain virtually continuous during the early part of the new king's reign but:

…within the space of ten years Edward IV had almost succeeded in convincing the world that he was no more capable of governing England than the rival he had deposed. Never did a gambler throw away a fortune with more recklessness than Edward threw away the advantages which had cost him and his friends so much hard fighting to secure.

Since Warwick the Kingmaker's 'policy throughout seems to have been selfish and treacherous', his defeat and death in 1471 was 'an unquestionable blessing to his country'. Unfortunately, in the years that followed, the house of York irresponsibly:

…abused their triumph, became intolerant of rivals, and imbrued their hands in the blood of princes. Hardened by degrees in acts of cruelty and perfidy, they grew faithless even to each other. Clarence rebelled against his brother Edward, and, though forgiven, was finally put to death by Edward's order. The court was split up into factions. The old nobility were jealous of the queen and her relations. It was a world which, as Edward foresaw before his death, was not likely to hold together very long after him.

In 1878 James Gairdner published a major biography of Richard III, destined to remain the 'standard' academic study of the king until the 1980s. He emerged from his very extensive researches, moreover, convinced of 'the general fidelity of the portrait of Richard with which we have been made familiar by Shakespeare and Sir Thomas More'. Indeed, declared Gairdner:

The scantiness of contemporary evidences and the prejudices of original authorities may be admitted as reasons for doubting isolated facts, but can hardly be expected to weaken the conviction – derived from Shakespeare and tradition as much as from anything else – that Richard was indeed cruel and unnatural beyond the ordinary measure even of those violent and ferocious times.

Yet even Gairdner had reservations about Tudor portrayals. The prevailing notion of Richard III, he remarked at one point in his biography, is:

…of a cold, deeply politic, scheming and calculating villain. But I confess I am not satisfied of the justice of such a view. Not only Richard, but all his family, appear to me to have been headstrong and reckless as to consequences.

Gairdner himself was certainly prone, from time to time, to employ notably colourful phraseology about Richard III as, for instance, a man who was prepared to 'make use of every available prejudice, calumny and scandal to advance his own pretensions', as 'a hypocrite in many things', as 'cruel and unnatural', as a 'tyrant', and even as 'not the kind of villain Machiavelli would have recommended'. As for the nature of his rule, the 'three short months of violence and terror which compose the reign of Edward the Fifth', punctuated as they were by 'acts of tyranny', culminated in a positive 'reign of terror' once Richard made his bid for, and obtained, the throne. Yet Gairdner's biography also contains a great many positive judgements on the king's behaviour and policies, both before and after he seized the throne. For a start, the full-blown Tudor hunchback found no favour with him; rather, he believed, Richard III's bodily deformity, 'though perceptible, was probably not conspicuous', and certainly did not prevent him exhibiting 'great bravery on the field of battle'. The 'good rule of Gloucester' in the north of England during the 1470s and early 1480s was 'remembered long after his day as a very model of efficiency'. Until April 1483, moreover, he showed himself 'the zealous champion of his brother's rights', not least in leading a 'remarkably successful' campaign into Scotland in 1482. When Richard became protector 'no apprehensions disturbed the public mind'. Indeed, 'a reign of peace and prosperity was believed to have begun'. Even his usurpation of the throne was an event 'in which the nation, at first, tacitly concurred' and, once king, Richard III:

> ...seems really to have studied his country's welfare; he passed good laws, endeavoured to put an end to extortion, declined the free gifts offered to him by several towns, and declared he would rather have the hearts of his subjects than their money.

Even so, their hearts were just what he lost, not least as a result of his 'greatest crime' – the murder of the Princes in the Tower – until, in August 1485, the battle of Bosworth brought the 'final measure of his punishment'. Like most Victorian historians, moreover, James Gairdner found 1485 a highly satisfactory turning-point in English history:

> The Middle Ages, as far as England was concerned, may be said to have passed away with Richard III... There was now a strong anxiety to heal old sores, to reunite rival families, to see an end of bloodshed. And no one was better fitted for the work than the conqueror of Bosworth.

James Gairdner apart, William Stubbs' Oxford came to dominate the scholarly study of fifteenth-century English history in late Victorian times. Among its dons, Charles Plummer, a Fellow of Corpus Christi College, concluded in 1885 that 'the overgrown power and insubordination of the nobles', the sheer lawlessness of the mid-fifteenth century aristocracy indeed, was the prime cause of the Wars of the Roses. Charles Oman, who eventually became Chichele Professor of Modern History at Oxford, ended a short biography of Warwick the Kingmaker, published in 1891, convinced that, if Richard Neville had been 'born in a happier generation, his industry and perseverance, his courage and courtesy, his liberal hand and generous heart, might have made him not only the idol of his followers but the bulwark of the commonwealth'. As it was, 'cast into the godless times of the Wars of the Roses, he was doomed to spend in the cause of a faction the abilities that were meant to benefit a whole nation'. Sir James Ramsay, also an Oxford academic (at any rate until disqualified by marriage), published his substantial two volume narrative history of *Lancaster and York* in 1892. Covering the period from the usurpation of Henry IV in 1399 to Henry VII's triumph at Bosworth in 1485, Ramsay certainly benefited greatly from, and made notably productive use of, all the historical resources Victorian scholarship had now made available. Nevertheless, his conclusion that 'the house of York fell as much from the repugnance excited by the lives and conduct of its sons [especially the 'treacherous Richard Crouchback'] as for any definite offences against the nation' was nothing if not traditional.

JOHN RICHARD GREEN, WILLIAM DENTON AND THE VICTORIAN LEGACY

During later Victorian times, as university-based academic history developed, men like William Stubbs and his Oxford successors tended to address most, if not all, of their writing towards fellow scholars and the burgeoning number of students opting to study history. Stubbs, in particular, seems to have had little or no interest in reaching out to a wider public; he saw no need to provide English translations of the many Latin texts he edited; and he even seems to have been unmoved by the fact that his lectures on constitutional history at Oxford attracted but sparse audiences. Yet, as the level of literacy in later Victorian England rose dramatically, so did the potential mass market for history and, if professional historians rather baulked at catering for it, there was no shortage of amateurs only too willing to do so, Among them, John Richard Green – perhaps the most accomplished popular historian England has ever produced – shines like a beacon.

Although Green graduated from Jesus College, Oxford, in 1859, he soon became a practising Anglican priest and, for much of the 1860s, devoted himself to the religious and pastoral duties of a clergyman in London. Apparently he met William Stubbs on a train in 1863 and, according to Stubbs himself, 'for twenty years he and I were close friends'. However, although Green was certainly a serious historian and, indeed, dedicated his four volume *History of the English People* (published between 1877 and 1880) to 'two dear friends, my masters in the study of English history, Edward Augustus Freeman [Stubbs' successor at Oxford and author of both a five volume *History of the Norman Conquest* and a two volume study of *The Reign of William Rufus*] and William Stubbs', his own perspective on history and his motives in writing it could hardly have been more different. As early as 1862 he determined to become England's historian because his reading had convinced him of 'the utter blindness of all and everyone to the real subjects they profess to treat – the national growth and the development of our country'. It took him more than a decade to bring the project to fruition and, clearly, he did not always find the going easy. In a letter of 1865, indeed, his gloom is only too palpable:

> Sick – ill – suicidal – blank – ignorant – can't write anything – GONE TO POT.

Nevertheless, the *Short History of the English People* did at last appear in print in 1874 and, in the preface, Green provided an unequivocal statement of his aims:

> ...it is a history, not of English Kings or English Conquests, but of the English People... I have preferred to pass lightly over the details of foreign wars and diplomacies, the personal adventures of kings and nobles, the pomp of courts, or the intrigues of favourites, and to dwell at length on the incidents of that constitutional, intellectual and social advance in which we read the history of the nation itself... Whatever the worth of the present work may be, I have striven throughout that it should never sink into a 'drum and trumpet' history. It is the reproach of historians that they have too often turned History into a mere record of the butchery of their fellow-men.

Even so, Green did recognise the importance of England having had capable and effective rulers, and his comments on them are generally vivid and often perceptive. Indeed, he did not entirely reject the usefulness of studying wars and battles, at any rate as a means of introducing history to the young, as he made clear in a letter to Edward Freeman in 1878:

> ...though I say it who shouldn't, boys like fighting, and it's through war and the picturesqueness of war that we can best get them to follow out and understand the historical and larger aspects of things.

The *Short History of the English People* was certainly a huge success, rapidly and rightly becoming the most widely read history of its times. There had been nothing to compare with it since Macaulay's *History of England* and, insofar as it was Green's ambition to supersede Hume, he did so with a vengeance in an immensely readable, well-researched narrative, rich in vivid thumbnail sketches of past personalities as well as an imaginative and sustained attention to the social and cultural matters so dear to its author's heart. Moreover, although Green remained firmly within the Whig tradition of English historical writing, he gave it a dimension never before achieved, both in the *Short History* and the later, much larger *History of the English People*. Even William Stubbs admitted, after Green's death (in 1883), that he:

>...possessed in no scanty measure all the gifts that contribute to the making of a great historian. He combined, so far as the history of England is concerned, a complete and firm grasp of the subject in its unity and integrity, with a wonderful command of details and a thorough sense of perspective and proportion. All his work was real and original work.

Indeed, Stubbs conjectured, even when the *Short History* 'comes to be superseded it will be by a history on the lines of Green rather than on the lines of his critics'.

The fifteenth century was clearly not J.R. Green's favourite period and, when working on his four volume *History* in 1877, he himself was notably critical of what he had written a few years earlier:

>I have just been finishing and giving the last touches to the close of volume one, that is Joan of Arc and the Wars of the Roses. It is a mercy to have really got down so far. This last part from Richard II to 1460 has been a stiffer job than I counted on. It is so scandalously done in my Little Book that I got no help there and had to work wholly afresh. I think my greatest gain in these last years is a will and capacity to work at periods I don't like as much as periods I do. It wasn't so when I wrote Little Book, [where] I did such shameful bits of work as the page in which I hurried over Henry the Fourth. This was the real fault of the book, its inequality of treatment, its fitfulness and waywardness...

In his 1877 volume Green certainly extended considerably the coverage afforded to 1399-1461 and, in the next (published in 1878) he did the same for 1461-1485. Yet there is a clarity of vision and interpretation in the *Short History* (however misguided!) rather lost in Green's later work. 'There are few periods in our annals from which we turn with such weariness and disgust', he declared in 1874, 'as from the Wars of the Roses'. Moreover, he added:

>Their savage battles, their ruthless executions, their shameless treasons, seem all the more terrible from the pure selfishness of the ends for

which men fought, the utter want of all nobleness and chivalry in the struggle itself, of all great result in its close.

Even so, he stressed that fifteenth-century civil strife had only a limited impact on the country at large:

The ruin and bloodshed were limited, in fact, to the great lords and their feudal retainers. Once or twice indeed, as at Towton, the towns threw themselves into the struggle, but for the most part the trading and agricultural classes stood wholly apart from it.

Nevertheless, in terms of the Whig prospectus of England's political and constitutional progress through time, the wars had a truly stark significance:

The Wars of the Roses did far more than ruin one royal house or set up another. If they did not utterly destroy English freedom, they arrested its progress for more than a hundred years. [With their ending] we enter on a period of constitutional repression in which the slow work of the age that went before was rapidly undone… [The] character of the Monarchy from the time of Edward the Fourth to the time of Elizabeth remains something strange and isolated in our history.

For Green, in fact, this was the 'New Monarchy' (a term he invented) and its creator was the first Yorkist king. Edward IV, he believed, was 'the most pitiless among the warriors of the civil war', even if his 'winning manners and gay carelessness of bearing' were instrumental in securing him 'a popularity which had been denied to earlier kings'. Even more ominously, the king's 'indolence and gaiety' were:

…mere veils beneath which [he] shrouded a profound political ability. While jesting with aldermen, or dallying with his mistresses, or idling over the new pages from the printing press at Westminster, Edward was silently laying the foundations of an absolute rule which Henry VII did little more than develop and consolidate.

And, since Richard III was not only ambitious, ruthless and pitiless but also, when he deemed it necessary, prepared to throw off any pretence of constitutional rule as well, he too had little to recommend him to any Whig historian.

If the third volume of William Stubbs' *Constitutional History* provided the standard Victorian interpretation of fifteenth-century history at English universities by the end of the nineteenth century, his fellow cleric William Denton's *England in the Fifteenth Century* (published posthumously in 1888) probably had the greatest impact after J.R. Green on a wider reading public. A graduate of Worcester College, Oxford, in 1844, ordained priest in 1845 and vicar of St Bartholomew, Cripplegate, for almost forty years, Denton's not inconsiderable researches led him to pen perhaps the gloomiest survey of fifteenth-century England ever written. The Wars of the Roses, he concluded, may have had their origins in 'the rival pretensions of the houses of York and Lancaster' but, in reality, they were 'a war of the barons'; they were 'neither waged to protect national interests nor to vindicate the national honour'; and they ended 'in the destruction of almost every scion of the families of Lancaster and York', after a slaughter of people 'greater than in any former war on English soil'. Denton's hyperbole knew no bounds when describing the material, and indeed the moral and cultural, impact of the wars on English society:

> The people of England, exhausted by wars at home and abroad, acquiesced in the despotism of Edward IV. They were prepared, indeed, to submit to any ruler who would secure to them the blessings of peace. They yielded readily to the salutary despotism of the Tudors. The country sighed for repose. The commerce of England had been almost destroyed by these incessant wars. Great part of the land formerly cultivated lay waste for want of hands to till them. Hamlets and villages had disappeared... All the towns in the kingdom, with the exception of London, had been well-nigh ruined.

Moreover, he commented darkly, 'this outer ruin was but a type of a deeper ruin', since:

> ...the licence encouraged by civil war, and the example of the dissolute barons, injured the moral tone of the nation. Lust, cruelty, dishonesty, and a shameless disregard for the sanctity of oaths, were paraded before the eyes of the people... The people of almost all classes appear to have broken away from most of the restraints of religion. Sensuality was encouraged by the example of men of station and influence, and private wars raged, [whilst] private revenge showed itself in acts of savage violence.

Even the cultural life of fifteenth-century England degenerated appallingly:

> What was true of morals and material wealth was also true of art. Architecture had yielded to the spirit of the age; it had lost much of its nobleness... The hand of the English sculptor had grown stiff... In metalwork the glory of the maker had departed. English glass was no

longer sought for to adorn the cathedrals of the Continent nor even to decorate the private houses of England... Art in all its forms had become debased with the debasement of the artist.

If the material, moral and artistic condition of fifteenth-century English society found no favour with William Denton, the reputation of England's last Plantagenet king did not fare much better at the hands of several other Victorian historians. Although the revisionist cause, so exuberantly embraced by Caroline Halsted in 1844, had been maintained by Alfred O. Legge in a two volume treatment of *The Unpopular King* in 1855 and, rather less vehemently, by John Jesse in his *Memoirs of Richard the Third*, published in 1862, J.R. Green, William Stubbs and, most compellingly, James Gairdner had all been inclined to line up behind Tudor tradition and William Shakespeare (whose *Richard III* enjoyed a renewed popularity as a result of Henry Irving's powerful portrayal of the king). In 1891, however, Sir Clements Markham took up the cudgels on Richard III's behalf with a vengeance in the pages of the recently established *English Historical Review*, where he vigorously crossed swords with James Gairdner on the vexed issue of the Princes in the Tower and set out his stall as an enthusiastic advocate of Henry VII's responsibility for their murder. When, in 1906, he published *Richard III: His Life and Character*, the book proved to be the most fervent and thorough vindication of the king ever to appear in print. Clearing Richard III of all crimes and in effect turning Tudor tradition on its head, Markham declared vehemently that Gairdner's Richard III defied belief:

> Such a monster is an impossibility in real life. Even Dr Jekyll and Mr Hyde are nothing to it

Markham's own Richard was whiter than white: before becoming king, he 'displayed brilliant courage as a knight and remarkable ability as a general, as well as being 'justly popular throughout the country' and 'beloved in Yorkshire'; once on the throne he soon demonstrated great administrative ability, vigorously suppressed insurrections, pursued a wise and judicious foreign policy, and 'anxiously sought the welfare of his people'. All the evidence against the king, Markham concluded, is tainted, and the real Richard, properly rescued from 'the accumulated garbage and filth of centuries of calumny', turns out to be one of the best rulers England has ever had. The great villain, for Markham, was the cold, cunning and merciless Henry VII.

10

TWENTIETH-CENTURY HISTORIANS AND THE WARS OF THE ROSES

C.L. KINGSFORD, EARLY TWENTIETH CENTURY HISTORIANS AND THE NARRATIVE TRADITION

By the end of the Victorian era a division had already opened up between professional academic history and historical writing for a wider, non-specialist audience. During the twentieth century the barrier between 'serious' history, very much the preserve of university historians engrossed in their own ever more narrowly-based research and firmly committed to notions of history as a training for the mind, and 'popular' history, often written by enthusiastic amateurs, solidified alarmingly. Oxford and Cambridge led the way and profoundly influenced history teaching at so-called 'red brick' universities such as Manchester, where the great medievalist T.F. Tout made a powerful mark, and Bristol, where Tout's daughter Margaret Sharp taught for many years. Most of their staff tended to be Oxbridge-educated and their syllabuses, too, often followed those of the ancient seats of learning (not least in taking on board the political and constitutional framework for medieval England bequeathed by William Stubbs). The new universities of the 1960s, and even the polytechnics of the 1970s, if they opted to teach history at all, also inclined to embrace much of the baggage of traditional academic history, albeit in more imaginative syllabuses. Even when, in the 1990s, higher education expanded more dramatically than ever before, the older universities and their bench-marks of quality, expressed, most obviously, in learned historical journals whose pages tended to be an exclusive preserve of academics, continued to set the standards of history teaching and research. Sadly, however, fifteenth-century kings, politics and the Wars of the Roses inspired little or no interest in departments often dominated by nineteenth and twentieth-century specialists.

Even during the early twentieth century, notwithstanding the onward march of professional history, Lancastrian and Yorkist England attracted but sparse attention: indeed, the fifteenth century became the most neglected era in English history. Historians tended to downgrade the century's importance, and marginalise its content, in comparison with the fourteenth and sixteenth centuries; it suffered from negative labelling as, for instance, the age of usurpations, bastard feudalism and economic recession; and the prevailing Whig interpretation of the era was seriously challenged only by C.L. Kingsford and the young Oxford scholar K.B. McFarlane.

Yet, clearly, the fifteenth century could not be ignored completely, particularly since textbook series covering the whole of English history from Roman times to the present increasingly came into vogue. As early as 1904 Charles Oman remarked that:

> ...the main characteristic of the last twenty years, from the point of view of the student of history, has been that new material has been accumulating much faster than it can be assimilated or absorbed... Meanwhile the general reading public continues to ask for standard histories, and discovers, only too often, that it can find nothing between school manuals at one end of the scale and minute monographs at the other.

Moreover, since historians 'will not sit down, as once they were wont, to write twenty-volume works in the style of Hume or Lingard, embracing a dozen centuries of annals', the answer lay in 'dividing up English history into periods that are neither too long to be dealt with by a single competent specialist, nor so short as to tempt the writer to indulge in that over-abundance of unimportant detail which repels the general reader'. Two years later Oman put his money where his mouth was when, in 1906, as the fourth volume in a series entitled *The Political History of England*, he published his *History of England 1377-1485*. In similar vein, in 1913, there appeared, as part of a seven volume series, *England in the Later Middle Ages 1272-1485* by Kenneth H. Vickers and, the following year, R.B. Mowat's *The Wars of the Roses 1377-1471*. Early twentieth-century textbooks covering the later Plantagenet era tended to take the form of chronological political narratives, very much concentrating on kings, magnates and wars. As far as the Wars of the Roses were concerned, their authors generally took on board the Yorkist perspective of so many contemporary and near-contemporary chronicles while, at the same time, being clearly influenced as well by both Tudor tradition and the gloomy conclusions of William Stubbs. Kenneth Vickers, for instance, declared that:

> During the days of Lancaster and York the blare of martial trumpets and the turbulence of liveried retainers compelled the average citizen to stand aside and watch the unprincipled quarrels of the great... The wars of Lancaster and York were in fact a drastic remedy for a fell disease. The health of the body politic had been threatened by the growth of a too powerful nobility...

Nevertheless, and here Vickers displayed his Whig credentials only too clearly, that:

> ...this nobility should spend thirty years in civil strife, till its manhood was slain and its possessions destroyed or forfeited, was but the fighting of the various germs within the body, which ultimately led to their own destruction and to the triumph of the patient's healthy constitution... The turmoils of the last fifty years [ending in 1485] had not really undermined the foundations of the nation... The spirit of growth was not quenched, the possibilities of development were greater than ever before.

Textbooks apart, the early twentieth century also saw the appearance of several substantial biographies, most notably Kenneth Vickers' own *Humphrey Duke of Gloucester* (1907), Mabel E. Christie's *Henry VI* (1922) and Cora L. Scofield's two-volume treatment of *The Life and Reign of Edward the Fourth* (1923). For Vickers it was a tragedy that all Humphrey of Gloucester's 'brilliant abilities' and immense potential were:

> ...thrown away because the fire of genius burnt only in fitful gleams. Moral stamina was denied to an otherwise promising character, and the concentration which might have moulded his life's work into a useful policy was lacking. [By the time of his death he] had done nothing to carry England further along the highroad to strength and fame, he had lived in a decadent age and had been overwhelmed by the spirit of his times.

Nevertheless, since 'the first page of the Renaissance in England consists of the life of Humphrey Duke of Gloucester, all who value the inspiration to be drawn from the new era in human thought which dates from that great movement must respect the memory of this great Lancastrian

Prince'. Mabel Christie certainly highlighted Henry VI's admirable Christian virtues, 'charity, long-suffering, gentleness, goodness, faith, meekness and temperance', but, as a man 'who would have been happy in a cloister', he could never comfortably occupy a throne:

> With his inherent weakness of character, he was influenced in turn by whichever of his lords had succeeded in insinuating himself into the royal favour... He had no power of self-assertion to check the turbulence of his subjects... Neither did he in the least understand the spirit of his own age, for he dwelt for the most part in a dreamy realm of his own, into which he only allowed the clamour of the outside world to penetrate at necessary intervals. He showed no power either of discerning the character of those about him, or of interpreting the signs of the times.

C.L. Scofield clearly found Edward IV an altogether superior king and her comprehensive reconstruction of the political history of the first Yorkist's reign is scholarly, detailed, accurate and reliable: indeed, not only is it a truly magisterial narrative but one very unlikely ever to be superseded. On Edward IV himself, Scofield believed that when the king entered London in May 1471:

> ...he must have felt that he was master of England as he had never been before, [and] the victory begun at Mortimer's Cross and Towton [in 1461] now appeared to be complete. But if out of the troubles of the last ten years Edward the king had come forth triumphant, Edward the man, sad to say, had gone down in defeat. Very different from the brave, frank, generous, well-intentioned youth who had taken the crown from Henry VI with Warwick's aid in 1461 was the man who came back to England in 1471 to slay Warwick on the battlefield and Henry in a dungeon in the Tower. Edward was still a young man in 1471 [and] a brave man still. But ten years of kingship had taught him many bitter truths, and adversity, instead of making him wiser and better, had coarsened and brutalized him...

Nevertheless, unlike his two predecessors – Henry V and Henry VI – and, indeed, his two successors – Edward V and Richard III – he did die peacefully in his own bed.

Alone among early twentieth-century historians, Charles Lethbridge Kingsford firmly broke the mould of Victorian doom and gloom portrayals of fifteenth-century England. Yet, although an Oxford graduate, he spent much of his life (he died in 1926) as a civil servant and never held a full-time university post. Perhaps, indeed, it was because he was an outsider that he was able to interpret the Wars of the Roses and their impact on society so much more originally than most professional historians of his time. His first major foray into fifteenth-century English history came in 1901 when he published *Henry V: The Typical Medieval Hero*, a book firmly founded on the study of original sources but essentially traditional in its interpretation. Henry V, for Kingsford, was 'the true type of the medieval hero-king' and, although he had reservations about the justice of the king's claims to France and the sheer cost of waging war there for so long, he did not seriously question William Stubbs' estimate of Henry V as a 'constitutional' monarch who very much reflected the will of the people in his undertakings. Thereafter, Kingsford devoted much attention to London chronicles, published several of them, and analysed their nature, content and value in a thoroughly scholarly manner; a series of lectures delivered at Oxford University in 1910 resulted in his *English Historical Literature in the Fifteenth Century* (1913), a critical exposition and analysis of literary sources ranging from chronicles, biographies and histories to letters, ballads and poems; and, in 1919, he published a two-volume edition of *The Stonor Letters and Papers 1290-1483*, a major family archive for English social history. By 1923, such was Kingsford's reputation as both scholar and historian that he was invited to deliver the prestigious Ford Lectures at Oxford University, resulting in *Prejudice and Promise in Fifteenth Century England,* published in 1925. His central theme was to expose the 'prejudice' of Tudor historians of the era culminating in William Shakespeare's cycle of history plays and highlight the 'promise' evident in the spirit of adventure, commercial enterprise, social growth and intellectual ferment of the age. 'The fifteenth century in England was certainly not a brilliant epoch', he declared, but 'it has an enduring attraction as the seed-time in which we can trace the birth and growth of those mighty forces which were to make the next age so memorable'; indeed, he continued enthusiastically:

> ...the study of fifteenth-century history in England is far from futile, and however much the chronicles may fail us, we have no lack of material for the study of social and economic history... It is not, I think, an exaggeration to say that in volume and variety [record] sources for our fifteenth-century history far excel those of any previous age. Chroniclers and later historians, absorbed in the sordid politics of the time, have shrouded it in a veil of prejudice which has obscured its real character. It is only when we turn to records set down without any ulterior motive, and come face to face with the life of the people, that we can discover the truth and discern the promise of the fifteenth century in England.

Specifically, Kingsford argued that the impact of the Wars of the Roses on most people's lives was less than traditionally supposed. Moreover, it is a 'cardinal error' to assume the wars were a main cause of the troubles of the times, not least since the period of just over eighteen months between the battles of Blore Heath (September 1459) and Towton (March 1461) was 'the longest during which warfare was in any sense continuous or more than sporadic', and the fifteenth century did see periods of political and social harmony as well – most notably, under Henry V and during the later years of Edward IV.

K.B. McFarlane, J.R. Lander and the Triumph of Post-Whig History

C.L. Kingsford not only began seriously to get to grips (for the first time) with the massive legacy of record evidence bequeathed by fifteenth-century England but he also bravely mapped out a new agenda for studying social history as well as kings, politics and the institutions of government. Yet, until very recently, his pioneering work has been shamefully neglected by most professional historians of the period. K.B. (Bruce) McFarlane, by contrast, has long been hailed as the 'founding genius' of 'the only school that fifteenth-century historiography has had'. In the same year that Kingsford's *Prejudice and Promise in Fifteenth Century England* was published, McFarlane completed his undergraduate studies at Oxford University. He became a Fellow of Magdalen College in 1928 and spent the rest of his life (he died in 1966) as an Oxford don. Clearly, throughout his long academic career, he made a deep impression on many of the undergraduates (and still more the postgraduates) who came into contact with him, not least the future playwright Alan Bennett. An Oxford history student in the mid-1950s, and for a short while one of McFarlane's research students (working on the royal retinue of Richard II 1388-99, apparently), Bennett has recently recollected that McFarlane, 'undoubtedly the greatest medievalist of his time', was a perfectionist in his teaching, research and writing, a man who shunned popularity and publicity (but loved cats), and a scholar widely feared for his acerbic responses to the academic endeavours of others. Moreover, according to Bennett, he himself had never before 'come up against so strong a personality'. Even so, McFarlane 'managed without effort to acquire a body of pupils who were both friends and disciples and who carried on his work and cherish his memory'. Rather less flattering was the judgement of A.J.P. Taylor, McFarlane's long-time colleague at Magdalen but poles apart from him both personally and academically, in his 1983 autobiography:

Bruce, though I am told a scholar of the first rank, put teaching first and published little during his lifetime whether because he was a perfectionist or because he shrank from criticism I could not decide. As a matter of fact I do not think he was quite of the first rank. He had great learning and took great pains, but it seemed to me that in the last resort he lacked judgement... Now I incline to think that his admiring pupils have built him up more than he deserved.

A.J.P. Taylor was certainly right to stress McFarlane's devotion to teaching and research. Moreover, although first coming to the fifteenth century via William Stubbs and his Oxford legacy, by the later 1930s McFarlane had become convinced that Stubbs' whole approach to, and interpretation of, the era was fatally flawed. Unfortunately, as he put it in 1938:

> ...we have failed to do what is the duty of every generation of historians to do, namely to rewrite the broad outlines of our subject in the light of those specialized studies which are our prime concern. To all intents and purposes the attempt to interpret the period begins, and has ended, with Stubbs.

For the greater part of his career, once he had finally abandoned institution-based history, he devoted himself primarily to the study of fifteenth-century political society (particularly the English nobility), accumulated a mass of potentially relevant historical evidence, and flew a range of interpretative kites. Unfortunately, he never himself produced the new synthesis he had so ardently called for in 1938. Indeed, he proved enormously reluctant to publish at all and, at the time of his death, his sparse printed legacy consisted of a narrative survey of the Lancastrian Kings 1399-1461 he had written for the *Cambridge Medieval History* as a young man, a short book on *Wycliffe and the Beginnings of English Nonconformity* and a string of academic articles he had contributed to various learned journals over the years. He had never even published the text of his 1953 Ford Lectures on the later medieval English nobility, let alone attempted to address a wider historical audience. 'For him', so one of his admirers recalled later, 'the pleasure and rewards of acquiring knowledge dangerously outweighed those of publishing it'. Fortunately, he did bequeath fully written out manuscripts of several series of lectures, including the texts of his Ford Lectures, and a number of these, carefully edited by sympathetic disciples, eventually found their way into print in two posthumously published books: *Lancastrian Kings and Lollard Knights* (1972) and *The Nobility of Later Medieval England* (1973).

Bruce McFarlane was far more interested in the Lancastrian than the Yorkist era and it was only towards the end of his career that he at last provided an overview of the Wars of the Roses and their significance in a public lecture delivered in 1964. Henry IV was a particular favourite and he delivered several series of lectures on the king between 1936 and 1953, regarding him as 'that comparatively rare combination, the man of action who was also an intellectual'. Firmly rejecting William Stubbs' notion that Henry IV inaugurated a Lancastrian constitutional experiment, McFarlane believed the king capably defeated all attempts to dislodge him from the throne he had seized in 1399, never willingly concurred in any diminution of the traditional royal authority he exercised and, in the end, bequeathed a peaceful realm to his son in 1413. Virtually all McFarlane's lectures were written for discriminating Oxford undergraduate audiences but a single curious exception did turn up among his papers: a lecture on Henry V delivered to the Oxford branch of the Workers' Educational Association in 1954 where, for once, McFarlane allowed himself the luxury of trying to engage a non-academic audience. Consequently, perhaps, it is the most readable and enjoyable piece he ever penned, not least on account of its startling conclusion that:

> ...by whatever standards he is judged, Henry was superlatively gifted... He was born to rule and to conquer... Take him all round and he was, I think, the greatest man that ever ruled England.

Henry VI, by contrast, was a disaster. In this king, McFarlane declared in 1938, 'second childhood succeeded first without the usual interval and under him the medieval kingship was in abeyance'. Similarly, in 1945, he remarked that the character of politics for forty years after Henry V's death largely reflected the fact that, in 1422, the crown had been placed 'upon the head of a baby who grew up an imbecile'. And, in 1964, McFarlane concluded that, 'since Henry VI's head was too small for his father's crown', the Wars of the Roses eventually resulted because 'the nobility was unable to rescue the kingdom from the consequences of his inanity by any other means'.

The contrast between K.B. McFarlane and J.R. (Jack) Lander could hardly be more striking. McFarlane was an Oxford man through and through, never leaving the university where he himself had been educated. Lander, although a Cambridge graduate, spent his entire teaching career abroad (in Africa in the 1950s, then in Canada where, for many years, he held a chair in history at the University of Western Ontario). Whereas McFarlane never showed much interest in the organs of central government and administration in fifteenth-century England, Lander's early work very much focussed on the Yorkist council. And, while McFarlane published sparingly and almost always for a specialist readership, Lander not only penned a series of meticulously researched and penetrating articles but also several books catering for a wider audience, despite the danger that 'outraged specialists' might in consequence seek 'to scatter his rash bones to whiten by the wayside.' His stylish prose, moreover, surely qualifies him as a man of letters as well as a distinguished historian. Most notably, he published *The Wars of the Roses* in 1965, a pioneering and largely successful dovetailing of extracts from contemporary sources and linking commentary into a coherent narrative of events, a task 'begun amongst the sweat-saddened distractions of West Africa and finished among the snowstorms of Nova Scotia'. Lander's justification for writing the book, and his choice of passages, is illuminating:

> The materials for English history in the mid-fifteenth century are notoriously intractable... Though government records oppress posterity by the hundredweight they are mainly concerned with administrative detail... Only occasionally are they suitable for quotation in a book of this kind... General histories give a deceptively clear account of the events of the mid-fifteenth century. In fact such narratives are a patchwork of legend and rumour mingled with, and all too often taken for, fact... Many of the letters and narratives quoted in this book purvey biased opinion, wild rumour, meretricious propaganda, the foulest of slanders as well as historical truth.

Yet, he declared, baffling though they are:

> ...the smears of unscrupulous politicians and the credulous misconceptions of London merchants and country gentlemen are not to be despised. What people thought, their affections and their prejudices, have often been as important in history as truth itself.

In 1969 Lander again highlighted the problems posed by the nature of surviving evidence for fifteenth-century politics and society:

> Research workers can accumulate a vast amount of comparatively insignificant detail about the lives and possessions – particularly the possessions –

of fifteenth-century statesmen, nobles and gentry; only rarely any statements which throw a sure light upon their motives. With rare exceptions their thoughts may be inferred only from their actions, and such inferences, without knowledge of the evasions and compromises which so often precede momentous political decisions, are, at best, an equivocal, and may be a completely misleading, guide to the springs of action.

Nevertheless, in his sparkling survey of *Conflict and Stability in Fifteenth-century England* he certainly rose to the challenge magnificently, as he did again eleven years later in *Government and Community: England 1450-1509* (1980), despite the 'jejeune chronicles' and 'distinctly unalluring' administrative records of the age. Moreover, as an admirer remarked at the time of his retirement in 1986, throughout his career Lander had successfully combined 'historical scholarship and learning with deep dedication to the concerns and problems of students and teaching'.

Clearly, Lander rarely admired fifteenth-century England's kings and supermagnates. Government under Henry VI, he declared, 'drifted to almost inevitable disaster in the nerveless hands of a saintly muff'; Richard of York was an ambitious opportunist and self-interested aristocrat who failed to win much committed support from his peers; Warwick the Kingmaker was 'a domineering malcontent' who 'supported the house of York to serve his own ends'; and as for that 'family liability and public nuisance' George Duke of Clarence, he not only demonstrated 'fantastic lack of political judgement' but, in the end, thoroughly deserved his fate. Edward IV did win Lander's strong approval in 1956, admittedly, but even that was rather waning by the time he penned his final verdict on the king in 1980. As for the dilemma facing the English aristocracy in 1485, Lander's judgement was stark indeed:

> The choice between candidates [for the throne] was far from inspiring. Richard of Gloucester's reputation was tarnished beyond repair. He was a usurper. Many people were convinced that he was a murderer and many, judging by the social and political standards of the day, regarded him as a tyrant. On the other hand Henry of Richmond, though free from moral stain, was nothing more than an inexperienced political adventurer, an almost pathetic rootless exile, in whom the powerful and rich could repose little, if any, confidence.

Nevertheless, despite such a bunch of second-rate leaders and the prevailing lawlessness of the times, Lander concluded that the degree of mayhem resulting from the Wars of the Roses had traditionally been much exaggerated.

176

During the 1950s, and still more the 1960s, interest in fifteenth-century England began to grow significantly, at any rate if the proliferation of textbooks is anything to go by. Tending to cover economic, social, religious and cultural aspects of the period as well as politics, government and war (which had dominated early twentieth-century surveys), these included A.R. Myers, *England in the Later Middle Ages* (1952), V.H.H. Green, *The Later Plantagenets* (1955), E.F. Jacob, *The Fifteenth Century* (1961), G. Holmes, *The Later Middle Ages* (1962), S.B. Chrimes, *Lancastrians, Yorkists and Henry VII* (1964), B. Wilkinson, *The Later Middle Ages* (1969); and M. Keen, *England in the Later Middle Ages* (1973) – an excellent summing up of post-war research on later medieval England and, indeed, the best textbook of the period produced during the twentieth century. Several influential monographs also appeared, most notably R.L. Storey, *The End of the House of Lancaster* (1966): drawing heavily on unpublished records of Henry VI's reign (deposited in the Public Record Office), he argued compellingly that, since central direction under the last Lancastrian king – 'a devout and kindly simpleton' always inclined to leave the work of government to others – was so patently lacking, private aristocratic feuds proliferated in the country and eventually fed into the Wars of the Roses. By the later 1950s and 1960s, too, a number of K.B. McFarlane's former research students, mainly holding posts in provincial universities, were seriously beginning to make their mark. It was not until the 1970s, however, that fifteenth-century studies took off with a vengeance.

CHARLES ROSS, RALPH GRIFFITHS AND THE BRISTOL CONNECTION

In 1970 S.B (Stanley) Chrimes, whose own biography of Henry VII was to appear in 1972, organised (in collaboration with Charles Ross and Ralph Griffiths) the first ever assembly of fifteenth-century historians at University College, Cardiff. Attended by some fifty specialists in fifteenth-century British history, drawn from twenty-nine universities and other institutions in the United Kingdom and North America, its proceedings (including papers by B.P. Wolffe on Henry VI, Charles Ross on Edward IV and S.B. Chrimes on Henry VII) were duly published in 1972. Cardiff proved but the first of a series of colloquia convened over the next thirty years. Most notably, in 1978, Charles Ross organised a symposium at Bristol University, with the avowed – and successful – aim of promoting 'an informal and friendly gathering in which some of the younger scholars would have the opportunity to read and discuss papers of their own'. Many who took part had formerly been students at Bristol University, including Ralph Griffiths, A.J. Pollard and Michael Hicks; others were invited out of friendship and common historical interests; and all, either directly or indirectly, drew inspiration from the late K.B. McFarlane. No less significantly, Ross persuaded his friend Alan Sutton to publish the proceedings. Indeed, Sutton's role in publishing the 1978 papers and those of several subsequent conferences, as well as reprinting sources and commissioning a range of secondary works, proved vital in stimulating the remarkable take-off of fifteenth-century studies in the 1980s and 1990s.

Charles Ross, a contemporary of J.R. Lander and former pupil of K.B. McFarlane, taught at Bristol University from 1947 to 1982 (he died in 1986), spawned the Bristol connection of fifteenth-century historians and penned authoritative biographies of *Edward IV* (1974) and *Richard III* (1981), as well as a notably readable and splendidly illustrated study of *The Wars of the Roses* (published in 1976). His inspirational teaching enthused countless numbers of undergraduates over the years, as well as producing a string of postgraduate research students, but, unlike McFarlane, he had little time for historians who refused to recognise the existence of a wider reading period beyond the lecture room, monograph or learned journal. Indeed, he confessed a frank personal enjoyment of good popular history. As befitted a former McFarlane student, however, Ross did show a lifelong interest in the fifteenth-century English nobility; however after several years devoted to editing medieval records, it was the Wars of the Roses and the kings whose reigns they so disturbed that increasingly came to fire his interest.

The Wars of the Roses, perhaps more than any of his published work, possessed to the full all those qualities that made Charles Ross such a compelling and accomplished lecturer while, in the biographies of Edward IV and Richard III, he managed effortlessly to combine deep scholarship, penetrating analysis and sheer readability. For Ross, as for K.B. McFarlane, the Wars of the Roses resulted fundamentally from 'personal and political factors, especially those stemming from the weakness of the King and the impossibility of finding a political, non-violent solution to the problems which this involved'. Henry VI, he believed, was a 'peace-loving man, who was notably more merciful on occasion than most of his contemporaries, and who did his limited best to heal the feuds among his great men'. He was a 'faithful husband and a loving father' and both deeply religious and genuinely interested in education. Indeed, his 'most positive personal achievements' were the foundations of Eton College and King's College, Cambridge. Unfortunately, he entirely lacked the qualities necessary to command the respect of his great men and, in the 1450s, he seems to have become for most purposes 'a political cipher, more and more under the control of his counsellors and of his French wife, the high-spirited, autocratic and ruthless Margaret of Anjou.' No wonder England dissolved into civil war! Nevertheless, like Lander, Ross doubted if the Wars of the Roses had all that much impact on society:

> English life and civilization in general were remarkably little affected by thirty years of sporadic conflict. There was very little material devastation, little pillaging or plundering, certainly nothing to compare with the systematic devastation of people, buildings, stock and crops which the English armies had been wont to inflict on many parts of France during the Hundred Years War... England in the later fifteenth century was, in fact, the home of a rich, varied and vigorous civilization.

Charles Ross clearly felt a considerable empathy for Edward IV, as a man who combined a good deal of charm and affability, an uninhibited delight in the pleasures of life, and a firm commitment to the daunting task of ruling the realm effectively. Throughout his reign, Ross believed, Edward took his kingly duties seriously, kept a close personal control over the work of government and proved himself very active politically. Yet he was also notably inconsistent in his policies and not infrequently unsuccessful. Indeed, his political failings, not least his impulsive marriage to Elizabeth Woodville in 1464 and subsequent encouragement of the Woodville clan at court, led not only to the temporary restoration to the throne of Henry VI in 1470/71 but, ultimately, the downfall of the Yorkist dynasty altogether. Clearly, Edward IV's younger brother Richard of Gloucester did not have the same personal appeal for Ross although, when discussing his character, he achieved a greater degree of objectivity than most. Ross's Richard III, placed firmly in the context of his times, is an ambitious, determined and ruthless politician. He is also an effective political operator, however, who, having usurped the throne, disposed of his nephews and crushed a major rebellion, perhaps came nearer than is often allowed to establishing himself and his northern affinity permanently in the corridors and places of power in fifteenth-century England.

The Welshman Ralph A. Griffiths, himself a former research student at Bristol University, is perhaps the most eminent member of the Bristol connection still vigorously practising his craft. Indeed, it was he who organised a follow-up to Charles Ross's 1978 Bristol conference at University College, Swansea, in 1979, where the main participants were past and present Bristol and Swansea postgraduate students and the principal object, once more, was the encouragement of younger scholars to present the results of their researches (although Charles Ross himself was also prevailed upon to deliver a paper). Over a period of almost forty years, Ralph Griffiths has published extensively on fifteenth-century English and Welsh history, successfully addressing his fellow scholars, students and the more popular end of the historical market. He has assessed, among other things, Richard of York's intentions in 1450 and the origins of the Wars of the Roses, the importance of the sense of dynasty in Henry VI's reign, the role of the king's court during the fifteenth-century civil wars, and the pre-1485 history of the Tudor family. Most importantly, in 1981, he published *The Reign of King Henry VI*. Running to almost a thousand pages in length and as near a definitive history of the king's reign as we can ever hope to have, it was an awesome achievement. Rejecting K.B. McFarlane's contention that Henry VI progressed seamlessly from infancy to imbecility, Griffiths argued that the king, for all his shortcomings, did play an active role in government from the later 1430s until he suffered his nervous breakdown in 1453. Even though it is not possible to be certain of Henry's personal intervention (rather than passive assent to measures formulated by the men around him) nevertheless, Griffiths believed, the king did reject his father's militarism, proved himself extravagant and wasteful and, when demonstrably politically active, was also thoroughly incompetent. A well-intentioned man whose aspirations in those aspects of government that interested him – such as education, Anglo-French relations and rewarding his friends and servants – were laudable enough, he was also credulous, inappropriately compassionate to some, unnecessarily suspicious of others, and, most fatally, lacking foresight, prudence and political judgement. In particular, Henry VI 'showed little sagacity, subtlety or discrimination in his administrative acts, and none of the political astuteness necessary to achieve an acceptable balance among his subjects 'competing interests'.

At least two other members of the Bristol connection, A.J. (Anthony) Pollard and Michael Hicks, have also made an indelible contribution to our knowledge of fifteenth-century England. Both have organised fifteenth-century conferences and edited their proceedings, both have published extensively in historical journals and both have supervised postgraduate students of their own. Pollard, a research student of Charles Ross in the 1960s, has particularly concentrated his attention on the north of England in the fifteenth century, most notably penning a major study of *North-Eastern England during the Wars of the Roses*, published in 1990, that combined scholarship and readability in equal measure. For a wider audience, his short survey of *The Wars of the Roses* (1988) is an exceptionally stimulating and illuminating work of synthesis. On the origins of the wars, for instance, he concludes judiciously:

> In the mid-fifteenth century many circumstances combined to undermine the authority of the Crown – growing economic and financial pressures, material loss and humiliation in France, the lurking doubt concerning Henry VI's title. They made civil war more likely. In the last resort it was Henry VI's incapacity after 1453 which tipped the balance. In the end, to use a metaphor much favoured at the time, the ship of state was without a captain and, while the crew fell at each other's throats, she drifted onto the rocks.

On the personalities of the period, Henry VI, 'weak, vacillating, feckless and profligate', was quite simply 'the most unfitted to rule of all the kings of England since the Norman Conquest'; Margaret of Anjou was 'a strong-willed young woman prepared to go to any extreme to protect the inheritance of her only son'; Edward IV, a man of considerable personal magnanimity, succeeded, at any rate after 1471, in stamping his personality on the kingdom; and, as for Richard III, his career was 'more a tragedy than a melodrama in which he played the villainous uncle or virtuous hero'. The last Yorkist king, moreover, provided Pollard's subject for *Richard III and the Princes in the Tower*, a perceptive, entertaining and superbly illustrated book published in 1991. Michael Hicks, who graduated from Bristol University in 1970, also published his *Richard III: The Man Behind the Myth* in 1991, having earlier dissected the character and behaviour of the king's brother in *False, Fleeting, Perjur'd Clarence* (1980). Hicks' range of interests, and publications, over the years has embraced bastard feudalism, northern history and religious piety but he has always maintained, as well, an enduring fascination for personalities and their impact on politics during the Wars of the Roses. His conclusions, invariably based on detailed research (often into hitherto neglected or even unknown sources) have rarely been restrained. In 1979, for instance, he roundly condemned the 'growing power' of the Woodvilles following Edward IV's marriage to Elizabeth in 1464 since their advancement 'at the expense of others generated factions within the political consensus that ultimately undermined the crown'. George Duke of Clarence's 'behaviour is logical'; he was 'a conventional magnate' and 'certainly not mad'; and his reasons for drifting into opposition to Edward IV 'are not difficult to understand'. Unfortunately, he was 'temperamentally unsuited for the role in politics otherwise assigned by his royal blood, political power and personal ambition'. As for Richard III, he was an able, intelligent, well-organised man, a natural leader, and loyal and generous to his retainers; nevertheless, when it suited him, he could prove single-mindedly ambitious, aggressive and ruthless, his usurpation of the throne was the product of three months of calculated scheming and dissimulation, and his efforts, as king, to project himself as the man best suited to rule England failed to prevent his defeat and death at Bosworth.

During the 1970s and 1980s fifteenth-century studies flourished as never before, and not just as a result of the burgeoning Bristol connection. B.P (Bertram) Wolffe, for instance, published a biography of *Henry VI* in 1981, ironically enough the very same year as Ralph Griffiths' massive book appeared. Wolffe, however, was altogether more damning in his verdict. Henry VI, he argued, was neither so pious nor so enlightened in promoting education as traditionally supposed. Nor was he a simpleton. Rather, he was a positive, even sinister, political menace. From the end of his minority in 1437 until the early 1450s, Wolffe argued, the king was 'the essential unique feature of the reign': indeed, this was an era of truly personal rule. Henry VI's own unwise exercise of royal patronage seriously weakened the crown's financial position (as well as its political reputation) and, even worse, from 1444 until 1453 the king himself took the initiative frequently (and with dire consequences) in foreign policy. Henry VI's own 'wilful efforts', concluded Wolffe, 'divided, demoralised and hamstrung the English war effort in France, so that it dissolved in defeat and recriminations'. Moreover, the king's conduct simultaneously led to 'creeping paralysis in home affairs and a consequent collapse of respect for law and order by the great'. Once Henry VI suffered his dramatic mental breakdown in August 1453, however, Wolffe's king (like Griffiths') proved rarely, if ever, able to provide any real political leadership again. In his study of *The Wars of the Roses: Military Activity and English Society 1452-1497*, also published in 1981, Anthony Goodman certainly had the recent tendency to play down the impact of civil war on fifteenth-century English society firmly in his sights. Why the Wars of the Roses began concerned him little; rather, he aimed to show just what the conflicts were like through an analysis of the campaigns themselves, military organisation and methods, and the social consequences of civil strife. For Goodman, the wars were altogether more significant than either J.R. Lander or Charles Ross had suggested: the total period of campaigning lasted at least a year (rather than the twelve or thirteen weeks Lander had postulated); the cost of arming, feeding and billeting troops was considerable, not to mention the artillery and means of transport required; and, even if campaigns tended to be brief and localised, men had to be raised, fighting had to be done, and the resulting casualties, executions and forfeitures of land cannot but have had palpable social as well as political effects. Clearly, then, both Wolffe and Goodman sought to reinterpret the mid-fifteenth century along rather different lines than most of the Bristol connection but it was not until the 1990s that the spectre of rampant revisionism raised its head with a vengeance at Cambridge University.

CHRISTINE CARPENTER, JOHN WATTS AND THE CAMBRIDGE REVISIONISTS

Charles Ross, and most of the Bristol connection, had little time for the niceties of historical methodology, preferring a straightforward evidence-led approach to the past, untrammelled by theoretical models or paradigms about politics and society. By the early 1990s, however, Christine Carpenter and a coterie of Cambridge-trained revisionist historians were beginning to challenge their whole approach to fifteenth-century history and, in the process, claim to be the true intellectual heirs of K.B. McFarlane. Indeed, they overtly set themselves the goal of providing that new synthesis of fifteenth-century history McFarlane had called for way back in 1938 but never provided himself. Oddly enough, Cambridge had never before aspired to a high profile role in fifteenth-century studies. J.R. Lander had learned his trade at Cambridge University in the 1940s but then spent the whole of his own teaching career overseas. Rosemary Horrox, too, was a Cambridge-based research student in the 1970s but only belatedly obtained a full-time post at the university herself. Moreover, her doctoral thesis on 'The Extent and Use of Crown Patronage under Richard III', out of which grew *Richard III: A Study of Service* (1989), could easily have been inspired by Charles Ross himself (and was, in fact, supervised by another former McFarlane pupil G.L. Harriss) and, certainly, Horrox very much concentrated on royal patronage and the role of the king's servants during the turbulent years of the last Yorkist's high profile career. Yet patronage and its importance, ironically enough, was about to become a central target of the Cambridge revisionists. Christine Carpenter, like Rosemary Horrox, was a former postgraduate student of G.L. (Gerald) Harriss (whose own highly perceptive and thoroughly researched 1988 study of *Cardinal Beaufort*, incidentally, rather belies McFarlane's conviction that the fifteenth-century historian 'cannot honestly write biographical history at all'). Since the mid-1980s Carpenter herself has become firmly established as the intellectual guru of a group of young scholars whom, she tells us, 'I supervised as both undergraduates and research students'. John Watts, now a very well respected historian in his own right, certainly acknowledged his debt to her in 1996:

> ...how can I thank Christine Carpenter enough? Having been my teacher and friend for over a decade she has encouraged, cajoled, provoked and inspired me through every academic project I have tackled. I often feel that I owe almost everything to her support, both intellectual and personal.

Yet it was Colin Richmond, a member of the Bristol connection by proxy, who struck the first blow on behalf of serious revisionism in 1983. In particular, he rounded on the excessive attention paid by recent historians to patronage as the principal driving force of fifteenth-century political and social life. For instance, although the magnate affinity was indeed part of the normal fabric of society;

> ...it was only part, and patronage was not all that counted. Men were not Pavlovian dogs, jumping at the chance of a fee, a rent charge, a stewardship here, a parkership there. No more were lords puppet masters manipulating their marionette retainers to dominate the provinces or pack parliaments.

In 1989 the Cambridge historian Edward Powell, at a conference hosted by Manchester University, castigated even more strongly 'the reduction of constitutional history to politics, of politics to patronage, and of personal motivation to material self-interest' by too many of the post-McFarlane generation of historians. Then, at a colloquium held at Durham University in 1993, Christine Carpenter herself urged the need to 'put back into our subject that conceptual edge which it seems to have lost' and to do so 'by adding a constitutional dimension to our burgeoning knowledge of political events'; instead of concentrating on 'patronage and individual strivers', she insisted, we should devote ourselves to studying the 'political culture' of the age, 'the terms and currency of political action and beliefs'. For Cambridge revisionists, in fact, since fifteenth-century politicians thought and acted within a clearly established constitutional framework, the case for recognising the role played by principles and ideologies in politics (rather than simply stressing the personal ambitions and material self-interest of individuals) is overwhelming.

All this is heady stuff indeed, for intellectuals, but clearly best confined to the pages of learned journals and volumes of conference proceedings. For a wider – although not, perhaps, all that much wider – audience, John Watts published his monograph *Henry VI and the Politics of Kingship* in 1996. While freely admitting that his book 'does not begin to approach the range and depth of new information which Ralph Griffiths provided for us' in 1981, Watts nevertheless believed 'there is still room for a re-evaluation of our assumptions about the operation of fifteenth-century government and, indeed, for an attempt to apply the insights gained in the process to the muddled reign of Henry VI'. In the end, his opinion of the king could hardly be lower. Although Henry VI 'grew physically, and perhaps mentally', Watts concluded, 'he never came to perform the role expected of an adult king'. Not only are there good grounds for suspecting that the king's 'personal rule' was nothing of the kind, even the foundation of Eton and King's College, Cambridge, derived not from Henry's personal initiative but originated in plans formulated by his advisers. Throughout the 1440s (let alone the 1450s!) 'evidence accumulates to show that the king simply lacked the independence of will to make authoritative decisions and that this frustrated all forms of government which were focused upon him': indeed, his lords found themselves having to cope with 'forty years of virtual minority'. The Wars of the Roses, however, did not occur simply because Henry VI was a disaster, Edmund Beaufort Duke of Somerset corrupt and incompetent, and Richard of York brimming over with resentment at his exclusion from patronage and power. On the contrary, according to Watts, vital principles concerning the realm and its well being were at stake. The political conflicts of the 1450s, he argued, were fought over ideological issues: York continually justified his behaviour, even the use of force, on the grounds he was trying to promote the common good and interests of the country; his opponents, no less vehemently, proclaimed the overriding obligation of obedience to the crowned king; and, far from being merely the stuff of cynical populist propaganda, matters of principle were regarded as central to the very functioning of political society. Far from seeking to profit from the confusion generated by the king's incapacity, the nobility in the 1440s and 1450s desperately sought a consensus that would enable them to govern effectively on Henry VI's behalf; instead of a self-interested aristocracy pursuing financial advantage at court and territorial advancement in the provinces, Watts portrayed a mature and responsible political elite struggling, in exceptionally difficult circumstances, to maintain a unified and coherent government. Hence why the onset of full-scale civil war was so long delayed until, eventually, the king's prolonged and repeated failure to perform even a modicum of his royal functions made it virtually inevitable.

In 1997 John Watts' monograph was followed by Christine Carpenter's 'textbook' *The Wars of the Roses: Politics and the Constitution in England c.1437-1509*. On Henry VI, she barely dissented from Watts, believing the king cannot be held responsible for any part of the rule that occurred in his name, whether at home or abroad, during the 1440s and 1450s: the consequence of the last Lancastrian's 'nothing-ness', however, was not the triumph of 'evil counsel' (as traditionally supposed) so much as 'a concerted effort' by the nobility to 'put a semblance of monarchy in the void created by the absence of an active king' until, since there was 'no impartial figure powerful enough to constrain feuding magnates', politics moved during the 1450s 'from the precarious preservation of unity under a sham king to total disunity under a king about whom there could be no pretending any more'. Edward IV, by contrast, fared very well when judged by the criteria of Carpenter's paradigm of how fifteenth-century political society worked. Indeed, she concluded, the king possessed:

> ...an almost perfect instinct in the second reign [1471-1483] for the vital kingly balance between justice and mercy. If he had at times been a little casual during the first reign [1461-1470], he had learned to take greater care, and even the casualness was symptomatic of a tendency to trust and forgive that was essential in a medieval monarch, as long as it was allied, as in his case, with shrewdness and force of character. He should be acknowledged as one of the greatest of English kings.

Richard III, 'who had taken the throne in the name of continuity' with his brother Edward IV's regime, not only brought down the Yorkist dynasty but also propelled its aides 'into becoming the foundation of the new ruling house of Tudor'. As for Henry VII, although he became king 'under better circumstances than any other usurper in late-medieval England', he fatally mistrusted his nobility and showed 'a comprehensive misunderstanding of the nature of medieval kingship'. Carpenter, indeed, robustly declared herself 'an unrepentant critic' of a king who failed so dismally to conform to what was required of a polit-ically correct fifteenth-century monarch!

The Cambridge revisionists have certainly brought a breath of fresh air – or perhaps, even, a howling gale – into fifteenth-century studies and forced almost all later medieval historians to re-examine their own approaches to, and interpretations of, the period. Yet it is doubtful if the new Cambridge synthesis will ever win general acceptance as, bit by bit, it is dissected – even dismantled – by critics. Indeed, now John Watts is firmly ensconced in Oxford University, maybe even he might feel the need to reconsider his Cambridge inspired positions! William Shakespeare, certainly, would find himself bewildered in such strange and unfamiliar territory. The revisionists, at the very least, can surely be accused of overplaying their hand, even of caricaturing interpretations they so eagerly seek to demolish. Did any serious historian ever suggest, for instance, that patronage, personal ambition and the quest for land, wealth and office were the only motivations driving politically active men in the fifteenth century? Surely not. Yet to deny such aspirations existed, or seek to negate their powerful influence on the behaviour of the ruling elite, is equally absurd. Perhaps, too, revisionists have been too ready to accept fifteenth-century magnates' own justifications of their behaviour and even mistaken populist propaganda designed to win support during the Wars of the Roses for genuine enunciation of beliefs and principles. And, when it came to the crunch, did fifteenth-century politicians really react to events and situations so much more high-mindedly than their modern equivalents? Clearly, later medieval politics was not devoid of ideological content, but chivalry (arguably, the code of a culture of aristocratic and knightly violence, anyway) might well provide as good a guide to the behaviour of the ruling elite during the Wars of the Roses as concern for the realm's peace and well-being.

How have members of the Bristol connection, in particular, responded to revisionism? Certainly, Michael Hicks' perspective on fifteenth-century politics and society, as demonstrated in his *Warwick the Kingmaker* (1998), does not seem to have altered significantly. He firmly rejects the notion that, throughout his reign, Henry VI was a nullity: on the contrary, although the king lacked either the inclination or capacity for government, he was 'capable of occasional decisive action and secured obedient compliance from the political nation when he took it', and even after 1455 he was always more than a figurehead. As for Warwick the Kingmaker himself, Hicks very much ploughs his own interpretative furrow, regarding Warwick not as the traditional self-interested, greedy, power-hungry and turbulent 'last of the barons' so much as a charming, emotional and popular man, a man possessed of a strong sense of honour and family loyalty, and a man of extraordinary energy capable of relentless attention to his affairs. Indeed, declares Hicks:

There was nothing Warwick would not attempt and no obstacle that he would not overcome. He was indomitable, never surrendered, and never failed to recover until the very end. For twenty years he shaped events, his own career, and even history itself.

In 2000 A.J. Pollard published *Late Medieval England 1399-1509* (the best survey of fifteenth-century political history as a whole since Maurice Keen's in 1973) and, in 2001, a revised edition of *The Wars of the Roses*. Here, although he praised Watts' 1996 monograph as 'a thorough study of Henry VI's reign' in the context of contemporary expectations of kingship, he nevertheless rejected the argument that, even before his mental breakdown in 1453, the king was a complete nonentity. Carpenter's 1997 book he judged 'a lively and provocative account' of the period 1437-1509 while, at the same time, distancing himself from some of its more contentious conclusions, not least its author's verdicts on Edward IV and Henry VII. Moreover, whilst giving very fair coverage to the revisionist thesis that the importance of political patronage during the Wars of the Roses has been overstated and the role of ideology and principle seriously neglected, he firmly pointed out that, since the evidence is both 'incomplete and unreliable', the extent to which politicians really were influenced and guided by ideas and principles 'remains difficult to discern'. Perhaps most significantly, as far as the Wars of the Roses are concerned, Pollard's conclusions in 2001 remained largely unchanged from what they had been in 1988.

Paul Murray Kendall, The Richard III Society and the Wider Historical Market

The Cambridge revisionists, so far at any rate, have shown little or no interest in catering for a market beyond the confines of fellow professional historians and serious, preferably university, students of fifteenth-century history, at any rate if the early chapters of their recent books is any guide. John Watts' *Henry VI and the Politics of Kingship*, for instance, contains almost seventy pages (out of 366) on 'The Conceptual Framework' while, in *The Wars of the Roses*, Christine Carpenter devoted forty (out of 268) to a densely argued analysis of 'The Governance of England in the Fifteenth Century'. Fortunately, not all later twentieth-century academic historians were so narrowly focused. Over the years many have contributed to *The Ricardian* (journal of the Richard III Society) and the popular historical magazine *History Today*. Some books, too, have deliberately reached out to a wider reading public. Charles Ross clearly did so in *The Wars of the Roses* (1976), as did John Gillingham in 1981: indeed, his racy narrative treatment of

The Wars of the Roses, highlighting the curious paradox (for him) of just how peaceful later fifteenth-century England was despite the many battles of the time, combined vigour, wit and intelligence in almost equal measure. Ralph Griffiths, jointly with John Cannon (formerly a colleague of Charles Ross at Bristol University), produced *The Oxford Illustrated History of the British Monarchy* in 1988 where two scholars renowned for their scintillating lectures seamlessly fused erudition and readability. A.J. Pollard rose to the challenge no less magnificently in *Richard III and the Princes in the Tower* (1991) where, apart from an entertaining and academically flawless text, 'the tireless and frequently inspired picture research of Margaret Condon'(another member of the Bristol connection) helped make possible a splendid series of 'picture essays' covering Richard III's birth sign (Scorpio), pigs and boars (the white boar was the king's most famous badge), royal saints and books, portraits, cartoons and caricatures of Richard III, and the Princes in the Tower (featuring several highly sentimental nineteenth-century paintings of the boys). Nevertheless, during the last decade or so of the twentieth century, the gap between 'academic' and 'popular' history widened ever more alarmingly.

Perhaps the most renowned twentieth-century non-professional historian who published extensively on the Wars of the Roses era was the American Paul Murray Kendall (who died in 1973). For many years Professor of English (not history) at the University of Ohio, Kendall was a conscientious researcher who, despite an occasional penchant for over-the-top passages of purple prose and a tiresome tendency towards imaginative reconstruction in the face of inadequate evidence, often managed to beat the professionals at their own game. Perhaps his best book, published in 1962, was *The Yorkist Ages*, where he made his approach to the past abundantly clear:

> Like all historical writing, this is essentially an exercise of the imag-
> ination… As the novelist works imaginatively from the data of his
> experience, the historian works imaginatively from the more inert
> and 'outside' data of evidence preserved from the fangs of time…
> Facts are brute, recalcitrant matter; they must be rubbed together in
> the mind before they will assume the shape of meaning.

However, he added, 'I have invented no scenes, no conversations, no details of action' and, 'if the reader detects I have an enormous affection for these bygone people, I can but admit that, lacking such affection, I should not have been willing to spend so many months of my life in trying to live with them'.

Historical biography was Kendall's first love and, indeed, his *Art of the Biography* (1965) received a nomination for the Pulitzer Prize. In *Warwick the Kingmaker* (1957), he concluded that Warwick was 'a power unto himself' who 'acknowledged no bar or custom to his hopes': indeed, according to Kendall, 'Warwick's generation took him for granted like many another manifestation of God's unfathomable providence'. When reviewing the biography Charles Ross (an unashamed admirer of Kendall's work), while criticising its author's tendency to attribute to his subject 'too large a part in the great events of his day', nevertheless found it 'a very readable book' from which Warwick 'emerges as a human and understandable figure caught up in the consequences of his early and unusual success'. Yet, he added, 'not even Professor Kendall's persuasiveness can make a great man out of this touchy aristocrat who wrought his own downfall'. Ross was complimentary, too, about Kendall's earlier biography of *Richard the Third* as 'soundly based on a wide range of primary sources for which it shows a proper respect', despite an 'empurpled prose style' and the American's all too evident partisanship. 'When the picture of Richard's government is viewed in the frame of its actual brevity', Kendall concluded (in 1955):

> …the remarkable dimensions of his achievement leap into focus… Richard vigorously translated the idiom of his character into the language of kingship. In the course of a mere eighteen months crowded with cares and problems, he laid down a coherent programme of legal enactments, maintained an orderly society, and actively promoted the well-being of his subjects… Richard seems to have emerged from an earlier world… He had in him something of the first martyrs and something of the Germanic chieftain… If we cannot see his portrait clearly, we can at least choose its painter - not Holbein or even Rembrandt, but perhaps El Greco.

Splendid stuff!

Of all fifteenth-century English kings, in fact, none has attracted more interest - or been the focus of more controversy – than Richard III and, even in the twentieth century, he found both passionate defenders and harsh critics. Emotion has been generated in such diverse settings as our most famous public school (Eton), the privileged benches of the House of Lords, the journalistic ranks of both national and local newspapers, and even the programme producing fraternities of British radio and television. The 'In Memoriam' columns of *The Times*, *Guardian* and *Independent* never fail to carry at least one loving remembrance of the last Plantagenet on the anniversary of his untimely death on the battlefield of Bosworth on 22 August

1485 while, in 1984, London Weekend Television staged a four hour mock trial of Richard III (when, predictably, a jury found the king not guilty of the murder of his nephews). Can any other English monarch, moreover, boast so determined a champion as the detective novelist Josephine Tey? In her best-selling novel *The Daughter of Time* (published in 1951), we find Miss Tey's Detective Inspector Grant, anxious to combat the tedium of enforced idleness in hospital and inspired by an early sixteenth-century portrait of Richard III, turning his investigative talents to an unorthodox use: inevitably, he ends up clearing the king of all those crimes so unjustly credited to him by Sir Thomas More and William Shakespeare and casts his successor Henry VII in the role of murderer of the Princes in the Tower. Even more strikingly, Richard's enthusiastic rehabilitators, not only in England but elsewhere, have created flourishing societies specifically dedicated to defending his reputation against the dastardly charges of Tudor hacks (and anyone else who would blacken his name) and praise his achievements (whether as Duke of Gloucester or as king) in the highest of terms. In America during the 1930s, indeed, the Friends of Richard III Incorporated included among their ranks such distinguished figures as the writer James Thurber, the artist Salvador Dalí and the legendary Hollywood movie star Tallulah Bankhead. The English Richard III Society went one better, in 1980, when it enlisted as its patron the present Richard Duke of Gloucester. Originally founded in 1924 as the Fellowship of the White Boar, a vigorous and articulate pro-Richard III pressure group, it was reconstituted as the less vehement Richard III Society in 1956, with the declared aim of promoting 'in every possible way research into the life and times of Richard III, and to secure a re-assessment of the material relating to this period, and of the role in English history of this monarch'. *The Ricardian* (quarterly journal of the society) has, since 1975, become a respected academic periodical presenting the results of original research by amateur and professional historians alike. Unlike most learned journals, however, its long-time editor Anne Sutton has always strenuously sought to ensure contents that are not only scholarly but interesting and readable as well. The Richard III Society has also earned the gratitude of all fifteenth-century specialists by sponsoring the publication of major primary sources, most notably, in 1986, a new edition/translation of the *Crowland Chronicle*. In 1983, moreover, Jeremy Potter (the society's then chairman but no fanatic) published *Good King Richard?*, a readable and frequently perceptive survey of 'Richard III and his reputation 1483-1983', nicely enlivened by Potter's occasionally acerbic comments on the king's historians through the ages.

Sir Clements Markham, in 1906, had penned perhaps the most comprehensive whitewash of Richard III ever written, although Philip Lindsay ran it a close second in his study of *King Richard III* (published in 1933). Firmly addressing the memory of the king, as 'the kind of man whom we should turn to now that we move trembling towards the abyss of the future', he declared emotionally that:

> ...destiny could not break his spirit, the spirit that is England. Nothing could destroy that spark that Richard carried in his breast, the spark that kept him fighting, struggling on, when he could see nothing but blackness ahead. Indomitable, heroic, lovable, the great Richard, last of our English kings...

Even Paul Murray Kendall, in 1955, confessed he found it difficult to take Clements Markham's work seriously, since his 'white and black are as intense as those of the Tudor tradition'. As for Markham's Richard III himself, he is 'a sterling symbol of English pluck, mantled in the airs which blow upon the playing fields of Eton and the glorious reaches of the nineteenth-century British Empire'. Philip Lindsay's *King Richard III*, too, Kendall scathingly dismissed as 'a popular work'! Nevertheless, the king continued to have his ardent defenders: the very title of V.B. Lamb's *The Betrayal of Richard III* (1959) perhaps says it all; Audrey Williamson, in *The Mystery of the Princes* (first published in 1978), concluded that 'the ascription of the murder of the princes to Richard III is totally without any factual evidence whatever that would be accepted in any court of law'; and Elizabeth Jenkins, in *The Princes in the Tower* (also published in 1978), remarked that even if:

> ...it is admitted that Richard committed the crime, it becomes alarmingly clear how much reason he had to do it, and how much the circumstances of his past contributed to the doing. The story is not the sensational one of the crime of a habitual murderer, but the awe-inspiring one of a capable, strong-minded, dedicated king driven to a dreadful act from which he chose to think there was no escape.

In 1983, however, the Tudor saga returned with a vengeance in the pages of Desmond Seward's *Richard III: England's Black Legend*. Unashamedly hostile to his subject, Seward found Richard guilty of virtually every crime ever attributed to him and interpreted almost every event to his discredit. In what he proudly proclaimed to be 'the most hostile life of Richard III to appear for over a century', he concluded that the king:

...possessed the qualities of an Italian tyrant. He was the most terrifying man ever to occupy the English throne... His short life was filled with intrigue and slaughter [and if] certainly not a monster [he was] a peculiarly grim young English precursor of Machiavelli's Prince.

If Desmond Seward was content with Tudor tradition about Richard III, A.L. Rowse enthusiastically embraced it for the fifteenth century as a whole. Although once a reputable professional historian (a Fellow of All Souls College, Oxford, no less), he had largely ceased to be so by 1966 when he published *Bosworth Field and the Wars of the Roses*. For Rowse, in fact, the traditional picture of the Wars of the Roses remained 'in keeping with the best scholarship and the conclusions of common sense.' As for the battle of Bosworth, it did indeed bring to an end the 'long dynastic conflict', the 'brutal and fratricidal power-struggle', that had so dominated the fifteenth century, a conclusion which William Shakespeare could have heartily endorsed. Nevertheless, the book is very readable and Rowse's judgements on individuals, in particular, are certainly striking: since Henry VI was 'too good for this world', he declared, 'in the end he was put out of it'; Margaret of Anjou 'came to breathe the fire and slaughter of partisanship' as she 'fought like a tigress' on her son's behalf; Edward IV, 'a natural leader of men', proved himself a very successful ruler 'whatever people thought of his enjoying ease and sensuality'; and as for Richard III, he was 'a psychotic type', a veritable Adolf Hitler of the fifteenth century, heading a government no less repellent than that of the German Nazis. Hubert Cole's restrained and reliable narrative history of *The Wars of the Roses* (1973), and Alison Weir's more comprehensive treatment in *Lancaster and York: The Wars of the Roses* (1995), seem sadly mundane by comparison. Desmond Seward's *The Wars of the Roses* (also published in 1995), 'an attempt to evoke the world of the Wars of the Roses' through 'the lives of five men and women of the fifteenth century' (William Lord Hastings, a Yorkist loyalist, John de Vere Earl of Oxford, a stalwart Lancastrian, John Morton, a trimmer who ended his life as a cardinal, Jane Shore, Edward IV's mistress, and Margaret Beaufort, mother of Henry VII), is, by contrast, a compelling read (as well as lacking the venom of its author's earlier biography of Richard III). Otherwise, as far as popular history is concerned, military campaigns and battles seem to inspire endless interest and several books published in the 1990s specifically catered for this market. Much the best of them was Peter Hammond, *The Battles of Barnet and Tewkesbury* (1990), but *The Battle of Towton*, by A.W. Boardman, appeared in 1994 and, soon afterwards, two books by Philip A. Haigh: *The Military Campaigns of the Wars of the Roses* (1995) and *The Battle of Wakefield 1460* (1996). As for later medieval English kings, and William Shakespeare's portrayal of them and their turbulent times, they received well-informed and perceptive treatment in Peter Saccio's *Shakespeare's English Kings* (1977) and lengthier (if highly conventional) coverage in John Julius Norwich's *Shakespeare's Kings* (1999).

11

WILLIAM SHAKESPEARE'S PLANTAGENET HISTORY PLAYS IN PERSPECTIVE

THE PLAYS IN PERFORMANCE

During the twentieth century, as professional historians subjected contemporary and near-contemporary sources to ever more thorough and detailed scrutiny, our knowledge of fifteenth-century politics, society and the Wars of the Roses expanded enormously. Yet, ironically enough, William Shakespeare's portrayal of the age also became more familiar than ever before, as schools increasingly opted to teach Shakespeare, new editions of the Plantagenet cycle proliferated and, most importantly, so did performances of the history plays (especially *Richard II, Henry V* and *Richard III*).

All the Plantagenet history plays were written, and presumably performed, in the 1590s but we know virtually nothing of their early stage history. *Richard III* did make Richard Burbage's reputation as an actor, however, and he probably played the title role regularly until his death in 1619; *Henry V* almost certainly received its first performance at the newly opened Globe Theatre in 1599; and there is evidence of occasional revivals early in the seventeenth century: *Richard II*, for instance, was staged on the eve of Essex's rebellion in 1601 (and again in 1607), *Henry V* was acted at James I's court in 1605, and *Richard III* at Charles I's in 1633. For most of the seventeenth century, however, performances were extremely rare: history plays, especially if they dealt with kings, became ever more suspect in government circles during the politically turbulent years that preceded the outbreak of the English Civil War; theatres were closed in 1642 and remained so until the

Restoration; and, even after they reopened, risqué comedies, not serious dramas, seem to have been very much the flavour of the age. Towards the end of the century the actor-manager Colley Cibber cobbled together an extraordinary version of *Richard III*, cutting some two thirds of the playwright's original lines (including the king's famous opening speech) but adding a couple of hundred from other Shakespearian plays (as well as a thousand or so of his own). In 1700 he both published and staged the mangled result of his labours, playing the title role himself (although, apparently, his performance left a great deal to be desired). Nevertheless, Cibber continued to posture as Richard III, egomaniac *par excellence*, for almost forty years. Unfortunately, too, the play continued to be performed very much along the lines of Cibber's bizarre reconstruction throughout the eighteenth century and, indeed, for much of the nineteenth. David Garrick, great actor that he was, managed to make a success of it in 1741, played the role (*á la* Cibber) for some thirty-five years thereafter, and even chose to end his illustrious career with a performance of *Richard III*. John Philip Kemble, at the end of the eighteenth century, stuck to Cibber's adaptation as well; so did Edmund Kean in the early nineteenth; and, in 1857, so grotesque was his son Charles Kean's rendering that a contemporary critic scathingly judged 'the painter, the tailor and the upholsterer' to be 'Mr Kean's interpreters of Shakespeare'. Not until 1877 did Henry Irving at last make a real attempt to return to Shakespeare's authentic *Richard III* and it was only when Frank Benson made the part his own between 1886 and 1915 that Cibber's malign influence on the play was finally lifted. As for the other Plantagenet history plays, performances seem to have been either rare or non-existent before the later nineteenth century: both the Keans did, it seems, make a success of *Richard II*; the irresistible, if mythical, character of Sir John Falstaff occasionally resulted in highly garbled versions of the two parts of *Henry IV* being staged; and Henry V became a favourite role of both John Kemble and Charles Kean. It was only during the two or three decades prior to the outbreak of the First World War, however, that *Richard II* and *Henry V* (as well as *Richard III*) came to be regularly performed, the two parts of *Henry IV* enjoyed occasional revivals, and even the *Henry VI* trilogy was at last rescued from oblivion.

The twentieth century saw many memorable productions of Shakespeare's history plays and a number of outstanding performances: John Gielgud's portrayal of Richard II in 1937, for instance, proved pivotal in forging his reputation as a great classical actor; Donald Wolfit enjoyed real success playing Richard III as an Adolf Hitler look-alike in the early 1940s; and Peggy Ashcroft's Margaret of Anjou took Stratford-upon-Avon by storm in 1963. Even Ivor Novello abandoned romantic musical comedy roles for a time, in 1938, when he played Richard II. Most memorable of all was Laurence Olivier: indeed, if William Shakespeare and Tudor tradition profoundly influenced the treatment of fifteenth-century England by later historians, Olivier's portrayals of Henry V and Richard III had a similar impact on the acting profession. Of his 1937 performance of Henry V on stage, Olivier was later to remark (in his 1982 autobiography) that 'I was intensely shy of a great deal of it, being influenced by the 1930s dislike of heroism'. Nevertheless, in 1944, not least because of 'the pull of this play as popular propaganda', he both directed and played the title role in *Henry V* for the screen. Shot at Denham studios, and on location in Ireland (where Olivier himself was injured while filming the war scenes), and with splendid atmospheric music provided by William Walton, it proved a veritable blockbuster. Moreover, as Olivier recalled in 1982, 'the beyond-wildest-dreams acclaim' for *Henry V* 'established me indisputably as film director-actor-producer'. A few months before *Henry V* hit cinema screens in the autumn of 1944, Olivier learned he was to play Richard III for the Old Vic. He had no expectation of making a success of the part:

> I thought grimly of the lot that had befallen me; my Big One was to be *Richard III*, which was at this time a rather stale cup of tea; every old actor manager throughout history had played it and it bore that sort of stigma. Besides, it had been revived only eighteen months before by Donald Wolfit with great popular and critical success. Wolfit was a favourite with his own formidable public, as well as being a critics' pet. I obviously didn't have any chance of success with that one...

He need not have worried. His charismatic portrayal of the king as the very epitomé of evil, both on stage and, in the mid-1950s, on film, became the definitive performance of the twentieth century. The film script, helpfully beginning with a chunk of *3 Henry VI*, also cut a great deal of the play *Richard III* itself while, strangely enough, finding room for scraps of Colley Cibber's bastardised version. Nevertheless, this film (like *Henry V* before it) proved a great critical success and both have haunted actors ever since.

When, in 1984, Kenneth Branagh took on the role of Henry V at Stratford-upon-Avon, and Antony Sher that of Richard III, Sher recorded their first meeting in his journal (published as *The Year of the King* in 1985):

...I meet Ken Branagh for the first time. We share a common problem – living in the shadow of Olivier's films, *Henry V* and *Richard III*. Because they're on film, they have entered this century's consciousness in a way that is quite daunting for any actor or director approaching the plays.

Even so, both put in highly individual and critically acclaimed performances of their own. Branagh himself recollected, in 1988, that he found Henry V's character 'amazingly rich' and playing the king 'a remarkable experience' (and, indeed, he recaptured his stage performance on film soon afterwards). As for Antony Sher, once hooked on the Shakespearian image of Richard III as a 'bottled spider', he ended up playing the role on crutches! A few years later, on stage in 1990 and on film in 1995, Ian McKellen also achieved great critical success as the last Plantagenet king, memorably setting the action during the 1930s when (so McKellen believed) a tyrant reminiscent of Richard III might just conceivably have arisen once more in England. Otherwise, the later twentieth century saw a number of stagings of Shakespeare's Wars of the Roses cycle as a coherent tetralogy, most notably the pioneering productions of Peter Hall and John Barton at Stratford-upon-Avon in 1963 (captured, this time, for television).

THE PLAYS AND HISTORY: DRAMATIC LICENCE AT ITS MOST RAMPANT?

Although William Shakespeare's Plantagenet history plays received far more performances in the twentieth century than ever before, their historical content was never more thoroughly criticised. Indeed, Shakespeare's errors of fact, and the liberties he took with chronology and events, have now been catalogued in almost microscopic detail (most recently, in 1999, in John Julius Norwich's *Shakespeare's Kings*) and it would be tedious to repeat the exercise. Nevertheless, there are several departures from historical accuracy (even if perfectly justifiable for dramatic purposes) so striking that they cannot be ignored. In *Richard II*, for instance, the part assigned to the king's child-queen Isabel is entirely unhistorical, as is the introduction of Henry Percy Earl of Northumberland's son Hotspur as a mere boy (he was, in fact, rather older than Henry IV); the dramatic scene in parliament where Richard is publicly deposed (considered so dangerously topical in the later 1590s that it was deliberately cut out of early printed editions of the play) has no historical validity; and, splendid though it is, the story of the king's murder at the hands of Sir Pierce of Exton is just that, a colourful legend. In *1 Henry IV* the action very much revolves around the battle of Shrewsbury (1403), regardless of the complexity of events in the early part of the king's reign, while, in *2 Henry IV*, history is even more seriously distorted for dramatic purposes: much attention is devoted, for instance, to the young Prince Henry, Sir John Falstaff and their wild behaviour (most, if not all, of it highly dubious historically) and, as for the last few years of Henry IV's reign, they disappear altogether, as Shakespeare virtually leaps from Archbishop Scrope's rebellion (in 1405) to the king's last illness and death (in 1413). Much of the early part of *Henry V* lacks historical authenticity, too, and even more misleading is the strong impression conveyed that, as a result of the king's great victory at Agincourt, the whole of France now fell under his control.

From both a historical and dramatic perspective *1 Henry VI* is probably the weakest play in the Shakespearian cycle. It is thoroughly disorganised, often confusing and full of historical errors: most obviously, Shakespeare's chronology is wildly inaccurate; the importance of John Talbot Earl of Shrewsbury (in a drama that ends in 1444) is grossly exaggerated, while John Duke of Bedford's role is seriously underestimated; Joan of Arc is not only portrayed as a dabbler in the occult but even as Dauphin Charles' mistress; and as for the famous rose-plucking scene in the Temple garden, it is a complete fabrication. *2 Henry VI* is a much superior play dramatically and historically, too, it is altogether less cavalier in its treatment of known facts than *1 Henry VI*. Even so, there is much manipulation and misrepresentation: Richard of York did not concur in the downfall of Duke Humphrey of Gloucester, sponsor Cade's rebellion or begin plotting to take the throne as early as 1445; Margaret of Anjou was never Suffolk's lover, nor did she become a major player in politics from almost the very moment of her arrival in England; and, as in *1 Henry VI*, there is much telescoping of events. Perhaps inevitably, since it focuses on the Wars of the Roses themselves, *3 Henry VI* takes many liberties with both chronology and events, as well as exaggerating the degree of turmoil and prevalence of atrocities that resulted. Edward IV's twenty-two years on the throne, for instance, are severely compressed; dramatically inconvenient battles like Mortimer's Cross and second St Albans are downplayed so as to highlight Wakefield and Towton; and the events of 1464 and 1470 are ingeniously conflated. Yet the play is probably much better as a result.

Perhaps *3 Henry VI* is at its most unhistorical when dealing with the life and career of Richard of Gloucester before his brother Edward IV's death in 1483. Even at the end of *2 Henry VI* (when the historic Richard was not yet three years old), he appears as Somerset's killer at the first battle of St Albans in 1455 while, in the early scenes of *3 Henry VI*, he actively participates in the battles of 1460 and 1461 (not least as the slayer of Clifford). Moreover, although outwardly supporting Edward IV after Towton, it is 'not for love of Edward but the crown' (which he is already eagerly coveting for himself). After the battle of Tewkesbury in 1471 he shares in the murder of Prince Edward of Lancaster, stabs Henry VI in the Tower of London and even offers to kill Margaret of Anjou as well. All this has little or no justification in fact. Almost the whole of the first act of *Richard III*, with its dramatic intro-ductions of Anne Neville and Margaret of Anjou, is also unhistorical. Richard of Gloucester did not woo Anne Neville in the presence of Henry VI's corpse, nor did he engineer the arrest and execution of Clarence so as to smooth the path for his own long-planned seizure of the crown. Then, having ruthlessly compressed the events of twelve years (1471-1483) into a very few scenes, Shakespeare charts Richard of Gloucester's bloody progress to the throne, happily combining fact and fiction, and always focusing firmly on the character and behaviour of the new king himself. Most of Richard III's reign virtually disappears, however, since Henry Tudor's successful landing in the summer of 1485 immediately follows Buckingham's rebellion in the autumn of 1483.

The Plays and History: Underlying Truths Preserved?

Very few today would wish to claim, as John Churchill Duke of Marlborough apparently did in the early eighteenth century, that Shakespeare was 'the only History of England I ever read'. Clearly, our detailed knowledge of Lancastrians, Yorkists and the Wars of the Roses is immeasurably greater at the beginning of the twenty-first century than it was at the end of the sixteenth, Much painstaking historical research, particularly during the twentieth century, has seen to that. It is now more evident than ever before that Shakespeare's plays cannot be regarded as history. Yet was he, in the end, so very wrong about fifteenth-century English kings, magnates and the Wars of the Roses? When rejecting Shakespeare, and Tudor tradition, as vehemently as many have, can historians perhaps be convicted of throwing out the baby with the bathwater? After all, the playwright's stress on the political role of kings, the central importance of crown/baronial relations and the prevalence of warfare (both at home and abroad) during the later Middle Ages remains fundamentally sound; moreover, the personalities, ambitions and capacity to rule of individual monarchs were, indeed, vitally important.

How reliable, then, are Shakespeare's portrayals of fifteenth-century English kings? His stress on Richard II's acute awareness of his God-given regality and the high conception of kingship he held seems amply borne out by contemporary evidence, while the king's personal and political shortcomings do indeed go far towards explaining his failure to hang on to the throne. The notion that Henry IV's reign was dominated by the circumstances of his usurpation in 1399 and that, throughout his rebellion-dominated rule, he never felt fully secure on the throne, has also stood up to the test of time (and historical research) remarkably well. Most recent commentators on Henry V, too, have brought in favourable verdicts on the king, even if his epic and heroic qualities have become rather tarnished since Elizabethan times. Shakespeare's portrayal of Henry VI, so convincingly traceable back to contemporary and near-contemporary sources as it is anyway, squares very well with most modern verdicts on this pious, well-meaning yet clearly politically inept monarch; Margaret of Anjou is still generally seen as energetic, ruthless and single-minded in her determination to fight for her son's birthright; and Warwick the Kingmaker, if no longer quite the 'proud setter up and puller down of kings' of *3 Henry VI*, remains a pivotal figure in modern reconstructions of mid-fifteenth century politics and civil strife. Edward IV did receive less than fair treatment at Shakespeare's hands, and (at any rate after 1471) proved himself an able and effective ruler, but his life-long devotion to pleasure, his lack of wisdom in marrying Elizabeth Woodville and the dire (if temporary) consequences of his failure to retain Warwick's loyalty remain as evident as ever. And although Shakespeare's depiction of Richard III is over the top to say the least, he did ruthlessly secure the throne for himself in 1483; his defeat and death at Bosworth did open the way for Henry VII's seizure of the crown in 1485; and the Tudors did indeed then prove a highly successful dynasty for over a century.

As the Whig interpretation of history lost favour and the volume of historical research blossomed during the twentieth century, Shakespeare's notions of the Wars of the Roses as essentially dynastic in origins and nature came under ever more critical scrutiny; the impor-tance of bloodfeuds was seriously downgraded; and the Tudor vision of chaos and mayhem was largely abandoned. Yet 1399 did cast a long shadow over the fifteenth century; rival Lancastrian, Yorkist and Tudor claims to the throne certainly existed and their importance was only too clearly recognised by contemporaries; and the impact of the Wars of the Roses on society may well have been considerable. Perhaps, too, the relentless quest by professional historians for pseudo-scientific answers to the problems posed by fifteenth-century England and its sources has made them apt to forget that history is, and should be, a literary art as well as a painstaking search for truth (and here, surely, they have much to learn from amateurs!). Certainly, no mere historian will ever paint a more compelling and dramatic picture of England's Lancastrian and Yorkist kings, and the Wars of the Roses, than William Shakespeare.

BIBLIOGRAPHY

Allmand, C.T., *Henry V* (1992)

Austen, Jane, *History of England* (1791)

Bacon, Francis, *History of the Reign of Henry VII* (1622)

Baker, D. (ed), *Portraits and Documents: The Later Middle Ages* (1968)

Barron, C.M. and Du Boulay, F.R.H. (eds), *The Reign of Richard II* (1971), especially Aston, M., 'Richard II and the Wars of the Roses'

Bennett, A., 'K.B. McFarlane', *London Review of Books*, 4 September 1997

Boardman, A.V., *The Battle of Towton* (1994)

Branagh, K., 'Henry V', in *Players of Shakespeare 2*, ed. R. Jackson and R. Smallwood (1988)

Buck, George, *History of King Richard III*, ed. A.N. Kincaid (1982)

Bullough, G. (ed), *Narrative and Dramatic Sources of Shakespeare*, vol. 3 (1960), vol. 4 (1962)

Burrow, J.W., *A Liberal Descent: Victorian Historians and the English Past* (1981)

Carpenter, C., 'Political and Constitutional History: Before and After McFarlane', in *The McFarlane Legacy: Studies in Late Medieval Politics and Society*, ed. R.H. Britnell & A.J. Pollard (1995)

Carpenter, C., *The Wars of the Roses: Politics and the Constitution in England c.1437-1509* (1997)

Carte, T., *General History of England*, vol. 2 (1750)

Chrimes, S.B., *Lancastrians, Yorkists and Henry VII* (1964)

Chrimes, S.B., *Henry VII* (1972)

Chrimes, S.B., Ross, C.D. & Griffiths, R.A (eds), *Fifteenth-Century England* (1972)

Christie, M.E., *Henry VI* (1922)

Churchill, G.B., *Richard III up to Shakespeare* (1900)

Cole, H., *The Wars of the Roses* (1973)

Commynes, Philippe de, *Memoirs: The Reign of Louis XI 1461-1483*, ed. M. Jones (1972)

Crowland Chronicle Continuations 1459-1486, ed. N. Pronay and J. Cox (1986)

Curry, A., *The Hundred Years War* (1993)

Daniel, S., *The History of the Civil Wars between the Houses of York and Lancaster* (1609)

Denton, W., *England in the Fifteenth Century* (1888)

Dockray, K., *Henry VI, Margaret of Anjou and the Wars of the Roses: A Source Book* (2000)

Dockray, K., *Edward IV: A Source Book* (1999)

Dockray, K., *Richard III: A Source Book* (1997)

Fabyan, Robert, *New Chronicles of England and of France*, ed. H. Ellis (1811)

Flemming, J.H. (ed), *England under the Lancastrians* (1921)

Gairdner, J., *History of the Life and Reign of Richard III* (1878)

Gillingham, J., *The Wars of the Roses* (1981)

Gooch, G.P., *History and Historians in the Nineteenth Century* (1913)

Goodman, A., *The Wars of the Roses* (1981)

Gransden, A., *Historical Writing in England* c.*1307 to the Early Sixteenth Century* (1982)

Great Chronicle of London, ed. A.H. Thomas and I.D. Thornley (1938)

Green, J.R., *A Short History of the English People* (1874)

Green, J.R., *History of the English People*, vol. 1 (1877), vol. 2 (1878)

Green, V.H.H., *The Later Plantagenets* (1955)

Griffiths, R., *The Reign of Henry VI* (1981)

Griffiths, R., *King and Country: England and Wales in the Fifteenth Century* (1991), for reprints of Griffiths' articles

Griffiths, R. and Cannon, J., *The Oxford Illustrated History of the English Monarchy* (1988)

Guth, D.J., 'Fifteenth-Century England; Recent Scholarship and Future Directions', *British Studies Monitor*, vol. 7 (1977)

Habington, W., *History of Edward the Fourth King of England* (1640)

Haigh, C., *Elizabeth I* (1988)

Haigh, P., *The Military Campaigns of the Wars of the Roses* (1995)

Haigh, P., *The Battle of Wakefield 1460* (1996)

Hale, J.R. (ed), *The Evolution of British Historiography* (1964)

Hall, E., *The Union of the Two Noble and Illustrious Families of Lancaster and York* (1548)

Hallam, E. (ed), *Chronicles of the Wars of the Roses* (1988)

Halsted, C., *Richard III as Duke of Gloucester and King of England*, 2 vols (1844)

Hammond, P., *The Battles of Barnet and Tewkesbury* (1990)

Hanham, A., *Richard III and his Early Historians 1483-1535* (1975)

Harriss, G.L. (ed), *Henry V: The Practice of Kingship* (1985)

Harriss, G.L., *Cardinal Beaufort* (1988)

Hay, D., *Annalists and Historians: Western Historiography from the Eighth to the Eighteenth Centuries* (1977)

Hicks, M., *False, Fleeting, Perjur'd Clarence* (1980)

Hicks, M., *Richard III: The Man Behind the Myth* (1991)

Hicks, M., *Richard III and his Rivals: Magnates and their Motives in the Wars of the Roses* (1991), for reprints of Hicks' articles

Hicks, M., *Warwick the Kingmaker* (1998)

Holinshed's Chronicle, As used in Shakespeare's Plays, ed. A. and J. Nicoll (1927)

Holmes, G., *The Later Middle Ages* (1962)

Horrox, R., *Richard III: A Study of Service* (1989)

Hume, D., *History of England from the Invasion of Julius Caesar to the Accession of Henry VII* (1762)

Hurstfield, J. & Smith, A.G.R. (eds), *Elizabethan People* (1972)

Hutton, W., *The Battle of Bosworth Field* (1788)

Jacob, E.F., *The Fifteenth Century* (1961)

Jenkins, E., *The Princes in the Tower* (1978)

Jesse, J., *The Memoirs of Richard the Third* (1862)

Keen, M.H., *England in the Later Middle Ages* (1973)

Kendall, P.M., *Richard the Third* (1955)

Kendall, P.M., *Warwick the Kingmaker* (1957)

Kendall, P.M., *The Yorkist Age* (1962)

Kingsford, C.L., *Henry V: The Typical Medieval Hero* (1901)

Kingsford, C.L., *English Historical Literature in the Fifteenth Century* (1913)

Kingsford, C.L., *Prejudice and Promise in Fifteenth Century England*
   (1925), especially 'Fifteenth Century History in Shakespeare's Plays'

Kirby, J.L., *Henry IV of England* (1970)

Knights, L.C., *Shakespeare: The Histories* (1962)

Lamb, V.B., *The Betrayal of Richard III* (1959)

Lander, J.R., *The Wars of the Roses* (1965)

Lander, J.R., *Conflict and Stability in Fifteenth Century England* (1969)

Lander, J.R., *Crown and Nobility 1450-1509* (1976), for reprints of
   Lander's articles

Lander, J.R., *Government and Community; England 1450-1509* (1980)

Legge, A.O., *The Unpopular King* (1855)

Lindsay, P., *King Richard III* (1933)

Lingard, J., *The History of England from the first invasion by the Romans
   to the accession of William and Mary in 1688*, Vol. 3 (1819)

Longford, E. (ed), *The Oxford Book of Royal Anecdotes* (1989)

Lyly, John, *Euphues and his England* (1580)

Macaulay, T.B., *History of England*, Vol. 1 (1848)

Mancini, Dominic, *The Usurpation of Richard III*,
   ed. C.A.J. Armstrong (1936)

Markham, C., *Richard III: His Life and Character* (1906)

Mateer, D (ed), *The Renaissance in Europe: Courts, Patrons and Poets*
   (2000), especially R.D. Brown, 'The London Stage'

McFarlane, K.B., *Lancastrian Kings and Lollard Knights* (1972)

McFarlane, K.B., *The Nobility of Later Medieval England* (1973)

McFarlane, K.B., *England in the Fifteenth Century* (1981), for reprints
   of McFarlane's articles.

McKisack, M., *Medieval History in the Tudor Age* (1971)

Mirror for Magistrates, ed. L.B. Campbell (1938)

More, Thomas, *History of King Richard the Third*, ed. R.S. Sylvester (1963)

Moseley, C.W.R.D., *Shakespeare's History Plays* (1988)

Mowat, R.B., *The Wars of the Roses* (1914)

Myers, A.R., *England in the Later Middle Ages* (1952)

Myers, A.R. (ed), *English Historical Documents 1327-1485* (1969)

Norwich, J.J., *Shakespeare's Kings* (1999)

Olivier, L., *Confessions of an Actor* (1982)

Oman, C., *Warwick the Kingmaker* (1891)

Oman, C., *History of England 1377-1485* (1906)

Pollard, A.J., *The Wars of the Roses* (1988)

Pollard, A.J., *North-Eastern England during the Wars of the Roses* (1990)

Pollard, A.J., *Richard III and the Princes in the Tower* (1991)

Pollard, A.J., *Late Medieval England 1399-1509* (2000)

Pollard, A.J., *The Worlds of Richard III* (2001)

Potter, J., *Good King Richard?* (1983)

Powell, E., 'After "After McFarlane": The Poverty of Patronage and the Case for Constitutional History', in *Trade, Devotion and Governance*, ed. D.J. Clayton, R.G. Davies and P. McNiven (1994)

Ramsay, J.H., *Lancaster and York*, 2 vols (1892)

Rapin de Thoyras, P., *History of England*, ed. N.Tindall, Vol. 1 (1732)

Richmond, C., 'After McFarlane', *History*, Vol. 68 (1983)

Ross, C., *Edward IV* (1974)

Ross, C., *The Wars of the Roses* (1976)

Ross, C. (ed), *Patronage, Pedigree and Power in Later Medieval England* (1979)

Ross, C., *Richard III* (1981)

Rous, John, *History of the Kings of England*, in A. Hanham, *Richard III and his Early Historians* (1975)

Rous, John, *The Rous Roll* (1980)

Rowse, A.L., *Bosworth Field and the Wars of the Roses* (1966)

Saccio, P., *Shakespeare's English Kings* (1977)

Saul, N., *Richard II* (1997)

Scofield, C.L., *The Life and Reign of Edward the Fourth*, 2 vols (1923)

Seward, D., *Richard III: England's Black Legend* (1983)

Seward, D., *The Wars of the Roses* (1995)

Shakespeare, William, *King Richard II* (first performed 1595, New Arden edn, 1956)

Shakespeare, William, *King Henry IV Part 1* (first performed 1597, New Arden edn, 1960), *Part 2* (first performed 1598, New Arden edn, 1966)

Shakespeare, William, *King Henry V* (first performed 1599, New Arden edn, 1954)

Shakespeare, William, *King Henry VI Part 1* (first performed *c.*1590, New Arden edn, 1962), *Part 2* (first performed *c.*1590, New Arden edn, 1957), *Part 3* (first performed *c.*1590, New Arden edn, 1964)

Shakespeare, William, *King Richard III* (first performed c.1591, New Arden edn, 1981)

Sher, A., *Year of the King* (1985)

Schoenbawm, S., *William Shakespeare: A Compact Documentary Life* (1977)

Snyder, W.H. (ed), *The Crown and the Tower: The Legend of Richard III* (1981)

Steel, A., *Richard II* (1941)

Storey, R.L., *The End of the House of Lancaster* (1966)

Stubbs, W., *Constitutional History of England*, Vol. 3 (1878)

Taylor, A.J.P., *A Personal History* (1983)

Tey, J., *The Daughter of Time* (1951)

Thornley, I.D. (ed), *England under the Yorkists* (1920)

Tillyard, E.M.W., *Shakespeare's History Plays* (1944)

Trewin, J.C., *Shakespeare on the English Stage 1900-1964* (1964)

Turner, S., *The History of England during the Middle Ages*, Vol. 3 (1823)

Vergil, Polydore, *Three Books of Polydore Vergil's English History*, ed. H. Ellis (1844)

Vergil, Polydore, *The Anglica Historia of Polydore Vergil 1485-1537*, ed. D. Hay (1950)

Vickers, K.H., *Humphrey Duke of Gloucester* (1907)

Vickers, K.H., *England in the Later Middle Ages* (1913)

Walpole, Horace, *Historic Doubts on the Life and Reign of Richard III* (1768)

Watts, J., *Henry VI and the Politics of Kingship* (1996)

Weir, A., *Lancaster and York: The Wars of the Roses* (1995)

Wells, R.H., *Shakespeare, Politics and the State* (1986)

Wilkinson, B., *The Later Middle Ages in England* (1969)

Williamson, A., *The Mystery of the Princes* (1978)

Wolffe, B.P., *Henry VI* (1981)

LIST OF ILLUSTRATIONS

INDEX

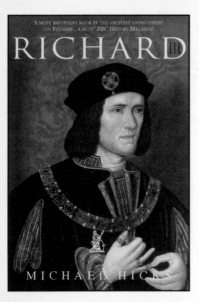
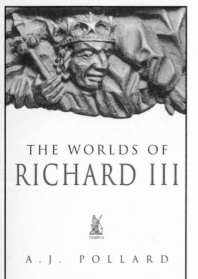